MODERN AMERICA

MODERN AMERICA

The United States from World War II to the Present

ALLAN M. WINKLER

University of Oregon

1817

HARPER & ROW, PUBLISHERS, New York
Cambridge, Philadelphia, San Francisco,
London, Mexico City, São Paulo, Singapore, Sydney

Sponsoring Editor: Marianne J. Russell
Project Editor: Susan Goldfarb
Cover Design: Wanda Lubelska Design
Text Art: Reproduction Drawings Ltd.
Photo Research: Mira Schachne
Production: Willie Lane
Compositor: Donnelley/Rocappi
Printer and Binder: R. R. Donnelley & Sons Company

Credits

p. 86: From the song "Little Boxes," words and music by Malvina Reynolds, copyright © 1962 Schroder Music Company (ASCAP). Used by permission. All rights reserved.

pp. 91–92: From "Howl," in *Collected Poems, 1947–1980* by Allen Ginsberg. Copyright © 1956, 1984 by Allen Ginsberg. Reprinted by permission of Harper & Row, Publishers, Inc.

p. 151: From the song "The Times They Are A-Changin'" by Bob Dylan. © 1963 Warner Bros. Inc. All rights reserved. Used by permission.

p. 178: Lyrics from "I Am Woman," lyrics by Helen Reddy, music by Ray Burton. Copyright © 1971 by Irving Music, Inc., Buggerlugs Music Company, BMI. All rights reserved. International copyright secured. Used by permission.

Modern America: The United States from World War II to the Present

Library of Congress Cataloging in Publication Data

Winkler, Allan M., 1945–
  Modern America.

  Includes bibliographies and index.
  1. United States—History—1945- . 2. World War, 1939–1945—United States. I. Title.
E741.W76 1985   973.9   85–7605
ISBN 0-06-047144-1

85 86 87 88 9 8 7 6 5 4 3 2 1

FOR JOHN MORTON BLUM

CONTENTS

PREFACE

This book deals primarily with the course of American history after the Second World War. But because I feel that the war had a profound impact in shaping the nature of postwar society, I have chosen to begin with a chapter dealing with World War II. That first chapter describes the tensions that culminated in the Cold War; the growth of presidential power; the development of more centralized economic planning; and the push for equality on the part of a number of social groups. All of those themes surface again and again in the chapters that follow.

Modern America is intended for use in courses dealing with the United States in the post–World War II period. It could also be used as one of several short texts in a course on the twentieth century or in a broader American history course. It is meant to provide an overview of the major social and political events of the recent past, to offer a mix of the important developments in all areas of American life. It deals with everything from cultural phenomena to diplomatic affairs. It is not intended to be exhaustive; it will provide a useful framework that can be supplemented with more detailed treatments of specific topics.

This book has grown out of all of the teaching and research I have done on the post–World War II period during the past ten years. It reflects my effort to understand a turbulent time. I hope it provides some insight into the roots of issues that continue to concern us today.

A number of people provided significant assistance at various points in this project. When I first began to write, I had the constant encouragement of members of the Noon Group, and in the long run, that made the effort easier.

Paul S. Holbo, John W. Jeffries, and Ken W. De Bevoise read an early draft and offered valuable suggestions. My sister, Karen Winkler Moulton, provided a thoughtful critique that made the process of rewriting easier. In the later stages of revision, Barbara Clarke Mossberg gave the kind of encouragement that made completion of the book possible. My wife, Alberta, and our children, Jenny and David, were, as always, basic sources of affection, stability, and support. Finally, this book, like all my work, benefited from the example of John Morton Blum—teacher, colleague, friend.

ALLAN M. WINKLER

MODERN AMERICA

chapter *1*

The United States and World War II

World War II ushered in a new age in the United States. The monumental struggle made enormous demands on the American people. It forced them to accept involvement with the world beyond, even as they mobilized at home to provide the resources that victory required. It made them confront new social and political issues as they adjusted to new trends in their own lives. The Second World War was, without question, a watershed in which the patterns of postwar America emerged.

For the world at large, the conflict was the final step on the road to total war. More extensive than the Great War that began in 1914, it became an epic struggle with a destructive force greater than any yet known. It brought tremendous casualties to soldiers and civilians alike and unleashed the specter of nuclear holocaust for the first time.

In America the war unfolded differently than it did elsewhere on the globe. The United States came to the struggle late, after other nations had been fighting for more than two years. Once engaged, Americans fought overseas but experienced no devastation at home. Though American soldiers lost their lives, their numbers never approximated the numbers of dead from other lands.

Even so, the war forged the patterns that guided the nation in the decades that followed. In the aftermath of the struggle, Americans were ready to assert a newfound authority both at home and abroad. World War II bred a confidence that the nation could deal with problems at any time, anywhere, on its own terms. That confidence came to be a two-edged sword, as over the years it brought not only triumph but tragedy as well.

The major concerns of the post-1945 years were all rooted in the experience of war. The Cold War confrontation with the Soviet Union stemmed from long-standing tensions that sometimes threatened to tear the Grand Alliance apart. The postwar sense of economic self-control rested on the awareness that wartime spending had finally brought the Depression to an end and on the assumption that similar fiscal practices could be used to maintain equilibrium in years to come. The reliance on the ever-larger federal bureaucracy grew out of the enormous expansion of the governmental system as it struggled to meet mobilization demands. The struggles of women, blacks, and other groups for equal treatment built on incremental advances made during the war. A new age was dawning, in which progress in all areas could easily come—or so Americans believed, with the same optimism they had shown during the war.

WARTIME DIPLOMACY

At the diplomatic level, the United States was intimately involved with its allies in the war. During the 1930s, as violence flared in Europe and in the Far East, Americans had hoped to maintain their distance. Slowly but surely, however, the nation was drawn into the European conflict as it came to the aid of the British, who were unable to resist the Germans on their own. The devastating Japanese attack on the American fleet at Pearl Harbor on December 7, 1941, finally drew the nation into a war on two fronts. Once a part of the struggle, the United States joined Great Britain and the Soviet Union in a Grand Alliance that sought to defeat the Germans, the Italians, and the Japanese. The coalition managed to remain intact, but not without constant friction, for the duration of the war.

Franklin D. Roosevelt and the War

Franklin Delano Roosevelt, president from 1933 until his death in early 1945, was the dominant American on the diplomatic front, and in other areas as well. As commander in chief in a cataclysmic struggle, he delighted in making major decisions about the course of the war. Assuming personal responsibility for important negotiations more than any president before him, he met his Russian and English counterparts in top-level conferences abroad. At the same time he sought to communicate to the public his own vision of American aims and his own confidence in the successful outcome of the war.

Throughout the conflict, Roosevelt conveyed the boundless optimism that had buoyed the nation in the desperate days of the Great Depression a decade before. A member of a wealthy old New York family, he was nonetheless able to persuade ordinary Americans that he had their interests in mind and that his New Deal would bring about improvement in their lives. Using his superb political skills, he helped the country weather the worst economic crisis it had ever known.

Elected more times than any other American president, he made people understand that he cared. Frances Perkins, his secretary of labor, observed that when he spoke to the public over the radio, "his face would smile and light up as though he were actually sitting on the front porch or in the parlor with them. People felt this, and it bound them to him in affection." With a voice that novelist John Dos Passos called "father-friendly, without strain," he managed to get others to follow his lead. Not all Americans supported FDR. Some members of the upper class cringed at the mention of "that man" and remained bitter opponents to the end. But millions more were willing to work with him and to do what he asked.

His popular appeal notwithstanding, Roosevelt was a complex and sometimes mystifying man. "I cannot come to grips with him!" complained one of his loyal Cabinet heads, and he spoke for all who had to work with FDR. The president could be exasperating in the extreme as he tried one approach, then another, or played one official against another for his own purposes. He frustrated his associates with his willingness to delay. Yet he had a superb sense of timing that more often than not vindicated him. "A second-class intellect—but a first-class temperament!" Justice Oliver Wendell Holmes once remarked, and that temperament carried the nation along.

Roosevelt's New Deal never really ended the Great Depression, but it did restore confidence, both in the business system and in the ability of the nation as a whole to deal with its problems once again. Roosevelt guided the country in the Second World War in the same way. Intuitively he understood the issues of the day and communicated them inspirationally. He made mistakes, to be sure, but he provided the spirit so necessary in the war.

The Grand Alliance and the Tensions of War

One of Roosevelt's major tasks was keeping the Grand Alliance from splitting apart. Although the United States, Great Britain, and the Soviet Union all sought to defeat the Axis, they experienced serious friction as they worked together. Each nation came to the struggle with its own aims and assumptions about how the enemy could be beaten, and those all too often led to contention, despite the common goal. The only thing worse than fighting with allies, British Prime Minister Winston Churchill once remarked, was fighting without them. Americans and Englishmen had long been suspicious of the Russians, and though public perceptions softened, the underlying tensions remained. The major powers accomplished a great deal by remaining together as much as they did.

The United States entered the war with its own definite aims. Victory was the essential concern, yet Americans argued that there was also a larger meaning to the struggle. Eleven months before the attack on Pearl Harbor, Roosevelt had spoken to Congress of the "four essential human freedoms"—freedom of speech and expression, freedom of worship, freedom from want, and freedom from fear. In the summer of 1941, he and Churchill had also laid out in the Atlantic Charter their conception of the world to come, in which the self-determination of nations, equal trading rights for all, and a system of general security would prevail.

The charter summed up general American assumptions about the war. The United States hoped to shape economic forces according to its vision of the postwar world. The war would create a world where Americans could enjoy peace and prosperity again, where trade could flow freely without tariff walls, and where American businesses would be free to expand. In the aftermath of the struggle, the United States wanted to see a stable and unified world where equal economic opportunity would abound. American power, tempered by the experience of war, would predominate, for the benefit of all.

A number of American leaders sensed what the future could hold. Wendell Willkie, Republican presidential candidate in 1940, wrote of the "One World" the war was helping to create. Henry A. Wallace, FDR's vice-president for most of the conflict, hoped the war would bring the "Century of the Common Man." But Henry Luce, the noted publisher, summed up prevailing sentiment best of all in a 1941 editorial in *Life* magazine, in which he wrote about the "American Century" and called on fellow citizens "to assume the leadership of the world" for the good of people in every land.

The other nations of the Grand Alliance had visions of their own. The English were fighting the war to survive. Until the United States entered the struggle, Britain stood alone in its effort to withstand German might. England was under attack, unsure of just how long it could maintain the effort to hold out. "What is our aim?" Churchill asked. "I can answer in one word: It is victory, victory at all costs, victory in spite of all terror, victory however hard and long the road may be." Yet the British had other aims as well. Like the Americans, they acknowledged the need for a stable world with self-determination for all. The Anglo-American heritage of 300 years provided a common bond, and the Atlantic Charter expressed the vision of England as well as of the United States. At the same time, England hoped to maintain the economic and territorial advantages of the British Empire, even as the United States sought to undermine the imperial preference system with American gains in mind. "I have not become the King's First Minister in order to preside over the liquidation of the British Empire," Churchill said tartly. But the interests of Americans continued to conflict with those of English friends.

The Russians came to the war with aims of their own. For the Soviets as for the British, survival was necessary before all else. Russia had been attacked in mid-1941, when Hitler aborted the Nazi-Soviet Pact of 1939, and now found itself fighting a war that often seemed lost. In Stalingrad, Moscow, and elsewhere the Russians desperately sought to hold on in the face of German strength. When they turned their attention to the future, they envisioned a stable world far different from what the English and Americans had in mind. Uneasy about their vulnerability along their western flank, they hoped for friendly governments in eastern Europe to help shield them from attack. They wanted a sphere where their influence would prevail, even when that threatened the unified world Roosevelt and Churchill hoped to create.

Just as the general aims of the Allies varied, so did their strategic interests. The Americans alone fought the Japanese in the Pacific, aware that no help would be forthcoming until the European war was won. On the continent, the Russians were grappling alone with Germany on the eastern front and desperately wanted their partners to open a second front in western Europe to relieve the pressure they felt. The United States seemed willing at first but was soon dissuaded by England, which had lost a whole generation of young men through frontal attack in World War I and was unwilling to launch a direct, full-scale invasion until the prospects for success were assured. The United States hedged and finally followed the English plan, which involved attacks on North Africa and then Italy before a cross-channel invasion could begin. Militarily that made the most sense, but it infuriated the Russians, who felt that their allies harbored deep-rooted resentments and were simply trying to bleed them into a state of weakness in the war.

The Big Three in the War

The leaders of the Grand Alliance recognized the need to maintain some measure of cooperation in their fight. Each spoke for his own national means and ends, yet all knew they had to smooth out their differences to gain the victory they together sought.

Winston Churchill, the tough-minded English leader, helped maintain the fighting spirit of his people in the war. Eloquent and incisive in speech, the prime minister with the bulldog look was 66 when he came to power, but he worked tirelessly to keep his nation alive. He reflected British defiance of the dictators and refusal to capitulate in the face of overwhelming odds. "I have nothing to offer but blood, toil, tears and sweat," he told Parliament in mid-1940, but that was enough to carry the nation along.

On the other side, Joseph Stalin guided the Soviet Union in its struggle to survive. Ruthless and grim, the Communist leader had dominated his party and state for the last decade and a half. In the pursuit of both national and personal ends, he had presided over the monstrous purges of his enemies in the 1930s, but he now tempered his ideological bent in the interests of gaining help for Russia in the war. Paranoid perhaps in his earlier actions, he came to the war intent on gaining acceptance of Russian wartime demands. At one point, as Stalin sought to get Allied compliance in guaranteeing Russian borders as of 1941 and ran into opposition from the other leaders, who invoked the Atlantic Charter, he complained that it looked "as if the Atlantic Charter was directed against the USSR."

FDR mediated between Churchill and Stalin. Roosevelt enjoyed a comfortable and secure relationship with Churchill, based partly on a naval background both shared, partly on a sense of mutual respect that grew throughout the war. With Stalin, Roosevelt was on less familiar ground, yet he remained confident that he could treat with him as successfully as he had with others in his long political career.

Roosevelt shared American assumptions about the Russians in general and Stalin in particular. Uneasy about the Bolshevik Revolution of 1917, the United States had not extended diplomatic recognition to the Soviet Union until 1933 and remained suspicious even after relations began. With Russian entrance into the fight, that uneasiness began to dissolve. Still uncomfortable with communism, Americans persuaded themselves that the Russians had begun to change and were moving closer to the democratic side. In 1943 *Life* magazine put out a special issue on Russia and called the Russians "one hell of a people" who "look like Americans, dress like Americans and think like Americans." Roosevelt and others referred to Stalin as "Uncle Joe," while *Time* named the Russian leader its "Man of the Year." Americans were sympathetic to their counterparts in the East, hopeful that a new relationship had begun.

Well aware of the dictatorial nature of the Soviet regime, Roosevelt argued that it was less threatening than people believed. "I think the Russians are perfectly friendly," he said. "They aren't trying to gobble up all the rest of Europe or the world. . . . They haven't got any crazy ideas of conquest." When others challenged that view, he dismissed their arguments. Yet he remained practical and shrewd behind his optimistic mask. "My children," he remarked, "it is permitted you in time of grave danger to walk with the devil until you have crossed the bridge."

FDR believed that he alone could deal with Stalin. He came back from one wartime conference in 1943 to report that he "got along fine" with the Russian leader, and the next year he summed up his feelings to Winston Churchill when he said: "I know you will not mind my being brutally frank when I tell you that I think I can personally handle Stalin better than either you or your Foreign Office or my State Department. Stalin hates the guts of all your top people. He thinks he likes me better, and I hope he will continue to do so."

Conferences and Issues

The leaders of the Grand Alliance did their best to work together, but the tensions were visible from the start. Midway through the war, they recognized that the coalition was in trouble and needed repair if the Axis was to be brought to task. To that end they met together at a number of high-level conferences to grapple with the issues of war and peace that were seldom easy to decide.

The first meeting came at Casablanca, in Morocco, in early 1943. The United States and Britain had invaded North Africa at Churchill's insistence a few months before and had therefore delayed opening the Russian-sought second front. Angry at the strategy followed and preoccupied with the eastern war, Stalin refused to attend. Roosevelt met Churchill alone and reluctantly agreed to move toward Italy, the next step in the prime minister's plan. To reassure the Soviets, the Western leaders pledged at the same time to fight on until the "unconditional surrender" of their foe. They would see the war through to the end.

All three leaders met later the same year. At Tehran, in Iran, Stalin and Roosevelt insisted that an invasion across the English Channel be launched in the near future and got Churchill's approval to move ahead. They also spoke about the future of Poland, Germany, and other European areas and about the ultimate entrance of the Soviet Union in the Pacific war. The final meeting of

Churchill, Roosevelt, and Stalin came at Yalta, in the Crimea, in February 1945, where many of the same issues were discussed. Several months later Roosevelt was dead, and Harry Truman represented the United States at Potsdam, in liberated Germany, in the last summit conference of the war.

One source of disagreement among the Allies was the question of Germany's fate after the war. Germany was clearly the aggressor, and acknowledgment would be made of that fact. But was it better to divide the nation into component parts or leave it whole with the possibility of another fight? There was some talk of partition at Tehran, but because of disagreement the matter was deferred to a later date. For a time Secretary of the Treasury Henry Morgenthau, Jr., had Roosevelt's ear and proposed stripping Germany of its industrial capacity and making it into a pastoral land. Then support for the approach of eliminating Germany's capacity to wage war declined, and at Yalta the Allied leaders agreed instead on zonal occupation and on some reparations to be paid by the defeated foe. The sum of $20 billion was taken as a basis for discussion, with half of that to go to the USSR.

Churchill, Roosevelt, and Stalin at the Yalta Conference in February 1945. (*FDR Library*)

The question of Poland was troublesome too. More than that, it was a symbolic issue. The Russians had legitimate security interests on the Polish border, yet Great Britain had gone to war as a result of the German attack on Poland and was not ready to write the nation off. There was anti-Soviet feeling in the region, and by the provisions of the Atlantic Charter, the Western powers argued that Poland should have the right to determine its own fate. At Tehran, agreement on the Russian-Polish border was reached, but there was controversy over the line dividing Poland and Germany. Stalin wanted the border pushed farther west to encompass a large part of Germany, to which Churchill protested: "It would be a pity to stuff the Polish goose so full of German food that it died of indigestion." More serious was the controversy over the government of the revived Polish state. There were at the time two governments claiming to represent Poland: one in London, supported by Britain and the United States, and one in Lublin, supported by the Soviet Union. At Yalta Stalin insisted on recognizing the latter group but did agree that it would be reorganized to include representatives of democratic elements in Poland and Polish representatives abroad. He also agreed to "free and unfettered elections" at an indeterminate point in the future. Stalin, in a major confrontation, came out ahead. Roosevelt knew that the agreement, as one of his aides said, was so loose that Russia could "stretch it all the way from Yalta to Washington without technically breaking it." But he also knew that, with other pressing priorities, "it's the best I can do for Poland at this time."

Still another question that had to be decided was the nature of an international organization after the war. The United States had rejected entrance into the League of Nations two decades before. Now the American public was coming to accept the idea of some kind of a body for the years ahead. Roosevelt for a time seemed to consider the notion of "four policemen"—the three major powers and China—working together to keep the peace, but as the internationalist impulse developed in the United States, his thinking changed as well. He became willing to include smaller nations, as long as the larger ones had a greater voice. The issue was discussed at Tehran and again raised at Yalta, where the notion of a veto was defined to protect big-power prerogatives in a more open forum. Compromises were made so that a new organization, to be called the United Nations, could take shape. The world would have a chance to see if the countries of the globe could, in fact, work toward a common goal.

The United States, Great Britain, and the Soviet Union did work together to win the war and achieved the victory they had long sought. In Europe they ground their way across the continent after the D-day landings of June 1944 and finally secured the German surrender in May 1945. In Asia, the island-hopping campaign brought American forces closer and closer to Japan. Before a scheduled invasion could take place, atomic bombs dropped on Hiroshima and Nagasaki in August 1945 caused Japanese resistance to crumble and brought the Pacific war to an end.

Even as the Allies won, however, they learned how difficult it was to proceed as a group toward a given aim. Pursuit of victory held them together for the duration of the war, yet even then the leaders in both East and West were aware that the differences dividing them were going to be difficult to overcome. World War II was over; but in a very real sense, the Cold War had already begun.

HOME-FRONT REORGANIZATION

As the war unfolded on the military front, it had a decided impact at home. The enormous demands of the struggle brought pronounced changes in the size and structure of the government. More centralized than ever, it assumed responsibility for tasks it had never considered before. Presidential authority grew accordingly, and by the war's end an unmistakable power shift had occurred.

The Economy at War

During the war years the economy grew at a remarkable rate. After years of depression, the nation was prosperous once again as the full labor force sought to provide the materials necessary to win the war. The enormous effort, which began for reasons of defense even before the attack on Pearl Harbor, proved to be the stimulus the country had been lacking for so long. Once deliberate, sustained spending began to take place, the specter of depression vanished, just as English economist John Maynard Keynes had predicted it would. That successful demonstration of what spending could do fostered a confidence in the ability of government to regulate the economy that persisted for the next 30 years.

Keynes was the most influential economist of his age. His major work, *The General Theory of Employment, Interest and Money,* was published in 1936, but before then he had been lecturing about the same ideas to his students at Cambridge University. Keynes challenged the notion that depression was but one phase in the business cycle that would pass as a matter of course. Rather, he argued, depression was equilibrium at a very low level that would persist unless sufficient spending occurred to get the system moving again. Spending could come from the private sector in traditional forms. Business investment in sufficient degree could make the necessary difference. If that investment failed to materialize, however, the same result could come from aggressive government action. Either tax cuts or large-scale spending programs could increase the amount of money in circulation and bring an end to depression.

Keynes traveled to the United States and met Roosevelt in 1934, but neither man understood the other. When he left, Roosevelt observed, "He left a whole rigmarole of figures. He must be a mathematician rather than a political economist." Keynes, for his part, was disappointed too; he had "supposed the President was more literate, economically speaking." He saw that, for all the activity of the 1930s, his theory was never really tried. The various initiatives of the New Deal worked in conflicting and contradictory ways, and while those efforts brought relief to the hardest hit and reform to the system, recovery lagged behind.

Not until 1940 did the massive spending that Keynes had called for begin to take place. When the United States started to mobilize for defense, the economy began to improve overnight. The nation became, in Roosevelt's phrase, "the great arsenal of democracy." Americans knew the vast potential of their land, yet they knew too that it had to be mobilized if the war was to be won. Conversion to a war footing was a major task. Old industries began to produce new goods, and new industries came into their own. Cars and appliances gave way to tanks, planes, and ships. The United States, unlike other belligerents, never experienced total mobilization but nonetheless embarked on an effort greater than it had ever known.

The economic expansion was massive indeed. Manufacturing output in the war years almost doubled as production of all major resources increased. The airplane manufacturing plant at Willow Run, Michigan, was more than a mile long, and the airplanes produced there and elsewhere made the difference in the war. By the time the struggle was over, more than 300,000 had rolled off the lines.

That enormous effort had a major impact on the business system in the United States. Discredited by the crash of 1929 and the depression that followed, businessmen regained the stature they had had in the years before. The government needed them and was increasingly willing to work on their terms. Secretary of War Henry L. Stimson, familiar with the corporate world through-

Workers at the Boeing aircraft plant in Seattle, Washington, in mid-1944. They have just completed their five thousandth Flying Fortress. (*Boeing Aircraft Co.*)

out his career, understood what was necessary. "If you are going to try to go to war, or to prepare for war, in a capitalist country," he said, "you have got to let business make money out of the process or business won't work."

The administration therefore did what was necessary to get business involved. It provided incentives and tax breaks that effectively underwrote the expense of plant expansion. It developed the cost-plus system whereby the government guaranteed all development and production costs and paid a percentage profit besides on the wartime goods it needed for the fight. The government also subsidized the creation of new industries altogether when demanded by the exigencies of war. With shipping lines disrupted and natural rubber in short supply, the government spent $700 million to create a new synthetic rubber industry to provide the product instead.

The government, in short, became a major partner in the industrial process. It helped foster an early version of the "military-industrial complex" that grew after the war. Large businesses were favored at the expense of smaller ones; ten corporations held one-third of the war orders placed. Yet the administration justified that concentration on the grounds of efficiency in the military effort, and it was a price planners were willing to pay.

The key to the business revival was the massive and continued spending necessary to fight the war, and spending went on as never before. Federal expenditures from 1940 to 1945 rose from $9.0 billion to $98.4 billion. The final bill came to more than $330 billion, a sum ten times larger than the direct expense of World War I and twice as large as the total of all spending in the history of the United States to that point. The spending, moreover, entailed large-scale borrowing as the government paid out far more than it took in. Congress chose not to raise taxes to the level necessary to pay for the full cost of the war, and money therefore had to be found in other ways. Only 40 percent of the total came from taxes. The rest came from bond sales and other borrowing mechanisms, as the national debt jumped from $43 billion in 1940 to $259 billion in 1945.

As the economy expanded, the labor force grew larger too. Union membership rose from 8.50 million in 1940 to 14.75 million in 1945, yet the union movement encountered difficulties during the war. Organized labor had done well in the year before Pearl Harbor, when the United Automobile Workers had gained a contract from Ford providing for a union shop—requiring workers hired to join the union—and for a dues checkoff, and other unions had made similar gains. But once the United States entered the war, deep-rooted divisions surfaced.

The American Federation of Labor and the Congress of Industrial Organizations, which had split apart in 1935, remained hostile to each other, perhaps even more so than before. As assembly-line production made craft distinctions less meaningful, more jurisdictional disputes occurred. At the same time, there were disputes with management, as unions contended they were not benefiting from the profits of war. The National War Labor Board, created in early 1942, sought to preserve labor peace and to settle labor-management disputes, but it was not wholly successful. It did grant certain concessions to labor, including the maintenance-of-membership formula, which specified that a union member who failed to quit within 15 days of the signing of a contract would remain a member for the duration of the contract. Yet it proved unable to stop a wave of strikes.

Though labor and business officials had taken a no-strike pledge on December 23, 1941, it was not legally binding, and as labor frustrations grew, a number of strikes took place. In 1943, 3.1 million workers went out on strike, though usually for only a few days, compared to less than 1 million the year before.

None of that slowed down the massive industrial effort. Full-scale production continued for the duration of the war. The military needed massive amounts of material, and the American industrial machine cranked out all that was demanded. As ships and planes were lost in battle, the factories at home could produce more without worrying about supply exceeding demand. With the infusion of money, unemployment dropped, as Keynes had predicted it would. Although about 8 million Americans—14.6 percent of the work force—were still out of work in mid-1940, that level soon began to fall until it reached 670,000—1.2 percent of the total labor force—in 1944.

The wartime experience left its mark. Watching their economy grow stronger, Americans became confident that with proper fiscal measures, depression need not recur. The government could monitor spending levels to maintain prosperity and keep unemployment down. Full employment was possible, liberal economists believed, and they now felt they knew how to use their tools to achieve that end.

Bureaucracy at War

As the government spent more and more money and brought the economy around, it became far more centralized than it had been before. The process had begun during the New Deal, but it now continued at an ever-faster rate. Increasingly, the federal bureaucracy became the focal point for actions in countless areas the private sector had served in the past.

Wartime expansion built on the changes of the decade gone by. Facing crises when he took office in 1933, FDR had brought major changes to bureaucratic structure in Washington. During the New Deal, the White House became an initiator of legislation and worked hand in hand with Congress to get things done. New agencies administered the relief programs and recovery schemes. To an outsider, the acronyms for these programs could be confusing, but the people affected came to rely on the NRA, CCC, AAA, WPA, and other organizations. They touched the lives of Americans throughout the United States and became an accepted part of the administrative scheme.

The war brought an even greater centralization of command. Increasing numbers of Americans went to work at government jobs. Between 1940 and 1945, the number of civilian employees in government posts rose from 1.0 million to 3.8 million. These employees assumed powers not held before and provided very necessary coordination in an economy gearing for war.

Federal officials staffed an entirely new bureaucracy. As hostilities threatened, Roosevelt began to develop the American capability for defense. Even before the attack on Pearl Harbor, he established a number of agencies to take command. First there was a National Defense Advisory Commission, then an Office of Production Management, later a Supply Priorities and Allocations Board. In characteristic fashion, the president split lines of authority and allowed agencies to compete with one another in the task at hand. After Pearl Harbor, sensing the need for a tighter grip on the process of mobilization, Roosevelt created a new War Production Board to provide that direction. It oversaw the complex process of conversion from peacetime production to wartime demand. In the face of some resistance, particularly in the automobile industry, the WPB had to outlaw certain kinds of production but finally got the process under way. When further coordination was necessary in 1942, the president acted again, this time to create an Office of Economic Stabilization, and in the next year an Office of War Mobilization. At the head of both was James F. Byrnes, a Supreme Court justice and popular southerner who resigned from the bench to become "economic czar." With his office in the White House and the whole mobilization process under his command, Byrnes was in casual title as well as in fact the "assistant president" of the United States.

Not only did the government guide the productive process in the struggle; it imposed its coordination in numerous other areas as well. Because federal spending increased so rapidly during the war years, inflation threatened to get out of control. The natural result of more money chasing the fewer goods available was a rise in prices purchasers were willing to pay, and in the first half of 1942 the cost-of-living index climbed 7 percent. When Roosevelt received the advice that "a little inflation would not hurt," he responded with the story of "a fellow who took a little cocaine and kept coming back for more until he was a drug addict." He and the members of his staff remembered the experience of the First World War, when prices had risen 62 percent between 1914 and 1918 and another 40 percent in the years immediately thereafter. They were determined that such a spurt should not occur again.

The bureaucracy expanded to bring inflation under control. Initially the Office of Price Administration and Civilian Supply, established by executive order in April 1941 to prevent profiteering and price hiking that could raise the cost of living, had only the power of "jawboning." When that proved ineffective, another act in early 1942 gave the agency, now known as OPA, some teeth. There were selective price controls for a time, but then in April the General Maximum Price Regulation mandated a freeze on all retail prices at March levels. Another Price Control Act, passed in October, further extended the effort to hold the line.

The other side of the regulatory apparatus related to wage control. For prices to remain in line, the administration argued, wages too should stay within certain bounds. The War Labor Board (WLB) was the organization responsible for control. In July 1942 the WLB adopted the "Little Steel" formula. Faced with a wage demand by workers of the Bethlehem, Republic, Youngstown, and Inland steel companies, the board took January 1, 1941, as a starting point and allowed a 15 percent increase to meet the rise in living costs to May 1942. That measure, applied elsewhere as well, provided an element of restraint, but not enough. The October 1942 Price Control Act also provided for more stringent wage controls, and those, in time, kept inflation in check.

With all the regulatory machinery in the war years, how well did the process actually work? The productive effort was a major success. American enterprise produced the goods necessary to bring the Axis crashing down. Similarly, the economic controls worked to the desired end. There were violations of all sorts, as an illegal black market flourished for the duration of the war and provided items in short supply to those willing to pay any price. Nonetheless, the general system was successful. Scarce goods were distributed relatively fairly, and inflation remained in check. Over the last two years of the war, the cost-of-living index increased no more than 3 percent, and, paradoxically, though OPA was one of the most unpopular federal agencies, Gallup polls revealed that the American people supported the efforts to keep prices from getting out of hand.

The Politics of War

Operating at the top and overseeing the vast process, Franklin Roosevelt understood the implications of the changes taking place. He knew that the executive establishment was assuming added authority at the expense of the legislative branch. He knew too that the process of domestic reform had run its course as the 1930s came to an end. Hoping to avoid unnecessary antagonism, he cut back on New Deal initiatives during the war. At a press conference in late 1943, he declared that the New Deal had arrived when the patient—the United States—had suffered from a serious internal disorder. But then, at Pearl Harbor, the patient had been in a terrible external crash. "Old Dr. New Deal," Roosevelt said, "didn't know 'nothing' about legs and arms. He knew a great deal about internal medicine, but nothing about surgery. So he got his partner, who was an orthopedic surgeon, Dr. Win-the-War, to take care of this fellow who had been in this bad accident."

The New Deal remained on the back burner for the duration of the war. Roosevelt's implicit pledge indicated he would not push for further reform in return for support for his efforts to win the war. In foreign affairs, political opponents proved willing to follow his lead. On the domestic front, however, they gave him a hard time. They were not content simply to see the New Deal wind down; they wanted to roll it back altogether. In Congress a coalition of southern Democrats and Republicans, which had begun to coalesce in the late 1930s, now began to attack. Arguing that the return of prosperity made New Deal agencies unnecessary, legislators in 1942 and 1943 liquidated the Civilian Conservation Corps, eliminated the National Youth Administration, dissolved the National Resources Planning Board, and gave the Farm Security Administration just enough funding to limp along. There were still tasks that the various agencies could have done, but Congress was determined that they go.

That effort to circumscribe executive power only highlighted changes that had taken place. The power of the president was clearly expanding, and despite congressional efforts to limit the process, it was questionable if much could be done. Although Theodore Roosevelt and Woodrow Wilson had enhanced the powers of their office in the first decades of the twentieth century, not until the presidency of FDR did that expansion proceed in a systematized way from which there could be no turning back. The New Deal response to crisis cast the president in a major role, and in 1939 Roosevelt regularized the changes that had taken place. His creation of the executive office, with administrative channels and important agencies under his control, provided the mechanism for later expansion and gave the president the authority to move as he saw fit.

Roosevelt, meanwhile, assumed greater powers in other ways and provided a model for his successors. Committed to an activist role, he proved willing to act in the foreign as well as the domestic sphere. When Britain was struggling against Germany in the early days of the war, FDR chose to implement a deal trading destroyers to Britain in return for bases by executive order rather than by congressional vote. The need for national defense was his justification then as later, when he inaugurated a convoy system across the Atlantic and ordered the navy to respond to German vessels by shooting on sight even before the United States entered the war.

During the struggle itself, Roosevelt's approach only enhanced his powers. In the greatest conflict of all time, he helped provide the coordination necessary to win, and through his active participation in the major wartime conferences abroad he established an example for the postwar years. He relished the use of power and enjoyed the authority he had. Criticism notwithstanding, he used his power in the national interest, for he sensed that action was necessary if victory was to be won. In the end, government grew to an extraordinary degree, and presidential power grew at the same time. There as elsewhere, the war left a legacy that could not be denied.

At the war's end, Americans may have hungered for a simpler past and members of Congress may have looked for a scaling down of the executive role, but the country had changed. New channels of authority governed the patterns of the postwar years. The government had forged close relationships with industry in the war, and those ties had led to the development of the atomic bomb and numerous other implements of war. The basic research had come from scholars in American universities, now more thoroughly committed to the needs—and funds—of the military establishment than ever before. Those ties, in the face of increasing demands for defense in the Cold War period, meant that government would remain influential. There was no turning back.

With victory assured, Americans accepted, almost as a matter of course, the changes that had taken place. They looked to government to promote prosperity in ways that had not been possible before. Roosevelt sought to encourage that sense by his espousal of an "Economic Bill of Rights"—with guarantees of homes, jobs, and educational opportunities—for the years after the war. Congress was not yet ready to go that far, but did pass the G.I. Bill to provide those benefits to veterans of the war and thereby at least kept the vision alive for other Americans at home. The government had provided before and could provide again. The days of passive government had come to an end.

AMERICAN SOCIETY AT WAR

Americans welcomed the changes taking place. The war helped unify the nation, just as it allowed the unemployed to return to work. After years of depression, the revival of prosperity brought a sense of long-overdue relief. After years of debate over involvement in foreign struggles, people could now devote themselves enthusiastically to involvement in a just cause. As the military demanded more and more materiel, job opportunities opened up for women and members of a number of minority groups and provided hope for a greater voice in postwar society. Not all groups, however, fared comfortably during the struggle. Japanese-Americans in particular suffered real hardship in the United States.

The American Mood

Compared to other nations in the war, the United States was fortunate. Almost 400,000 Americans were military casualties, but the struggle left 2.8 million German soldiers and 7.5 million Russian soldiers dead before it had run its course. And with the addition of civilian losses to the military figures, an estimated 20 million citizens of the Soviet Union lost their lives. The United States entered the war late, was far from the major fields of battle, and never had to undergo the total mobilization experienced by some of the other fighting nations. Less than 10 percent of the American people fought in the struggle. By the middle of the conflict, nearly seven out of ten people in the United States indicated that they had not had to make any "real sacrifices" as a result of the war.

For most Americans the war brought a sense of uplift lacking in the decade before. It sparked the conviction that the nation was engaged in a righteous crusade. It gave people a sense of common cause. Unified and united, they were willing to work together to see the struggle through to victory. In 1942 anthropologist Margaret Mead observed that for Americans to make the necessary commitment, "we must feel that we are on the side of the Right." In World War II Americans felt strongly that virtue was on their side. Fascism was brutal and irrational and appealed to the worst in human nature. As poet Archibald MacLeish wrote, it was "in its essence a revolt of man against himself—a revolt of stunted, half-formed, darkened men against a human world beyond their reach and most of all against the human world of reason and intelligence and sense." Against that foe, American democracy stood ready to save the day.

Americans were confident that the Allied side would win. In his address requesting a declaration of war from Congress on December 8, 1941, Franklin Roosevelt proclaimed his abiding faith that "we will gain the inevitable triumph—so help us God." The Office of War Information, America's propaganda agency in World War II, put out for people at home and abroad the basic message "that we are coming, that we are going to win, and that in the long run everybody will be better off because we won." Americans believed that, and it gave them sustenance in their fight.

They marched off to battle in high spirits. "Goodbye, Momma, I'm Off to Yokohama," proclaimed one popular song. "Praise the Lord and Pass the Ammunition," echoed another. American magazines, correspondent Ernie Pyle wrote, saw the war as "romantic and exciting, full of heroics and vitality," and the soldiers he observed showed good morale throughout. Yet he saw too that they were often afraid, and he gave them credit for their successful effort on the front lines to overcome their fear.

The war changed those who fought it. Even more, it changed the face of American society at home. Working at well-paying jobs once again, young people who had chosen to postpone marriage or family during the Depression now ceased to wait. The American population, which had grown by only 3 million in the 1930s, rose by 6.5 million between 1940 and 1945. The baby boom, with its implications for the postwar years, was under way.

The war also led people to find new ways of spending their money. Consumer items were in short supply, just as materialistic values surfaced again. When rationed goods were unavailable, or when the black market could not provide, Americans spent their money wherever they could. They spent it on entertainment, on nightclubs and movies and resorts. They bought books in ever-increasing numbers. Wendell Willkie's *One World* sold faster than any book before it, and paperback editions began to abound. Americans purchased pharmaceuticals more than in the past; the $95 million spent in 1942 was $20 million more than in 1941. People were, of course, ailing no more than they had been earlier; they simply had money to spare. After the deprivations of the Depression, it was enjoyable to buy things just for the fun of spending again. And to make sure Americans did not forget, advertising men promised new and better items when civilian production resumed.

Americans searching for amusement remained intensely interested in professional sports. Baseball, the national game, was hit hard by the war, as more than 4000 of 5700 players in the major and minor leagues joined the military forces. Even so, baseball survived. Roosevelt recognized its value as a builder of morale and encouraged its continuation for the duration of the struggle. Major-league games were played in twilight, to allow working fans to attend while still honoring the ban on night contests in some parts of the country. They often featured teams whose rosters had changed dramatically since Pearl Harbor. Gone were Joe DiMaggio, Bob Feller, Ted Williams, Hank Greenberg, Peewee Reese, and scores of others. Instead, the lineups featured virtual unknowns. One such player was Pete Gray, who joined the St. Louis Browns in 1945. Gray played in 77 games and hit .218—with one arm. A good outfielder who caught the ball in his glove, then flipped it in the air, grabbed it with his bare hand, and threw it back, he was also proficient at the drag bunt. Crowds were interested in Gray, and he became a box-office attraction.

Americans responded to changed times by traveling more than in the past. Some set off to cities like Seattle and Los Angeles and Detroit to take available jobs. In the South and Southwest and on the Pacific Coast, the cities grew rapidly, often too fast. Mobile, Alabama, grew 33 percent in a three-year period. New Orleans, Louisiana, increased by 20 percent in 1942 and kept on growing. Other cities followed the same pattern. Not all movement, however, was for purposes of employment. Many people took vacations if they could not spend their money in other ways. With automobile travel restricted by gasoline rationing, they rode the railroads and buses more than before. Transportation was a profitable enterprise again.

Americans made some sacrifices, to be sure. Despite full employment, they often found conditions in crowded cities to be uncomfortable at best. Rural residents who had gravitated to urban regions where the jobs were located had the hardest time of all. They found the slums lonely and isolating, with none of the bonds they had known earlier. The Nevels family in Harriet Arnow's novel *The Dollmaker* suffered all of the dislocations real migrants endured. Coming from Kentucky, family members found the patterns of Detroit strange and hard to accept. They were misfits in their new home, and for them the human costs of the wartime struggle were high. One child ran away, and another died in an accident related to the strains of city life.

On balance, though, the war treated Americans well. Though they hungered for goods they had done without in the 1930s and resigned themselves to waiting a while longer until the war's end, they knew that prosperity was back and plenty beckoned once more. The better times they had longed for after the Great Crash of 1929 had finally arrived.

Women at War

Within the society as a whole, a number of groups took advantage of the necessities of war and made social gains. Women were without question second-class citizens at the start of the struggle. During the Depression, wives had found it difficult to work, for men trying to support families resented the competition they offered. Many jobs were closed to them, and in the jobs they did hold, the pay was usually much less than men received.

Production was the first priority at home, and with workers needed, it was undeniable that women constituted a major labor reserve. During the war 6.5 million women entered the work force and eventually made up 36 percent of the working population, compared to 25 percent in 1940. For the first time there were more married than single women workers. They gravitated initially to light jobs that men had given up, but midway through the war they moved into heavy industry too.

Women worked in steel plants, shipyards, and airplane factories for the duration; in some they did most of the work. They ran machines, cut dies, and operated large cranes. In short, they performed all kinds of industrial tasks. Women also joined branches of the service open to them: the Women's Auxil-

Women welders in New Britain, Connecticut, in 1943. (*Library of Congress*)

iary Army Corps (WAC) and the navy's Women Accepted for Voluntary Emergency Service (WAVES).

Women thoroughly enjoyed the experience of employment. "Some just love their jobs," one told the Office of War Information. "I think they for the first time in their life feel important." It often proved "vastly more stimulating and rewarding than housework," another found. Women who were working already finally had a chance at occupational mobility. Nearly 30 percent of the 2.5 million women entering the manufacturing force came from other jobs that were less attractive.

The male response to women working was mixed. Some men feared that women would become too strong, too much like men. They feared that women would reject, or at least neglect, their children as they found outside jobs more exciting than activities at home. When women entered military service they sometimes faced a cool response. On learning that women were being assigned to his camp, one marine officer was said to have grumbled: "Goddamn it all. First they send us dogs. Now it's women."

To encourage women to work at the necessary tasks, the government sought to glamorize the roles they could play. "Rosie the Riveter" became the media symbol of the woman at work. She could do a man's job—but still maintain her feminine qualities at the same time. In the newspapers and magazines and on radio programs, women at work were praised. A concerted propaganda effort helped change traditional attitudes in the interests of the war.

Even so, women faced problems in the labor force. While working they still had to provide for their families and homes, and that remained a major task. Despite a need for day-care facilities for children, the government never adequately met the demand. Although the government adopted the principle that women would receive equal pay for equal work, in fact men continued to earn a good deal more. In 1944 the average weekly wage for women was $31.21, compared to $54.65 for men.

Nonetheless, the experience was a good one that few women regretted. At the war's end, some women happily returned home, but others wanted to continue to work. Various surveys between 1943 and 1945 revealed that 61 to 85 percent wanted to stay in their jobs. They faced pressures, however, from returning servicemen and from other male workers who had their own positions in mind, and many women drifted away as a result. By 1947 the female part of the work force had fallen to 28 percent. Yet even for women who did not remain employed, the experience of the war stayed in mind. It created a new sense of independence and demonstrated opportunities for future work. The status of women changed little in the war, but the labor experience encouraged many women to move into previously closed areas and to build on that start in the postwar years.

Blacks at War

Blacks, too, were able to use the demands of war to bring about social change. Engaged in a long-standing struggle for equality, they were interested in advancing their own cause as they participated in the larger war. Conditions in the 1940s reflected the gulf between the American dream and the American reality for blacks in the United States. Rigid patterns of segregation had developed in the late nineteenth and early twentieth centuries, and the Jim Crow system separating the races was particularly entrenched in the South. Separate schools for blacks and whites were the norm. Separate hotels, restaurants, and other facilities kept the races apart. In the North segregation was less legally entrenched, but residential patterns, with blacks congregating in urban ghettos, produced the same result. Racial tension in northern cities was often equally pronounced. Organizations such as the National Association for the Advancement of Colored People (NAACP) resisted in whatever ways they could, yet progress came all too slowly for the individuals concerned.

There had been but minimal change in the decades before World War II. Blacks who supported the American effort in the First World War were disillusioned to discover in the subsequent peacetime years that there was little inclination on the part of either the government or the public to support them in their own fight for equal rights. The New Deal of the 1930s for a time seemed to give hope for change, yet with other pressing political priorities, little was done for the black race as a separate group during the Great Depression, and some New Deal programs, in fact, only perpetuated preexisting patterns of separation. Even so, blacks benefited from other efforts that assisted the poor in general, and they responded by starting to vote for the Democratic party for the first time since the Civil War.

At the start of World War II, blacks found themselves slighted on a variety of fronts. They faced continued discrimination as they sought jobs or positions in the military forces. Blacks were not allowed to join the air force or marine corps. In the navy they were permitted to enlist only in the all-black messmen's branch. In the army they were restricted to the few regular black units that had been created after the Civil War.

There were other indignities too. Blacks who did join the army sometimes found prisoners of war treated better than they were. They had to watch the army, in a decision endorsed by the American Red Cross, segregate the blood plasma of whites and blacks, even though there was no difference at all. Frustrations mounted, especially since the administration seemed unwilling to move toward change.

The secretary of war had strong views on the question of race. Henry L. Stimson, a crusty old Republican who had served as secretary of war under William Howard Taft and secretary of state under Herbert Hoover before returning to head the War Department again under FDR, considered blacks inferior, for they had scored lower than whites on intelligence tests in World War I. Those tests measured education rather than intelligence, but Stimson's mind was set. Blacks were unfit for flying, he believed, and in the same vein he declared: "Leadership is not imbedded in the negro race yet and to try to make commissioned officers to lead men into battle—colored men—is only to work a disaster to both."

Other Americans seemed to agree, and even more felt there was no real problem at all. A poll in 1942 showed that six out of ten Americans believed that blacks accepted their place in society. Roosevelt himself was unwilling to act. Preoccupied by the war, he also knew that southern members of Congress had votes he needed for other things. "I don't think, quite frankly," he said at the end of 1943, "that we can bring about the millennium at this time."

Faced with those conditions, black Americans were determined to wage their own two-pronged attack. They launched a "double V" campaign—V for victory in the war against the dictators overseas and V for victory in their own struggle for fair treatment at home.

One of the more important leaders, even before the United States entered the war, was A. Philip Randolph, head of the Brotherhood of Sleeping Car Porters. Respected by other black leaders, he decided that it was time to press the government to uphold the rights of American blacks. In January 1941 he proposed a massive march on Washington under the slogan WE LOYAL NEGRO AMERICAN CITIZENS DEMAND THE RIGHT TO WORK AND FIGHT FOR OUR COUNTRY. The demands included an end to discrimination in employment, an end to discrimination and segregation in the federal government, and an end to segregation in the armed forces. Randolph wanted to mobilize the black masses, to "create faith by Negroes in Negroes" in working to attain their own ends. The movement frightened FDR, for he feared the possibility of violence if masses of blacks descended on Washington. After his attempts at sweet-talking failed, he finally got Randolph to call off the march in return for an executive order establishing a President's Fair Employment Practices Committee (FEPC).

The FEPC was from the first underfunded and understaffed. It lacked rigorous powers of coercion and had to rely on persuasion alone. When war production was clearly threatened by manpower shortages resulting from the drafting of white workers, the agency could press firms to upgrade blacks to more responsible positions and to hire others to fill jobs previously closed to them. In other situations, though, the record was less good.

Even so, the war itself brought change. Blacks moved up to better jobs and eventually gained greater opportunities in the military services. More important, they showed a determination to take matters into their own hands. The March on Washington movement showed a new mood of militancy on the part of American blacks, a mood underscored by other actions as well. While the older NAACP worked through legal and political channels, the new Congress of Racial Equality (CORE) stressed the tactics of nonviolent resistance, and those began to show results. In Chicago and Washington, activists brought about the integration of previously segregated restaurants. In Baltimore and Yellow Springs, Ohio, they opened up theaters that had been previously closed to blacks.

More ominous was the increasing incidence of violence at home. Black migration from the rural southern areas to the urban centers of war production caused terrible crowding and competition for scarce services in the cities. Racial confrontations were often the result. In the summer of 1943 there were racial explosions in nine army training camps. Far more serious riots erupted in Detroit and Harlem that showed vividly the depth of the frustrations that were growing all the time.

The Detroit riot grew out of long-simmering tensions. Earlier there had been a struggle over a housing unit built for blacks, then demanded by whites to ease the crowding they also felt. Black protests finally led to their regaining the complex, but not without ill will on both sides. Conditions continued to deteriorate until one extremely hot Sunday evening in June 1943, when matters got completely out of control. Scuffles between blacks and whites led to more serious violence. Rumors on both sides fanned the flames. Before long a full-scale race riot was under way. By the time the riot was over several days later, 25 blacks and 9 whites were dead, approximately 700 people were injured, and about $2 million of property had been destroyed.

In Harlem, in New York City, a similar uprising occurred at the beginning of August. In response to a rumor that a policeman had killed a black soldier, the community erupted. Sweeping through the business district, people smashed windows, entered stores, and took goods. Though there were no battles between blacks and whites as in Detroit, 6 blacks were nonetheless killed and 300 injured. And the uprising reflected the same frustrations and resentments against oppression that were felt by blacks throughout the land.

Those episodes provided vivid evidence of an explosive force that could not be contained forever. As Walter White, head of the NAACP, wrote: "A wind *is* rising—a wind of determination by the havenots of the world to share the benefits of freedom and prosperity which the haves of the world have tried to keep exclusively for themselves. . . . Whether that wind develops into a hurricane is a decision we must make."

Hispanics and the War

Like women and blacks, Hispanics faced discrimination during World War II. In 1940 there were about 1.5 million Spanish-speaking people in the United

States. Some lived in eastern cities; many more resided in the West and Southwest. Chicanos—Mexican-Americans—were the most numerous. Chicanos often found themselves grouped together with blacks, separated by skin color, with the further disadvantage of a different language as well. "For Coloreds and Mexicans," a sign outside a Texas church declared. Deprived of decent jobs, they were frequently forced to live in run-down areas. Without political influence there seemed to be no way to break the poverty cycle.

Labor shortages again made the crucial difference. Needing manpower, the government drafted Chicanos into the armed forces in large numbers. Farm workers, like other rural Americans, gravitated to the cities in search of better-paying jobs. They were able to get work in the major war-production centers, and settled in Seattle, San Diego, Chicago, Detroit, and other places where Spanish-speaking migrants had gravitated before.

At the same time, the war caused an acute shortage of farm labor, and the United States looked to Mexicans to help meet the need. Faced with the problem of providing food for home-front as well as for Allied forces, American growers sought to import Mexicans to work in the fields. They initially wanted simply to open the border and to hire at the lowest possible wage, but Mexico insisted on contracts that guaranteed basic rights. A program begun in 1942 led to the entrance of several hundred thousand braceros over the next few years.

Despite protective agreements and new jobs, Mexicans and Mexican-Americans continued to suffer discrimination in the United States. Braceros complained of withheld wages and dismal working conditions. Industrial workers often found themselves overlooked for the supervisory or skilled jobs that whites got. Like women, they sometimes received lower wages for the same work.

Chicano tensions, like black frustrations, were most visible in the crowded cities. Many young Mexican-Americans belonged to neighborhood groups or gangs and favored a distinctive costume. The zoot suit consisted of trousers flared at the knees but tighter at the ankles, a long key chain, and a felt hat. It set them apart and posed an ostensible threat to members of the middle class who associated the costume with gang activity.

In early June 1943, sailors based in Los Angeles entered Mexican sections of the city to seek revenge on Chicanos who had allegedly attacked them in their search for women. Rampaging throught the streets, the sailors entered bars and movie theaters and tore the zoot suits off the Chicano youths. Law enforcement officials either stood aside or arrested Mexican-Americans without cause. The press, long critical of Chicanos, only fanned the flames. Eventually naval personnel were ordered out, and the riot came to an end. Like the black-white confrontations in other cities, however, it left a surge of anger in its wake.

Native Americans

Indians in the United States became actively involved in the war effort too. The treatment they had received over the past 150 years "could hardly be expected to produce loyal citizens devoted to the Nation's welfare and willing to defend it against its enemies," John Collier, commissioner of Indian affairs, observed. Yet Native Americans sensed the larger stakes of the struggle and willingly offered their military and industrial support.

Though Indians in three states were denied the right to vote, they were still subject to the draft. Approximately 25,000 Native Americans served in all branches of the military, most of them in the army. Indians from tribes with a warrior tradition proved especially willing to enlist. The Mission Indian Federation of California sent "a message of loyalty and readiness to serve our great Nation." The Crow tribe of Montana enthusiastically offered the government all of its manpower.

Native Americans served valiantly in combat. Ira H. Hayes, a Pima from Arizona, was one of three survivors of the episode at Mount Suribachi on Iwo Jima where marines managed to raise the American flag. Some Navajos worked as code talkers. Their language was so obscure that it served as a vehicle for transmitting marine corps messages by radio and phone.

Indians still faced some discrimination. On occasion they were limited to clerical duty or other support work behind the lines. Traditional stereotypes also remained. In units with only one Indian, he often found himself called "chief." Still, military service went smoothly, and Native Americans were decorated for their deeds.

Indians provided substantial home-front service as well. They worked in war industries throughout the country. Two thousand Navajos helped build a sizable ordnance depot in New Mexico. Other Indians constructed aircraft on the West Coast and all kinds of other military items in the major centers of war production.

The war sped up the process of Native American assimilation into the larger society. As thousands left the reservations for military or industrial jobs, they had to make adjustments to the outside world. Indians who served abroad or moved to other parts of the nation were less likely to settle back into older patterns when the war came to an end. Some made the transition more easily than others, but all had to confront a change.

Italian- and Japanese-Americans

Some ethnic or racial groups had even more difficulty during the war. Those who came from nations with which the United States was fighting had the worst time. Major foreign crises have often caused hysteria at home, and World War II was no exception. In the First World War, German-Americans had borne the brunt of hostility in America. Two decades later those tensions were forgotten, as Germans had assimilated more fully into the mainstream of American life. Other groups found themselves targeted this time.

For Italian-Americans conditions were harsh and grim. In the 1930s many of the immigrants, uneducated and unskilled, had trouble finding jobs. Outsiders in their new home, they looked on Benito Mussolini and the "New Italy" with a sense of pride. They were caught in the middle between two cultures, yet no choice was necessary until the United States went to war. Then they embraced the American cause, but the government nonetheless branded noncitizen Italians as "enemy aliens" in the nation they called their own. That designation was finally lifted, and Italian-Americans fought valiantly in the struggle, but for some a sense of alienation remained.

For Japanese-Americans the situation was even worse. As of 1940, they numbered slightly more than 125,000 in the United States, roughly one-tenth of one percent of the population of the country. Concentrated on the West Coast, largely in California, they became the focus of hostility soon after the Pearl Harbor attack. "Don't kid yourselves and don't let someone tell you there are good Japs," Representative Alfred Elliot of California declared in Congress in early 1942. "A good solution to the Jap problem," the governor of Idaho said, "would be to send them all back to Japan, then sink the island. They live like rats, breed like rats and act like rats."

Since that solution was not practicable, a newly created War Relocation Authority, acting with presidential and congressional approval, brushed constitutional niceties aside and moved Japanese-American citizens and noncitizens alike to camps in the interior. There, deprived of property and possessions, most had to remain for the duration of the war. Some were segregated still further in concentration camps for refusing to renounce their loyalty to the emperor of Japan.

The treatment of the Japanese-Americans was the worst violation of civil liberties on the American side of the struggle. Authorities used military neces-

Japanese residents of Los Angeles preparing to depart for the evacuation reception center at Manzanar in 1942. (*UPI/Bettmann Newsphotos*)

sity and national security as justification for what they did, but even they later had to acknowledge that their actions had gone too far. The Japanese-Americans were clearly casualties of the war.

THE UNITED STATES AND THE WAR

World War II changed the United States. It brought a stronger government role, a stronger presidential role, and an understanding that the economy could be guided more aggressively than before. It opened up new opportunities for women, blacks, Chicanos, and other groups as they filled empty jobs and produced the implements of war. It revived a sense of optimism that shaped American policy and mood for the next 20 years.

The changes were not totally new, of course. Government had been growing larger and stronger since the first days of the New Deal. The proliferation of new agencies and the centralization of executive authority were well under way when the war began. A women's movement had been voicing demands for more than half a century. Black organizations had been active in their pursuit of equality for decades. The optimistic, materialistic mood that characterized the home front in the 1940s and fed into the future reflected a similar heady mood in the 1920s before the Great Crash. There were certain continuities, to be sure, but the war helped to crystallize the patterns of the postwar years.

Once committed, Americans embraced their cause in an expansive way. On all fronts they worked for the victory they knew lay ahead. When the war was over, the United States stood ready for a new age. With the Axis powers devastated, with the Soviet Union exhausted, and with the western European Allies depleted by the fight, the United States by contrast was vital and eager to assert its enormous strength. The economy was healthy, and the people were ready for the "American century" they knew lay ahead. While millions of inhabitants of the far corners of the globe faced starvation, Americans were well fed; in fact, obesity was beginning to be viewed as a public health problem in the United States. Militarily, America was strong and now had possession of the secret of atomic energy, which had helped bring the war to an end. Resources seemed abundant, and the nation had the scientific and technological talent to use them in ever more exciting ways.

The United States emerged from the war confident, perhaps too confident. Americans had performed in the war with a mission, and that sense of mission remained. Propaganda had trumpeted the American virtues at home and abroad, and Americans believed what they saw and heard. They had expectations for the future, related to their acceptance of success in the past, that might prove hard to fulfill in the postwar period ahead.

SUGGESTIONS FOR FURTHER READING

There is a voluminous literature dealing with the military side of World War II. A. Russell Buchanan, *The United States and World War II,* 2 vols. (1964), serves as a good starting point. Martha Byrd Hoyle, *A World in Flames: A History of World War II* (1970) is a brief but useful overview of the struggle.

On the diplomacy of the war, Gaddis Smith, *American Diplomacy During the Second World War* (1965) is the best short account. For fuller descriptions, see Herbert Feis, *Churchill, Roosevelt, Stalin: The War They Waged and the Peace They Sought* (1967); William Hardy McNeill, *America, Britain, and Russia: Their Cooperation and Conflict, 1941–1946* (1970); and Gabriel Kolko, *The Politics of War: The World and United States Foreign Policy, 1943–1945* (1970).

For the human side of the front lines, see correspondent Ernie Pyle's *Here Is Your War* (1971) and cartoonist Bill Mauldin's *Up Front* (1945).

For the home front, John Morton Blum, *V Was for Victory: Politics and American Culture During World War II* (1976) and Richard Polenberg, *War and Society: The United States, 1941–1945* (1972) are essential for understanding the changes taking place. Geoffrey Perrett, *Days of Sadness, Years of Triumph: The American People, 1939–1945* (1973) provides a narrative overview of the war at home. Richard Lingeman, *Don't You Know There's a War On? The American Home Front, 1941–1945* (1970) is another readable assessment of developments inside the United States.

On selected topics, Bruce Catton, *The War Lords of Washington* (1948) describes the process of mobilization. Nelson Lichtenstein, *Labor's War at Home: The CIO in World War II* (1982) deals with labor's side of the war. Philip J. Funigiello, *The Challenge to Urban Liberalism: Federal-State Relations During World War II* (1978) is a useful assessment of the government's role. Alan Clive, *State of War: Michigan in World War II* (1979) is an outstanding state study. John W. Jeffries, *Testing the Roosevelt Coalition: Connecticut Society and Politics in the Era of World War II* (1979) is a perceptive account of political change during the war.

Regarding women's roles in the war, Susan M. Hartmann, *The Home Front and Beyond: American Women in the 1940s* (1982) and Karen Anderson, *Wartime Women: Sex Roles, Family Relations, and the Status of Women During World War II* (1981) are perceptive and thorough.

Literature about other groups is growing. On blacks, Neil A. Wynn, *The Afro-American and the Second World War* (1975) provides a good place to start. On the Japanese-American experience, see Roger Daniels, *Concentration Camps U.S.A.: Japanese Americans and World War II* (1971).

Harriet Arnow, *The Dollmaker* (1954) is a moving fictional account of the dislocations of war.

chapter *2*

Cold War and Containment

The Cold War was the greatest single force affecting the United States after World War II. Following the Axis defeat, the alliance between East and West fell apart and was replaced by an adversary relationship that dominated Soviet-American relations in the succeeding years. The new struggle stopped short of erupting into a major shooting war, yet still had a profound impact on American affairs. It led to ever more intensive efforts to restrain the Russian foe and provided the framework within which all other issues unfolded. The increased spending for defense encouraged economic growth but frequently shortchanged social programs and slowed the course of reform at home. Even more important, the Cold War altered American attitudes about the Communist threat, as it sparked an ill-advised attempt to ensure a new standard of loyalty within the United States.

The Cold War between the Soviet Union and the United States had its origins in the tensions of the Second World War. The major allies had worked together for a common end, yet were only too aware of how fragile the Grand Alliance was. As the conflict drew to an end, each side insisted on its own priorities even more vigorously than before, and agreement became increasingly difficult to attain. Hope for cooperation faded as friction grew, and international suspicion proved to be the enduring legacy of the war.

THE SOVIET UNION AND THE UNITED STATES

In 1945, and for the next few years, the Soviet Union and the United States were the major Cold War protagonists. The United States remained closely tied to Great Britain, but the British had been devastated by the European conflict and were unable to provide much support. Though the United States sought Britain's advice and maintained a united western front, the real initiative came from Washington. A similar situation held in the East, where the Russians claimed the allegiance of Poland, Czechoslovakia, and other nearby lands, yet dictated policy on their own. Even after the Chinese joined the Russian camp, the Soviet Union remained the dominant force.

American Goals

The United States emerged from World War II supreme and strong. It had fought hard but now found that it was in far better shape than any of the other powers. Its economy was healthy, and its industrial capacity was greater than ever before. Having weathered both the ravages of the Depression and the challenges from abroad, Americans now looked forward to the better times to come. In the war itself they had provided materials for all members of the Grand Alliance, and American planes and ships and tanks had made the difference in the end. Now ready for reconversion and a return to peacetime production, they hoped to continue selling their wares around the globe.

Implicitly, the United States viewed the world as an interdependent whole in which each nation played a necessary part. Americans wanted to eliminate trade barriers and economic restraints wherever they were found so that the fruits of their industry could be accessible to all. More than altruism was involved. Unless foreign markets could be found, Americans feared that they might face the prospect of decline and the horror of depression once more. "We've got to export three times as much as we exported just before the war if we want to keep our industry running at somewhat near capacity," Under Secretary of State William L. Clayton told a congressional committee in March 1945. Continued prosperity depended on access abroad.

It was not an entirely selfish vision that Americans shared. They were proud of their democratic system and what it had achieved. With a sense of mission deeply rooted in their past, twentieth-century Americans shared the old Puritan notion that their state should be as a city upon a hill for the rest of the world to see. That sentiment had manifested itself in the expansionary fervor of the 1840s and the imperial escapades of the 1890s, then even more dramatically in the two world wars. Victorious at last in the latest crusade, Americans hoped to generalize from that experience and offer their principles of liberty and free enterprise abroad. They genuinely believed that these concepts would benefit other people, wherever they were. And by assisting them, the United States would benefit too, for as President Harry Truman observed, "We ourselves cannot enjoy prosperity in a world of economic stagnation."

Russian Goals

The Soviet Union had an altogether different notion of what lay ahead. Worn out by the war, the Russians were concerned, almost obsessively, with their own security. Stalin feared that the Germans would recover quickly. "Give them twelve to fifteen years and they'll be on their feet again," he remarked. "And that's why the unity of the Slavs is important." The Soviets were determined to head off another attack, and with the German invasion firmly in memory, they insisted on defensible borders and friendly regimes on their western flank. They wanted and needed stable and submissive governments in the eastern European states that would be receptive to their military and political demands. Whereas the United States hoped for access to all corners of the globe, the Soviet Union insisted on absolute authority in its part of the world and was unwilling to compromise there at all.

The Russians had moved toward their goal while the war was still under way. In October 1944, Stalin and Churchill had come to a secret agreement allotting influence in the Balkan states. At a meeting in Moscow, the British prime minister had opened the matter by proposing that the Russians have a 90 percent predominance in Rumania, 75 percent in Bulgaria, 50 percent in Yugoslavia and Hungary, and 10 percent in Greece, with Britain—and the other Allies—having the remainder of influence in those lands. After Churchill put the proposal on paper, he later recalled, Stalin "took his blue pencil and made a large tick on it, and passed it back to us." The matter was settled "in no more than it takes to set down."

That agreement reflected the Soviet intention to remain supreme in those areas where Russian interests were paramount. In the war itself, the Soviets had muted their ideological line as they downplayed the notion of world revolution and mobilized support for more nationalistic goals. They still feared capitalist encirclement, still had confidence in the triumph of communism in the end, but the message was trumpeted less aggressively than before. As the war drew to a close, Stalin for a time seemed to maintain the same position. He pointed less toward world conquest and more toward support of socialism in Russia itself and in the areas nearby. But in those areas he was determined to stand firm. The Russians would brook no interference in their region.

In the immediate postwar period, the Russians generally made good on their guarantees. They stripped their zone of Germany of remaining industrial might as they followed their own interpretation of an agreement that had been left intentionally vague. At the same time, however, they allowed non-Communist governments in a number of neighboring states. In Finland, Stalin permitted an independent regime as long as the Finns remained friendly to the Russians in foreign affairs, while in Hungary a Soviet-sponsored election led to a non-Communist government. Russian authority was more visible in Poland. In June 1945, Stalin allowed several pro-Western Poles to enter the government in fulfillment of the Yalta accords, but the regime remained Communist nonetheless, and the elections agreed to in 1945 never took place.

Regardless of how cautiously Russia moved, its basic position still conflicted with that of the United States. Soviet dominance in eastern Europe denied American access to economic involvement there and led to some concern about the future expansion of trade. So too were American hopes for democratic self-determination being denied. The pattern was not a promising one. Barriers erected in one part of the world might soon appear elsewhere. Economic interests and missionary impulses both were being thwarted from the start.

Harry S Truman

A new American president faced the Russians as the Second World War came to an end. Harry Truman, who had assumed power on Franklin Roosevelt's death in April 1945, was not particularly well prepared for the job. A Missouri politician who drew support from the notorious Pendergast machine while managing to avoid its taint, he had only recently developed a national reputation. After service in the Senate as a New Deal Democrat, he had gained a broader following with his fair-minded conduct as chairman of a Senate investigating committee that sought to eliminate inefficiency and waste in the war production effort. That exposure, and his border-state background and party regularity, helped gain him the vice-presidential nomination in 1944 when the Democrats were looking for a compromise choice. Yet his three months in office after the general election had done little to ready him for the highest office in the land. Roosevelt never took him into his confidence, and Truman was no better informed than before on the major issues.

President Harry S Truman bidding for political support. (*UPI/Bettmann Newsphotos*)

No wonder Truman felt inadequate at the start. The day after he became president, he told reporters: "I don't know whether you fellows ever had a load of hay fall on you, but when they told me yesterday what had happened, I felt like the moon, the stars and all the planets had fallen on me." To a former Senate colleague he groaned, "I'm not big enough. I'm not big enough for this job." Others shared that view. Tennessee Valley Authority director David Lilienthal spoke for many when he said, "The country . . . doesn't deserve to be left this way."

Yet Truman soon felt more comfortable at his new task. He was a feisty politician who was able to respond to the challenge he faced. Once he got over the insecurity of his role as an accidental president, he proved willing to take matters into his own hands. Truman was impulsive; he enjoyed making quick decisions and made a virtue out of rapid response. Under Secretary of State Joseph C. Grew was delighted with Truman's brisk manner. "When I saw him today," Grew wrote in early May, "I had fourteen problems to take up with him and got through them in less than fifteen minutes with a clear directive on every one of them. You can imagine what a joy it is to deal with a man like that." A sign on Truman's White House desk read "The Buck Stops Here," and he was willing to take immediate stands on issues, even though associates sometimes wondered if he understood all the implications. Roosevelt had shown a masterful sense of timing and had often been willing to delay wartime decisions if that seemed the best course. Truman took a different approach.

The major issues Truman faced revolved around the war, yet the new president came to office with no sense of foreign affairs. His chief concerns had been domestic ones, and he had little understanding of the nuances of diplomacy. He held traditional American attitudes about self-determination and free expression and choice, but he was not fully conversant with the problems involved. Suspicious of the totalitarian powers, in July 1941 he had said, "If we see that Germany is winning we ought to help Russia, and if Russia is winning we ought to help Germany." Now that Germany had been defeated, he still had to deal with the Soviet Union.

Truman and the USSR

Truman took a hard line from the start. Not long after he assumed office he declared that it was time to "stand up to the Russians," to teach them to behave. His advisers encouraged him in that view. Averell Harriman, ambassador to the Soviet Union, warned that the United States faced a "barbarian invasion of Europe" unless the Russians could be checked. He and others urged the president to be tough at all costs. Truman's attitude was that he was "not afraid of the Russians" and that he would stand firm. He understood that he might not get all he wanted, but "on important matters . . . we should be able to get 85 percent."

Truman took an uncommonly blunt approach in his first meeting with Soviet Foreign Minister Vyacheslav Molotov. In office less than two weeks, Truman was concerned that the Soviets were taking liberties in Poland that were not sanctioned by even the elastic Yalta terms. Though Molotov appeared conciliatory, Truman insisted sharply that the Russians act according to the pact. When Molotov protested, "I have never been talked to like that in my life," Truman retorted, "Carry out your agreements and you won't get talked to like that." Soviet-American relations went downhill from there.

Other actions reflected an increasing American determination to resist the Russians. Six days after V-E Day signaled the end of the European war, Truman issued an executive order cutting off lend-lease supplies to the Allies. The struggle in the Pacific dragged on, and Russia had agreed to assist there, but even so, the action held. Ship loading in the United States was halted, and ships at sea bound for the Soviet Union and the United Kingdom were ordered to reverse course. Secretary of State Edward Stettinius felt the action was "particularly untimely" in view of the delicate state of the Grand Alliance affairs. Truman had been warned of the consequences of his actions and later realized that a phased end to shipments would have been preferable. By then, however, the damage had been done.

The United States also sought to use economic pressure in other ways to attain its ends. Russia desperately needed financial assistance as it looked to the years ahead, and in January 1945 it had requested a $6 billion loan to use for postwar reconstruction. Roosevelt, generally amenable, had hedged, in the hope of gaining certain concessions in return. In August the Russians renewed their request, this time for only $1 billion. Now conditions had changed. Truman, not Roosevelt, was at the helm, and the tensions that had long been smoldering were more visible. The United States first lost the Soviet request, or so the government claimed, then in March 1946 indicated a willingness to consider the matter if Russia pledged "non-discrimination in international commerce." In short, the United States wanted to see the Russians open themselves to access on the part of such agencies as the World Bank and the International Monetary Fund, which relied heavily on American support. Stalin refused the offer and launched his own five-year plan instead.

THE COLD WAR AND CONTAINMENT

Soviet-American relations deteriorated quickly after 1945. Gone were the hopes of a cooperative world order that had guided the Grand Alliance during the war. Rhetoric became increasingly shrill on both sides, and more rigid policies followed the inflammatory public statements. The United States undertook to contain Soviet expansion wherever it could and began to establish alliances to counter what was perceived as a growing threat. Even before the start of the next decade, the world was divided once again into two camps.

The Cold War Declared

By 1946 positions on both sides had hardened. In early February Stalin declared in a speech that Marxist-Leninist dogma, downplayed during the war, was as valid as it had always been. Capitalism and communism were on a

collision course, and a series of cataclysmic disturbances would tear the capitalist world apart. In the United States, policy became increasingly rigid too.
Officials who argued for a more cautious approach soon found themselves out
of favor. Secretary of Commerce Henry A. Wallace was one of the casualties. In
a public address in September he claimed that America's hard line was preclud-
ing any peaceful settlement of world affairs. The Russians, he asserted, had
legitimate security concerns in eastern Europe and were only trying to "social-
ize their sphere of interest just as we try to democratize our sphere of interest."
The two nations needed to embark on a policy of "mutual trust." That view ran
counter to the position of Secretary of State James F. Byrnes, then negotiating
with the Russians in Paris. Backed into a corner and forced to decide between
members of his team, Truman reponded by firing Wallace from his Cabinet
post. He was "tired of babying the Soviets," he wrote privately that year, and
was ready to stand firm.

Support for a firmer stance came from George F. Kennan, the second
ranking officer at the American embassy in Moscow. He sent a long telegram to
the State Department not long after Stalin's February 1946 speech, later up-
dated it, and the next year published his argument for public scrutiny under the
pseudonym "Mr. X" in the journal *Foreign Affairs.* Kennan claimed that the
Russians had "no real faith in the possibility of a permanent happy coexistence
of the socialist and capitalist worlds." Any policy based on an assumption of
friendly ties was but idle fantasy that would bring no good. Stalin and his
associates had long been fanatical in their views and could not be trusted to
change. Indeed, "the whole Soviet governmental machine, including the mechanism of diplomacy, moves inexorably along the prescribed path, like a persistent toy automobile wound up and headed in a given direction, stopping only
when it meets with some unanswerable force."

With others in the administration feeling much the same way, the public
proclamation of the Cold War came as no suprise. But the announcement came
not from an American or a Russian but from an Englishman. Speaking in
Fulton, Missouri, in March 1946, with Truman on the platform, former Prime
Minister Winston Churchill declared that "from Stettin in the Baltic to Trieste
in the Adriatic, an iron curtain has descended across the Continent." To
counter the threat he called for an association of English-speaking peoples to
remain vigilant at all times. Cold War had come, and with it an American
determination that Soviet pressure, in Kennan's phrase, "be contained by the
adroit and vigilant application of counter-force at a series of constantly shifting
geographical and political points."

Containment in Practice

The first major application of containment policy came in 1947 with the development of the Truman Doctrine. East-West confrontations in a number of
areas persuaded the United States that it was time to stand firm.

The Middle East was one such region. During World War II the Big
Three had together occupied Iran to ensure that supply lines to the Soviet

Union remained clear. In 1946, when the Russians ignored the agreement to leave the oil-rich land, the United States first complained to the United Nations, then threatened to respond if the Russians did not move. Faced with public embarrassment, the Soviet Union backed down.

But if the Russians had eased off in one area, they had no intention of shifting course elsewhere in the world, and the eastern Mediterranean became the next trouble spot. The Soviets renewed pressure on Turkey for joint control of the Dardanelles, a strait between the Black Sea and the Mediterranean. And while they were not directly involved in Greece, a civil war there pitted Communist elements against the English-aided monarchy, and revolutionary pressures threatened to bring the government down.

In February 1947 the British ambassador informed the American State Department that his country could no longer afford to support Greece and Turkey with economic and military aid. Britain was in a state of decline after enormous efforts in two world wars. A harsh winter in a still unsettled time caused British industry to falter and finally led the English to draw the line. Would the United States now move into the void?

Truman was willing, and the step seemed an obvious one. The United States had recently resisted the Soviet Union in Iran. It had been following the events in the Mediterranean and had sent observers and economic representatives to the region. East-West positions had already hardened. The administration was ready for a full-fledged Cold War.

Quickly the State Department worked out a proposal for American aid when Britain pulled out, but the administration still needed to persuade resistant legislators that the national interest would best be served in that way. Congress, more conservative than before, was concerned with cutting budgets and taxes and was hardly excited about a massive aid program that lawmakers felt the country could ill afford.

Meeting with congressional leaders, Under Secretary of State Dean Acheson warned that "like apples in a barrel infected by one rotten one, the corruption of Greece would infect Iran and all to the east." A Communist victory, he argued, would "open three continents to Soviet penetration." The major powers were now "met at Armageddon" as the Soviet Union pressed for whatever advantage it could get. Only the United States had the power and will to resist. Acheson was persuasive, yet Senator Arthur Vandenberg of Michigan, one of the key Republicans whose support was necessary for any bipartisan move, warned that the administration had to develop a public base of support if it hoped to act. Quite literally, government officials needed to begin "scaring hell out of the country" if they wanted to attain their ends.

Truman was ready to oblige. On March 12, 1947, less than three weeks after the British request, he went before Congress and made a forceful case. "I believe that it must be the policy of the United States to support free peoples who are resisting attempted subjugation by armed minorities or by outside pressures," the president said. Unless the United States was willing to act, the free world might not survive: "If we falter in our leadership, we may endanger the peace of the world—and we shall surely endanger the welfare of our own

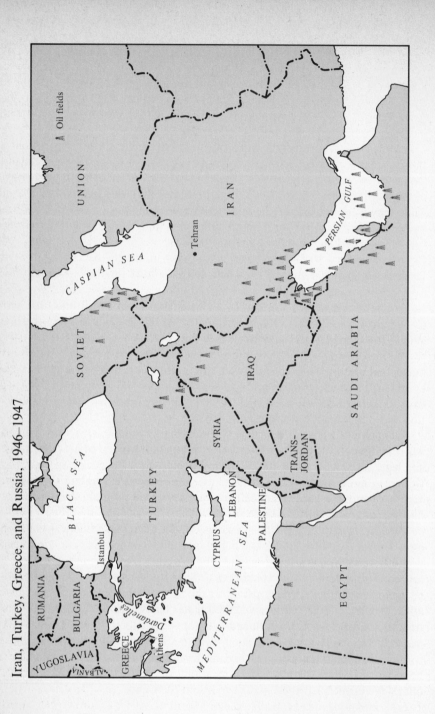

Iran, Turkey, Greece, and Russia, 1946–1947

nation." To avert calamity, Truman asked Congress to appropriate $400 million for Greek and Turkish military and economic aid.

There was a measure of resistance to his stand. Greece and Turkey were hardly democratic regimes, some critics observed. Others, like commentator Walter Lippmann, warned that the United States could not by itself stop encroachment in all parts of the globe. Nonetheless, Congress was willing to follow the administration's lead, and the requested aid bill quickly passed.

The Truman Doctrine was a major step in the Cold War. Truman's own address, Bernard Baruch observed, "was tantamount to a declaration of . . . an ideological or religious war." The president himself understood that the turning point had been passed. The United States was now actively committed to resisting the Soviet Union. The era of containment had begun.

The next step came before too long. Much of Europe was in trouble in the aftermath of the war. Economic disruption threatened to cause political instability as well as aggravate the Communist threat. Already the signs could be seen. In France and Italy, for example, large Communist parties were growing stronger and ceasing to cooperate with established governments as they had done before. In such circumstances, administration officials believed, it would be easy for Russia to move in. Something had to be done fast, for as new Secretary of State George C. Marshall commented, "The patient is sinking while the doctors deliberate."

On June 5, 1947, at the Harvard University commencement ceremony, Marshall revealed the administration's willingness to assist. He called on the European nations to come together and draw up an economic aid program that the United States could support. The kind of program he had in mind was to be "directed not against any country or doctrine but against hunger, poverty, desperation, and chaos." It would help the ravaged nations, even while it helped the United States by creating markets for American goods. And it might ward off depression that could recur unless stability was maintained around the world.

At the same time Marshall and others in the administration had broader ideological interests in mind. American assistance, Marshall observed, would permit the "emergence of political and social conditions in which free institutions can exist." The Cold War dimension was central, and the Marshall Plan and the Truman Doctrine, Truman acknowledged, were "two halves of the same walnut."

The European nations moved quickly to respond to Marshall's charge. In the summer of 1947 they worked out the details of a huge request. The Soviets attended the first planning meeting, but since Marshall had specified that the program be open and Russian economic information was rigidly closed, they ceased to cooperate and moved to develop their own plan for aid. When the multinational proposal was finally hammered out, the United States pared it down a bit but agreed to provide $17 billion over a period of four years to 16 cooperating nations.

Not all Americans were pleased with what was going on. Some members of Congress feared spreading American resources too thin. Henry Wallace termed the scheme the "Martial Plan" and argued that it was but another step toward war. Still, supporters won out, and in early 1948 Americans committed themselves to European revival as the containment policy moved forward another step.

While engaging in the reconstruction of Europe as a whole, the United States was particularly concerned with rebuilding Germany. The balance of power had shifted, and with the Soviet Union increasingly strong in the East, there seemed to be a vacuum in central Europe that had to be filled. At Yalta, as the European war had drawn to an end, the Allied leaders had agreed on the creation of four zones, occupied by the Russians, Americans, British, and French. Near the end of 1946 the Americans and British merged their zones for economic purposes and began to assign administrative duties to the Germans. By mid-1947 the effort to rebuild German industry was under way.

The Soviet blockade of West Berlin in June 1948 spotlighted the German issue. The city, located within East Germany, had been split when the country itself had been partitioned. Now the western section faced isolation from outside. A United States and Royal Air Force operation began to fly needed goods to the beleaguered Berliners. Operation Vittles brought in more than 2 million tons of supplies and ultimately led to the lifting of the blockade.

The Berlin crisis, and the extension of Communist control over Rumania and Czechoslovakia, underscored the need for a more organized means of meeting the Soviet threat. To that end, in 1949 the United States helped establish NATO—the North Atlantic Treaty Organization. Twelve nations formed the alliance, in which an attack against any one member would be considered an attack against all, to be met by appropriate armed force.

The American Senate, reluctant to make such pacts in the past, proved willing to go along with public opinion this time, and the United States established its first formal alliance with Europe since Revolutionary days. Congress then went further than authorizing mere membership alone when it voted to give military aid to its NATO allies. The Cold War had changed traditional American attitudes and softened the long-standing reluctance to become closely involved in European affairs. The United States was now willing to take a stronger stand.

The Fall of China

Also in 1949, a major shock in Asia strengthened American resolve to remain vigilant at all times. China, one of the Allied powers in the Second World War, had waged a debilitating struggle against the conquering Japanese, while at the same time fighting a bitter civil war. The Nationalist regime of Jiang Jieshi (Chiang Kai-shek)* was exhausted by the foreign struggle, far from the sources of supply, and was hopelessly inefficient and corrupt. It was no match for the Communist faction of Mao Zedong (Mao Tse-tung), which sought to seize control. World War II ended with no end to the continuing internal conflict.

* Chinese names have been rendered in the modern *pinyin* spellings. The older Wade-Giles spelling is given in parentheses at the first occurrence of a name.

Cold War Europe in 1950

ICELAND

NORWAY

SWEDEN

FINLAND

BALTIC SEA

NORTH SEA

U S S R

DENMARK

UNITED KINGDOM

IRELAND

NETHERLANDS

GERMAN DEM. REP.

POLAND

Berlin 4–Power Occupation

British Zone

FED. GERMAN REP.

U.S. Zone

CZECHOSLOVAKIA

BELGIUM

ATLANTIC OCEAN

LUXEMBOURG

French Zone

FRANCE

AUSTRIA

HUNGARY

RUMANIA

SWITZERLAND

BLACK SEA

YUGOSLAVIA

BULGARIA

PORTUGAL

SPAIN

ITALY

ALBANIA

TURKEY (joined NATO 1951)

GREECE (joined NATO 1951)

MEDITERRANEAN SEA

NATO nations

Communist nations

Neutral nations

0   Miles   500

The resolution finally came in 1949. In the aftermath of the war, the United States seemed to favor some sort of coalition between the Nationalists and the Communists, and a variety of high-ranking American officials—among them General George C. Marshall—sought to bring about a reconciliation, but to no avail. The Nationalists hoped they could win the struggle; the Communists were committed to the idea of control. As the Communists' successes mounted, American officials who watched what was happening reported that the United States could be of little help unless drastic reforms occurred first. But Jiang was hardly interested, and the end drew inexorably nearer. As of early 1949 the Nationalists had abandoned Beijing (Peking) and Tianjin (Tientsin). Shanghai fell next, then Guangzhou (Canton). By the end of the year Jiang's regime had left entirely for the island of Formosa (now Taiwan), where the defeated leader nursed the illusion that his was still the rightful government of all China, to which he would someday return.

What was the United States to do? The American attitude toward China had never been clear. Franklin Roosevelt had earlier hoped that a strong China could help ensure stability in the Far East and considered the nation one of the "four policemen" that could help preserve the postwar peace. But his view was as naive as that of Senator Kenneth Wherry, who once declared, "With God's help we will lift Shanghai up and up, ever up, until it is just like Kansas City."

As friends of the Nationalist regime argued that the United States should have provided aid to avert Jiang's defeat, the Truman administration issued its response. Dean Acheson, secretary of state after 1948, claimed in a 1054-page "white paper" that the result was far beyond the control of the United States. Jiang himself was wholly responsible for his defeat, and only full-scale intervention could have bailed him out; but that would have involved intercession to support a government no longer respected by its own troops or people. "Nothing this country did or could have done within the reasonable limits of its capabilities would have changed the result," Acheson said, "nothing that was left undone by this country has contributed to it."

Acheson for a while considered granting diplomatic recognition to the new regime, but he backed off after the Communists seized American property, harassed American citizens, and then signed a mutual-assistance pact with the Soviet Union. The United States withheld recognition with the argument that the new Communist government had not met traditional American requirements for diplomatic accord.

At the same time, the United States withheld aid from the Nationalists on Formosa on the assumption that the Communists on the mainland would soon conquer the island as well. That position, and indeed the entire American stance, infuriated the largely Republican China lobby in the United States, made up of friends of Jiang Jieshi. They called the administration's explanation a "whitewash of a wishful, do-nothing policy" and blamed Truman for having "lost" China. The charge was absurd, for China was never America's to lose, but it reflected the increasing concern over the expanding Communist threat.

Harry Truman's response was to call for a full review of America's foreign and defense policy. The National Security Council, organized in 1947 to provide policy coordination, undertook the study, with most of the work done by the departments of State and Defense. NSC-68, the paper that resulted, was an immensely important document that, though highly classified, gave shape to American policy for the following 20 years.

Presented to the National Security Council in 1950, NSC-68 viewed the international arena in polar terms, with conflict endemic between East and West. As new and better weapons emerged, the stakes grew higher. "The issues that face us are momentous," the document declared, "involving the fulfillment or destruction not only of this Republic but of civilization itself." Russian objectives conflicted with American ideals and had to be resisted at all costs. NSC-68 considered the alternatives America faced. The nation could continue on its present course, with relatively limited military and defense budgets, but if it hoped to resist the Soviet threat, it would have to make a far more massive effort. Defense spending should increase drastically from the $13 billion level set for 1950 to as much as $50 billion per year. The nation should increase the percentage of its budget allotted to defense from 5 percent to 20 percent. The cost would be large, the document acknowledged, but for the free world to survive, the United States had to move unilaterally to stem the Red tide.

ATOMIC AFFAIRS

The atomic bomb was still another variable in the unfolding Cold War. Developed during World War II, the bomb helped end the struggle, only to become a bargaining chip in international affairs. The United States hoped to use the threat of the bomb to get its way in the diplomatic arena. That effort proved unsuccessful, as the Soviet Union resisted the pressure and developed its own weapon instead. In the early 1950s both nations devised new hydrogen bombs and began to build ever-larger nuclear arsenals. Before long a dangerous arms race was under way.

Background of the Bomb

America's effort to develop the bomb began long before the nation entered the war. In August 1939 Albert Einstein, the eminent physicist, wrote Franklin Roosevelt a letter in which he observed that "it is conceivable . . . that extremely powerful bombs of a new type may . . . be constructed," and he hinted that the Germans were interested in the possibility too. Roosevelt responded by forming a committee to look into the matter. After several bureaucratic reorganizations, the task became known as the Manhattan Project. The quest lasted until the end of the war, cost $2 billion (at the time a huge sum of money), and included the construction and use of 37 installations in 19 states and Canada. The task involved much of the nation's scientific and engineering talent and employed 120,000 people. After producing the first self-sustaining atomic chain reaction in history, American scientists had to find a way to amass or produce the particular kind of uranium that could be molded into a bomb.

The United States worked on the project with British help. Scientists were exchanged and information was shared, as both nations dedicated themselves to the common goal. For a time American scientists sought to limit the cooperation, for they felt that the United States was doing most of the developmental work, but the British fought to remain involved. Prime Minister Churchill saw the bomb as a form of postwar insurance against the Soviet Union, and to that end he and Roosevelt moved to exclude other parties from the project. At the Quebec Conference of August 1943, the two leaders signed a secret agreement stating that the United States and Great Britain would not use the bomb against a third party without the other's permission and would not communicate atomic information to others except by mutual consent.

Where did the Soviet Union fit into the equation? In some ways that was one of the fundamental questions of the war. It was clear that the bomb would change the nature of military power and could well start a massive armaments race. It was also evident that several choices could be made. The United States could exclude Russia entirely from the process of atomic development. That might strengthen the American position after the war, but it would only lead to Russian distrust of American intentions. Alternatively, the United States could tell Stalin and the Russians what American scientists were doing, in the hope of securing cooperation after the war in developing a plan for international control.

With the matter unresolved, Truman became president of the United States. He had known nothing about the bomb before he assumed the presidency, but now he was informed about the whole process of development and about the bearing the bomb might have on relations with the Soviet Union, which were deteriorating all too fast.

While Truman, Churchill, and Stalin met together at Potsdam in July 1945, American scientists finally tested their bomb for the first time at Alamogordo, in the New Mexico desert. It was a stunning success. The crash broke windows 125 miles away. A blind woman saw the light. At the conference Truman was clearly exhilarated and became more assertive in his dealings with the others. Taking lightly the suggestion that the Russians be informed, he "casually mentioned . . . that we had a new weapon of unusual destructive force." But for that offhand comment, the secret remained officially intact.

In early August 1945 the bombs were dropped on Hiroshima and Nagasaki, and World War II came to an end. Why did the United States use the terrible bombs and not try alternative means of toppling Japan? Some policymakers feared that an invasion would cost an unacceptable number of American lives. Others argued that the Soviet Union wanted to play a more active role in the Pacific and its entrance into the Asian war would allow it to gain an unacceptable foothold there. But the most important reason the bomb was dropped was quite simply the fact that no influential officials seriously considered not using the weapon. They had assumed its wartime use from the start, and though it was initially intended for Germany, the European war was over and the Pacific war was still going on. Franklin Roosevelt had worked on the assumption that the bomb would be employed when ready. Uninformed and unsure of himself, president only because of his predecessor's death, Truman was not prepared to overturn a decision made when the expensive process of development was begun.

Hiroshima, destroyed by an atomic bomb in 1945. (*AP/Wide World*)

The Question of Control

Now, however, with the bombs revealed, the United States had to confront the even more ticklish question of how much of the secret should be shared. Some Americans felt that the bomb was the product of American ingenuity and enterprise and should remain in American hands. They were persuaded that it would take the Russians years to duplicate their feat. But scientists knew that once others saw that the feat could be accomplished, it would take far less time for another power to accomplish the same task. They wondered if it might not be better to deal with the question of sharing before it was too late.

Secretary of War Henry L. Stimson first took a hard-line stance, then came to favor a more sympathetic approach to the Soviet state. Earlier, in June 1945, he had considered possible concessions the United States might gain with the bomb as a negotiating weapon and had wondered if it might not be used to help settle some of the diplomatic problems developing with the Russians. By the end of the struggle, though, Stimson saw the matter in different terms. Old, tired, and ready to leave government service, he showed new insight as he dealt with atomic affairs. It would not work to try to cajole the Russians while "having this weapon ostentatiously on our hip," he observed, for "their suspicions and their distrust of our purposes and motives will increase." International cooperation depended on mutual accommodation. "The chief lesson I have learned in a long life," Stimson declared, " is the only way you can make a man trustworthy is to trust him, and the surest way you can make a man untrustworthy is to distrust him and to show your distrust."

On the question of trust, the United States never followed Stimson's advice. After leaving office, Truman recalled that "it was important to retain the advantage which possession of the bomb had given us" until the creation of a "foolproof method of control," and most Americans agreed. A poll in September 1945 revealed that 85 percent of those questioned wanted the United States to retain sole possession of the bomb for as long as possible. Another survey showed that 73 percent of the sample opposed placing the weapon under United Nations control. Congress shared the public view. Thirty-nine Republicans and 37 Democrats wanted to retain the secret of the bomb; only 5 Democrats were willing to turn it over to the UN.

Something had to be done, however, and in early 1946 the United States was ready to act. It had seen that mere possession of the bomb was not making the Russians any more malleable in eastern Europe, so a new approach had to be tried. Truman and his advisers therefore agreed to try to work through the UN. One plan, drafted by Dean Acheson and David Lilienthal, proposed an international agency that would move by stages toward full ownership and control of atomic weapons. The United States would retain its advantage until the UN took over.

Financier Bernard Baruch, on his appointment as ambassador to the UN Atomic Energy Commission, proposed a modified version of the plan. In his scheme there would be international inspection and an agreement to abstain from using the veto in the Security Council in discussions of managerial controls. That meant penetration of Soviet secrecy, and the Russians rejected the plan and countered with one of their own. They called for destruction of all atomic weapons, then a discussion of controls. Despite Baruch's awareness that they all faced "a choice between the quick and the dead," negotiations bogged down. For the Americans it was either their plan or none at all, and the Russians felt the same way. The United States therefore moved toward its own internal mechanism of control as hope for international cooperation and disarmament came to an end.

The United States gave up on the process of sharing with the passage of the Atomic Energy Act of 1946. It provided that a new Atomic Energy Commission would supervise all atomic energy development in the United States and, under tightest security, authorize all activity in the nation at large. The United States had decided to press on alone, as hope for international cooperation in this sphere, as in others, disappeared.

Nuclear Proliferation

For several years the secret remained secure as the United States retained its nuclear monopoly. Then, in September 1949, reporters were summoned to the White House office of the presidential press secretary, who passed out a mimeographed announcement that took them by surprise. In it the president declared, "We have evidence that within recent weeks an atomic explosion occurred in the U.S.S.R."

The Russians had not publicly proclaimed their achievement. An air force weather reconnaissance plane on a routine mission had picked up air samples showing higher than normal radioactivity counts. Other samples confirmed the first findings. Scientists analyzing them carefully were soon certain that there had been a Soviet nuclear test.

The American public was shocked. Suddenly the security of being the sole atomic power in the world was gone. Wondering why they had been caught unaware, some people suspected subversion. Others anticipated a possible Russian attack. Tension was evident on all fronts. At a meeting of the Joint Committee on Atomic Energy at the Capitol, legislators who had just heard the announcement were startled by the loud thunderclap. "My God," someone said. "That must be Number Two!"

There was no denying that the world had changed. Harold C. Urey, an atomic scientist and winner of the Nobel Prize, spoke for many Americans when he observed that he was "flattened" by Truman's announcement. "There is only one thing worse than one nation having the atomic bomb—" he went on, "that's two nations having it." Despite all efforts to the contrary, the atomic genie was out. The nation had to accept the fact that its monopoly no longer existed, that its terrible secret was no longer secure.

Truman now considered developing a new superbomb potentially far more devastating than the atomic bomb. Scientists debated the advisability of taking that course. Edward Teller, a physicist who had worked on the Manhattan Project, was intrigued by the novelty of the puzzle. During the war, as other scientists struggled with the problem of fission, he began to consider the possibility of fusion, which might release energy in still greater amounts. He envisioned an atomic explosion detonating another reaction of even larger force. As Cold War tensions become more intense, he saw a chance to proceed.

Other scientists opposed Teller. J. Robert Oppenheimer, head of the successful effort to build the bomb during the war and a major figure in the atomic establishment, resisted pushing on. He feared the consequences of the new weapon Teller had in mind. Truman, however, chose to follow Teller's lead. In early 1950 he authorized the experimental development of a hydrogen bomb.

Before long, both the United States and the Soviet Union succeeded in their quests. Hydrogen bombs could be built, just as Teller had predicted. Far more powerful than the primitive weapons that had devastated Hiroshima and Nagasaki, they provoked even greater fears. The government remained quiet about MIKE, the first test of a hydrogen device at Eniwetok in the Pacific in November 1952, but rumors circulated that it had created a hole 175 feet deep and a mile wide in the ocean floor. A year and a half later, after the March 1954 BRAVO test in the Bikini atoll, Lewis Strauss, Atomic Energy Commission chairman, admitted that "an H-bomb can be made . . . large enough to take out a city," even New York. Pictures in the popular press revealing the impact of weapons tests in Nevada and in the Pacific gave a vivid sense of the damage that could occur.

Both the United States and the Soviet Union stockpiled new weapons, and an arms race was the result. Scientists had feared such a possibility ever since 1945. Now their fears were realized as the nuclear equation complicated the pattern of the Cold War.

THE KOREAN WAR

The Cold War heated up in 1950 as active fighting broke out in a far corner of the globe. In Korea, the United States underscored its commitment to contain the Communist threat. The basic outlines of American policy had been established with the Truman Doctrine, the Marshall Plan, and the North Atlantic Treaty Organization and had been emphasized in NSC-68. Now the administration had the chance to demonstrate its determination to stand firm.

Background of the War

The Korean War was rooted in divisions that had occurred during World War II. Long a pawn in the Far East, under Japanese control since 1905, Korea had hoped for freedom after the war. Roosevelt, Churchill, and Jiang Jieshi had pledged their support for an independent state at the Cairo Conference of 1943, but the rapid end of the Pacific war in 1945 had allowed Soviet troops to accept the Japanese surrender north of the 38th parallel, while American forces did the same south of that line. From the exigencies of war grew the rigid line of demarcation that became more permanent as time went on. As in other areas of the world, temporary partition became established fact.

After the war both sides professed support for a unified regime, but as relations deteriorated, unification became impossible. When a tentative agreement at the Moscow Conference of December 1945 broke down, both sides set up dependent governments in their zones. In the south, the American-educated Syngman Rhee emerged supreme, while in the north the pro-Russian Kim Il Sung led the regime. Each side received arms and aid from its patron state and sought reunification on its own terms. The major powers entertained the same dreams. As one economic adviser observed, the basic American hope was that the leaders in the south would "institute a whole series of necessary reforms which will so appeal to the North Koreans that their army will revolt, kill all the nasty Communists, and create a lovely liberal democracy to the everlasting credit of the U.S.A.!" His cynicism notwithstanding, he summed up a basic American view that mirrored the reverse vision on the Soviet side.

In 1949, as both the United States and Russia pulled out of their respective zones, the standoff remained. But now the United States had to decide how strong its commitment to Korea really was. At first it seemed ambivalent and vague. In January 1950, Secretary of State Dean Acheson declared that the American defense perimeter in the Pacific ran from the Aleutian Islands through Japan to the Philippines and therefore seemed to exclude Korea itself. In fact the policy outlined reflected a hope that peace and stability would come without a positive military guarantee, though Acheson also indicated that aggression in Korea would be resisted by the United Nations.

Attack and Response

On June 25, 1950, North Korean forces moved across the 38th parallel and into the south. Following Soviet-built tanks, the northern troops pressed their advantage and pushed opposing soldiers farther and farther back. Was the invasion undertaken at Soviet command? Kim Il Sung had visited Moscow earlier and spoken to Stalin of his problems at home. The Russians may well have acquiesced in the idea of an attack, but both the planning and timing seem to have come at the initiative of North Korea.

The United States was taken completely by surprise. Acheson himself later acknowledged that the administration expected the Communists to attain their objectives "through guerrilla and psychological warfare, political pressure and intimidation" rather than through military force. But the attack had come, and now the Americans had to respond. Virtually all commentators saw the conflict in global terms. They were certain that the Russians had masterminded the attack and came to believe that American national security and world peace were at stake.

Korean War, 1950–1953

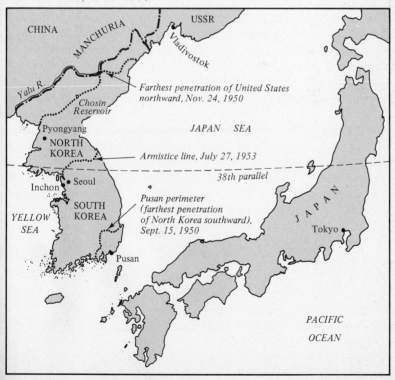

Truman responded quickly. The day after the attack, the president declared, "Korea is the Greece of the Far East. If we are tough enough now, if we stand up to them like we did in Greece three years ago, they won't take any next steps. But if we just stand by, they'll move into Iran and they'll take over the whole Middle East." Later he argued that the lessons of the past were clear: "In my generation this was not the first occasion when the strong had attacked the weak. I recalled some earlier instances: Manchuria, Ethiopia, Austria. I remembered how each time that the democracies failed to act it had encouraged the aggressors to keep going ahead. Communism was acting in Korea just as Hitler, Mussolini, and the Japanese had acted ten, fifteen, and twenty years earlier. . . . If this was allowed to go unchallenged it would mean a third world war, just as similar incidents had brought on the second world war." Truman, Acheson, and other advisers saw the invasion as a turning point in the Cold War. "The attack upon Korea makes it plain beyond all doubt," Truman said, "that Communism has passed beyond the use of subversion to conquer independent nations and will now use armed invasion and war."

In response Truman readied American naval and air forces. He directed General Douglas MacArthur in Japan to provide supplies to the South Korean troops. At the same time, the United States went to the Security Council of the UN and got a unanimous resolution branding North Korea the aggressor. The Soviet Union failed to veto the resolution because it was boycotting the organization as a protest against the exclusion of the People's Republic of China. Another resolution two days later called for UN members to assist South Korea in repelling aggression and restoring the peace. Truman meanwhile ordered American air and naval forces into battle south of the 38th parallel, and when those did not appear to be enough, he ordered in American ground forces as well. The defense effort was theoretically a UN venture, but in the end the United States provided half the ground troops and most of the sea and air support. Furthermore, commands came from the United States, not from the UN.

At first the war went poorly for the United States. The South Koreans and Americans suffered one defeat after another and were driven steadily toward the south end of the peninsula. Eventually UN forces held, and MacArthur decided on a daring gamble. Landing forces behind Communist lines, he began a major counterattack at Inchon on the western shore. In the face of intimidating odds, the gamble paid off, and soon the UN forces had pushed the North Koreans back to the former boundary line and fulfilled the initial American aims in the war.

Now, however, the United States decided to go beyond the 38th parallel, to push on to the Chinese border, and to settle the Korean problem once and for all. Reunification became the major war aim. Although the Chinese sent signals through diplomatic representatives in India that American movement toward their border would constitute a security threat, the United States chose to dismiss the warning. Acheson sought to demonstrate that Chinese interests were not threatened, while MacArthur argued that the Chinese could not or would not mount effective resistance and claimed that he would "have the boys home by Christmas." He was wrong. In late October, as UN forces marched through North Korea, Chinese troops briefly appeared in battle, then disappeared, as if to signal a determination on China's part to resist. At the end of November, five months after the start of the war, a full-fledged Chinese counterattack came and, in terrible winter fighting, threw the UN forces back toward the 38th parallel.

The Truman-MacArthur Controversy

As the struggle led to stalemate, a bitter conflict ensued between MacArthur and his civilian commander in chief. MacArthur, an arrogant, imperious man with unmatched self-assurance, had not been back to the United States for 14 years, but he had his own pronounced ideas about the direction American policy should take. While the administration was most concerned about the containment of Communism in Europe, MacArthur stressed the need for even stronger resistance in Asian lands. While Truman was trying to direct a limited war and to prevent the conflict from getting out of control, MacArthur wanted to push harder and deal the enemy a decisive defeat. He proposed allowing hot pursuit of attacking aircraft, using atomic weapons against China, unleashing the Nationalist Chinese against the Communist troops, and blockading the mainland of China itself. To all suggestions Truman and his advisers said no. They feared total war that might involve the Soviet Union and weaken American strength elsewhere in the world. As General Omar N. Bradley, army chief of staff, observed, it would have been "the wrong war, in the wrong place, at the wrong time, and with the wrong enemy."

General Douglas MacArthur, American leader in Korea before he was relieved by President Truman. (*AP/Wide World*)

Nevertheless, MacArthur pressed his point. He issued controversial statements in the field and then, in April 1951, as the war dragged on with no end in sight, sent a letter to Joseph W. Martin, minority leader of the House of Representatives. "It seems strangely difficult for some to realize," he wrote, "that here in Asia is where the Communist conspirators have elected to make their play for global conquest. . . . that here we fight Europe's war with arms while the diplomats there still fight it with words." He argued that if Asia fell, Europe would fall too, and he closed by asserting, "There is no substitute for victory." When Martin made the letter public, Truman had no choice but to relieve MacArthur.

Though the president had the full support of the Joint Chiefs of Staff, his decision was still an immensely unpopular one. The public was outraged. Republican Senator Joseph McCarthy of Wisconsin echoed a common sentiment in attacking the president when he declared, "The son of a bitch ought to be impeached." MacArthur returned home to a parade and a hero's welcome, and in an address before a joint session of the House and the Senate, he repeated his arguments about the Asian war and concluded by proclaiming, in the words of an old army ballad, "Old soldiers never die, they just fade away."

Once the emotion subsided, Truman was able to press for his more limited aims. After a year of war, the administration was willing to settle for an armistice at the 38th parallel again, and a long process of negotiation began that was to last for years. In July 1953, with a new president in the White House, an agreement was finally reached, and the Korean War came to an end.

Consequences of the Korean War

The war was an inordinately frustrating one for the United States. It began and remained a limited conflict, and indeed, Truman had early termed the UN response merely a "police action" to check aggression that had occurred. He had allowed MacArthur to proceed north, but when the easy victory sought was denied, the president became determined to avoid a major war that would have far-reaching military and diplomatic consequences and might lead to pronounced disruption at home. And yet, to many Americans, MacArthur's position seemed to make sense. If a war had to be fought, why not seek victory? The United States had the power to bring the North Koreans to their knees. Why could it not be used? Limited war was a difficult concept to comprehend, and it led to increasing anxiety on the domestic front.

Despite its limited nature, the Korean War resulted in 54,000 American deaths and an even larger number of American soldiers wounded. It also brought significant change within the United States. It led to economic regulation again, though not to the same degree as in World War II. An Office of Defense Mobilization was active, and an effort was made to control inflation, which spurted in the first year of the war. Even more important were major spending shifts. Military expenditures soared, from $13 billion in the 1949–1950 fiscal year to just under $60 billion in 1952–1953. Military retrenchment came to an end as defense spending followed the guidelines proposed in NSC-68. That shift strengthened the military voice in national affairs and diverted both money and attention from the process of domestic reform.

There were important political consequences as well. The war poisoned relations with China and entrenched the diplomatic standoff that lasted more than 20 years. It led the United States to sign a treaty with Japan to ensure that the former Pacific enemy would now serve as a barrier to the Chinese. The rehabilitation of Japan paralleled the rehabilitation of Germany as the Cold War encouraged new alliances. In Southeast Asia, Americans now saw movements for independence not as nationalistic strivings but as examples of the Communist conspiracy at work. The policy of containment had expanded to meet what seemed like an ever-enlarging Communist threat.

Finally, the war served to enhance presidential authority, and that expansion of power set important precedents for the future. Roosevelt earlier had moved in the same direction, and Truman built on his start. When the North Korean invasion occurred, Truman made a unilateral decision to intervene. He obviously felt the need to respond quickly and to avoid divisive debate, yet the fact remains that he moved with neither congressional approval nor a declaration of war. Only after he had authorized American force did he meet with Congress to inform members about what he had done. That approach similarly characterized later conduct of the war. After the struggle, the expansion of executive power continued.

ANTICOMMUNISM AT HOME

The Cold War affected more than American foreign policy. The commitment to containment and the mounting frustration over the military struggle to resist communism abroad led to a greater effort to check communism at home. There had been a program established even before the Korean War began, but the military conflict caused the domestic effort to get out of hand.

The Roots of Fear

Anti-Communist anxieties in the United States had roots deep in the past. Americans had feared radical revolt ever since the days of the Russian Revolution, and the Red Scare after World War I was one result. Suspicions of the Soviet Union had been submerged during the Second World War, but with the breakdown in relations, the old fears revived. Before American entrance into the war, as Germany and Russia fought each other on the eastern front, there was a tendency to see the two dictatorships as much alike. The *Wall Street Journal* commented, "The American people know that the principal difference between Mr. Hitler and Mr. Stalin is the size of their respective mustaches." And William C. Bullitt, former ambassador to Russia, called the struggle one between "Stalin and Lucifer." Sentiments warmed for a time, but after the war the equation of Hitler and Stalin, Germany and Russia, revived. *Life* magazine summed up the growing sentiment when it observed that the alarming figure of "Big Brother" in George Orwell's *Nineteen Eighty-Four* was an amalgam of Hitler and Stalin, and others picked up on the same theme.

In the early Cold War period, a series of disclosures lent substance to American fears. In February 1945, government agents found numerous classified documents in the offices of the allegedly pro-Communist *Amerasia* magazine. A year later, a Canadian commission revealed a number of spy rings and pointed to subversion that had occurred during the war. There were calls to do something to protect the security of the United States.

The Truman Loyalty Program

As Harry Truman sought to mobilize support for his containment program, the rhetoric of his administration became increasingly shrill. The president heeded Senator Arthur Vandenberg's demand to "scare hell" out of the American people if he hoped for congressional support. The president and his staff pictured Cold War issues in black and white as they set American virtues against Russian designs. For Truman, "the issue which confronts the world today" was one of "tyranny or freedom." Godless communism was a "threat to our liberties and to our faith." Worst of all, according to Attorney General J. Howard McGrath, were the "many Communists in America" who each bore "the germ of death for society."

At the same time, Truman moved to deal with the threat of subversion. Apprehensive about Republican gains in the midterm elections of 1946 and fearful of a congressional loyalty probe that could be used for partisan ends, he sought to head off such an investigation by starting one of his own. At the end of 1946 he appointed a Temporary Commission on Employee Loyalty. On the basis of its report, he established a Federal Employee Loyalty Program by executive order in March 1947. The FBI was to check through its files for evidence of threatening activity, and cases then would move through the respective agencies to a new Civil Service Commission Loyalty Review Board. Initially the program was meant to have certain limits and safeguards. Dismissal could occur only when "reasonable grounds exist for the belief that the person involved is disloyal to the Government of the United States." Those limits did not last long, for the Loyalty Review Board assumed more and more power, and as it did so it came to overlook individual rights. The burden of proof shifted as the new standard for dismissal became that of whether there was a "reasonable doubt as to the loyalty of the person involved."

The Truman loyalty program examined several million employees and only ended up with the dismissals of several hundred. But it helped foster the largely unwarranted fear of subversion, led to the assumption that absolute loyalty could be achieved, and legitimated investigatory tactics that became even more threatening in other hands.

The House Committee on Un-American Activities

Truman was not alone in his loyalty quest in the early years of the Cold War. Congress, too, was determined to get into the act. In 1947 the House Committee on Un-American Activities (HUAC) took aim at the motion-picture industry and began asking questions about the political leanings of those working there. HUAC had been suspicious of Communist involvement in a number of labor disputes in Hollywood two years earlier and now wanted to prevent Communist inroads in the movies.

Though HUAC never proved that Communists in Hollywood got anything of substance into the pictures they helped make, the committee left its mark. A number of figures called to testify under oath resisted succumbing to the scare tactics and refused to cooperate. They were hit with severe penalties and scapegoated for their stand. The Hollywood Ten, including Ring Lardner, Jr., and Dalton Trumbo, were cited for contempt and sent to federal prison. Hollywood then capitulated, established a blacklist of industry members with even marginally questionable pasts, and caused still more people to suffer as a result.

HUAC made an even greater splash with the Hiss-Chambers case. Whittaker Chambers, a former member of the Communist party who had broken with it in 1938 and become a successful editor of *Time* magazine, charged that Alger Hiss, among others, had been a Communist in the 1930s. Hiss was a highly distinguished New Dealer who had served in the Agriculture Department before moving on to become assistant secretary of state. He had worked at the controversial Yalta Conference and had served at the San Francisco Conference organizing the UN. Now he was out of government, president of the Carnegie Endowment for International Peace. Hiss denied Chambers's charges, and the matter might have died there had not freshman congressman Richard Nixon decided to press on. He finally extracted from Hiss an admission that he had known Chambers in earlier years. Outside the hearing room, Hiss sued Chambers for libel, whereupon Chambers embellished his story and charged that Hiss was a Soviet spy. With controversial evidence, including several rolls of microfilm that Chambers had hidden in a pumpkin patch at his Maryland farm, HUAC pressed on. In December 1948 a federal grand jury took the case a step further. Since the statute of limitations precluded an espionage indictment, the grand jury indicted Hiss for perjury instead, for lying under oath about his relationship with Chambers.

The case was a troubling one. Chambers was unstable, prone to change his story, and not wholly truthful at all times. Yet Hiss, too, seemed contradictory in his testimony and never adequately explained how copies of stolen State Department documents had been typed on a typewriter he had once owned. The first trial ended in a hung jury, the second in a conviction in January 1950 that sent Hiss to prison for almost four years.

The Hiss case for many Americans seemed to show the existence of a real Communist threat. It "forcibly demonstrated to the American people," Nixon declared, "that domestic Communism was a real and present danger to the security of the nation." It also led people to question the Democrats' approach to the problem. After Alger Hiss's conviction but before his appeal, Dean Acheson asserted his support for his friend. Regardless of what happened, he said, "I do not intend to turn my back on Alger Hiss." Decent though his affirmation of support was, it caused the secretary of state trouble with political foes. Harry Truman had earlier called the case a "red herring," but the court had decided otherwise. Now the loyalty program, for all its excesses, faced charges of laxity at home. The case therefore had broad ramifications for the anti-Communist crusade. It helped justify the witch-hunt that followed.

McCarthy

The key figure fighting communism in the 1950s was Senator Joseph R. McCarthy of Wisconsin. McCarthy had come to the Senate in 1946, where he voted for the most part with the conservative members of his Republican party on domestic affairs. In that election he had demonstrated his capacity for duplicity, calling himself "Tail Gunner Joe," although he had done mostly desk work in his service in the war. In office he was sometimes known as the "Pepsi-Cola Kid" for his efforts on behalf of the soft-drink company to end sugar rationing at the war's end. But his early years were undistinguished. Though he had occasionally touched on the issue of communism, he never seized on it with full force.

All that changed in 1950 as he looked toward reelection two years hence. Worried because Truman had carried Wisconsin in 1948, McCarthy knew he had to take the offensive and settled on the Communist question as his means of attack. He first gained national attention with a speech before the Wheeling (West Virginia) Republican Women's Club in February 1950, not long after the conviction of Alger Hiss. In that address he charged that he had in his hand a list of 205 known Communists in the Department of State. When pressed for details, McCarthy said first that he would release his list only to the president, then reduced the number of names to 57.

Early reactions to McCarthy were mixed. Richard Nixon initially questioned his effectiveness. A subcommittee of the Senate Foreign Relations Committee, upon investigation, called the charge a "fraud and a hoax." Yet McCarthy refused to stop, for he found a public primed by the Hiss case and, after July 1950, frustrated with the task in Korea of waging limited war. Republicans began to understand his partisan value and urged him on. Senator John Bricker of Ohio allegedly told him, "Joe, you're a dirty s.o.b., but there are times when you've got to have an s.o.b. around and this is one of them." "Mr. Republican," Robert Taft, Ohio's other senator, also encouraged his colleague from Wisconsin; he said, "If one case doesn't work, try another." McCarthy did.

He took on various targets. In the elections of 1950, he set out against Millard Tydings, the Democrat from Maryland who had chaired the subcommittee that dismissed McCarthy's first attack. A doctored photograph showing Tydings with deposed Communist party head Earl Browder helped bring about Tydings's defeat. McCarthy called Dean Acheson a "pompous diplomat in striped pants, with a phony British accent" and termed him the "Red Dean of the State Department." He was even more brutal in his attack on George C. Marshall. A man with a sterling reputation throughout his distinguished career, Marshall had helped work out Truman's policy in the Far East. Now McCarthy called him "a man steeped in falsehood . . . who has recourse to the lie whenever its suits his convenience," who was part of "a conspiracy so immense and an infamy so black as to dwarf any previous venture in the history of man."

McCarthy was a demagogue with great skill. He played on his tough reputation and did not mind appearing disheveled, unshaven, half sober. Obscenity and vulgarity were all part of his ruthless manner as he spoke of the "vile and scurrilous" objects of his attack. He boasted of lessons he had received in Wisconsin from one Indian Charlie, who had directed him to go straight for his opponent's groin whenever he found himself in trouble.

McCarthy employed a variety of methods that helped his reputation grow. He understood that accusations often seemed more credible the greater they became. Some of his charges might be proved false, but there were always others he could press, and the very process of repetition strengthened his attack. He constantly carried documents that he claimed proved beyond the shadow of a doubt that his charges were true. It mattered little what they contained; he used the papers themselves for visible effect. He knew how to play the press, how to make news when none existed. He issued statements to meet reporters' deadlines and provided the leads they could use. Often he called press conferences in the morning to announce that fresh disclosures would be forthcoming at other press conferences in the afternoon. He got the publicity he needed, and the publicity fueled his attacks.

McCarthy really came into his own when the Republicans won control of the Senate in the election of 1952. Chairman of the Government Operations

Senator Joseph McCarthy making his case at the Army-McCarthy hearings in 1954 as attorney Joseph Welch looks on. (*UPI/Bettmann Newsphotos*)

Committee and head of its Permanent Investigations Subcommittee, he now had a stronger base from which to operate. With two young assistants, Roy Cohn and G. David Schine, doing much of the staff work, he attacked the State Department's overseas information program. In response, the diplomatic establishment directed that the works of Communists and even fellow travelers be banned from American libraries abroad. Cohn and Schine, with the same ruthless determination shown by their leader, went on a quick tour of Europe and began pulling volumes off the shelves. Sometimes even officials who approved of the scattershot approach wondered how far it would go.

McCarthy finally pushed too far. In 1953 the army drafted Schine, then refused to allow the preferential treatment requested by Cohn. Angered, McCarthy began to investigate army security and even top-level army leaders themselves. He humiliated Secretary of the Army Robert Stevens. When the army charged that McCarthy was going too far in his quest for special treatment of Schine, the Senate began to investigate the complaint. The Army-McCarthy hearings began in April 1954 and lasted 35 days. Televised to a nationwide audience, they gave Americans a firsthand glimpse of the savage tactics McCarthy employed, even when there was no threat at hand. McCarthy came across to viewers as an irresponsible and destructive man, particularly in contrast to Boston lawyer Joseph Welch, who argued the army's case with a quiet eloquence that put McCarthy in his place. When the hearings were over, McCarthy's mystical appeal was gone. In broad daylight the tactics no longer made sense, and his support began to fade.

The Senate, fearful before of McCarthy's power and unwilling to take him on, now finally moved to condemn him for bringing the Senate into disrepute. He remained in office, but his movement was spent. Three years later, at the age of 48, he died a broken man.

Yet for a time he had exerted a powerful hold in the United States. At the height of his influence, polls showed that McCarthy had half the public behind him, with far fewer people opposed. "To many Americans," radio commentator Fulton Lewis, Jr., said, "McCarthyism is Americanism." Why did McCarthy have such an appeal? Largely because of the way he capitalized on Cold War anxieties. Americans were increasingly concerned with the spread of communism abroad, and the Truman loyalty program helped persuade them that there was a corresponding threat at home. Drawing on a popular following that included lower-class ethnic groups who supported the charges against established elites who could finally be brought to task, he also relied on a firm political base. McCarthy had the support of conservative Republicans, who saw him as a useful means to reassert their authority in the country. In the Senate his dominance rested on his colleagues' perception of his strength. Some, like George Aiken of Vermont, Margaret Chase Smith of Maine, and J. William Fulbright of Arkansas, did speak out, but most others did not. Dwight D. Eisenhower, president from 1953 on, disliked the senator from Wisconsin, yet said that he would "not get into the gutter with that guy." Richard Nixon, vice-president under Ike, acted as the administration's liaison to McCarthy as long as his value seemed assured. With that support behind him, McCarthy continued his campaign until the movement crumbled. During that time, he profoundly affected American life.

The Legacy of Fear

McCarthy and the others who joined in the anti-Communist crusade helped generate a pervasive sense of suspicion and fear in American society. In the late 1940s and early 1950s, it no longer seemed safe to dissent. Civil servants, government workers, academics, and actors all came under attack and found that the right of due process often seemed suspended during the Red Scare of the Cold War.

There were countless examples. In New York, subway workers were fired when they refused to respond to questions about their political actions and beliefs. In Seattle, a fire department officer who denied current membership in the Communist party but refused to talk about his past was dismissed just 40 days before he reached the 25 years of service that would have given him retirement benefits. Val Lorwin, a State Department employee who was on one of McCarthy's famous lists, faced agonizing hearings before finally clearing himself of trumped-up charges, but not without considerable emotional and financial expense.

Julius and Ethel Rosenberg were least lucky of all. Arrested in mid-1950 and charged with passing atomic secrets to the Soviet Union, they were tried and convicted when the Red Scare was at its peak. Exhausting appeal after appeal, they were finally executed in the electric chair in 1953. Though they never admitted their guilt, and might have been spared at another time, they became the unfortunate victims of a nation consumed by the passions of the Cold War.

THE UNITED STATES AND THE COLD WAR

America's aims and aspirations changed in the years after the Second World War. The hopes for cooperation faded as different perceptions of security emerged in the East and the West, and positions hardened as the years wore on. By 1947 the United States was determined to resist what it viewed as the savage and sustained Communist threat, and the American policy of containment began to take shape. As the nation girded itself, it moved to rearm, and the era of gigantic defense budgets began. The Cold War was always present in the background and never really faded away in the half decade that followed. As Americans became accustomed to military battles overseas, so they became accustomed to ideological battles in the United States. Communism was to be fought, whatever the consequences, wherever it appeared, at home as well as abroad. The Cold War became a way of life.

SUGGESTIONS FOR FURTHER READING

A number of outstanding books deal with the background and development of the Cold War. Walter LaFeber, *America, Russia, and the Cold War, 1945–1980,* 4th ed. (1980), is the best brief account of the Cold War and its effects. John Lewis Gaddis, *The United States and the Origins of the Cold War, 1941–1947* (1972) is a well-written and well-argued examination of the tensions that led to the breakdown in relations between the United States and the Soviet Union. Daniel Yergin, *Shattered Peace: The Origins of the Cold War and the National Security State* (1977) is another readable account of the start of the Cold War. Stephen Ambrose, *Rise to Globalism: American Foreign Policy Since 1938* (1980) and Gabriel Kolko and Joyce Kolko, *The Limits of Power* (1972) provide different perspectives on foreign policy in this period. Thomas G. Patterson, *On Every Front: The Making of the Cold War* (1979) is a brief but perceptive essay on foreign affairs in the Cold War years. Also see Adam Ulam, *The Rivals: America and Russia since World War II* (1971). Thomas H. Etzold and John Lewis Gaddis, *Containment: Documents on American Policy and Strategy, 1945–1950* (1978) is a useful collection of the major documents of the early Cold War years.

On atomic energy questions and their impact on diplomacy, see Martin J. Sherwin, *A World Destroyed: The Atomic Bomb and the Grand Alliance* (1975) and Gregg Herken, *The Winning Weapon: The Atomic Bomb in the Cold War, 1945–1950* (1980).

On the Korean War, David Rees, *Korea: The Limited War* (1964) gives a good assessment of the major foreign conflict in the 1950s. I. F. Stone, *The Hidden History of the Korean War* (1952) examines the struggle from an entirely different perspective. John W. Spanier, *The Truman-MacArthur Controversy and the Korean War* (1959) describes the heated battle between the president and his military commander in Korea. James A. Michener, *The Bridges at Toko-Ri* (1953) is a contemporary novel that provides a sense of the frustrations during the war.

On the anti-Communist crusade, Richard M. Freeland, *The Truman Doctrine and the Origins of McCarthyism* (1972) and Athan Theoharis, *Seeds of Repression: Harry S. Truman and the Origins of McCarthyism* (1971) locate the beginnings of hysteria in the Truman period. Richard H. Rovere, *Senator Joe McCarthy* (1960) is a short and readable account of McCarthy and his methods. Robert Griffith, *The Politics of Fear: Joseph R. McCarthy and the Senate* (1970) is a perceptive analysis of McCarthy's power base in the Senate and the forces that brought him down. Thomas C. Reeves, *The Life and Times of Joe McCarthy: A Biography* (1982) is a full-scale treatment of the anti-Communist crusader. David M. Oshinsky, *A Conspiracy So Immense: The World of Joe McCarthy* (1983) is a vivid examination of McCarthy and his times.

chapter *3*

The Fair Deal

The Fair Deal was Harry S Truman's program at home. Not formally named until 1949, the Fair Deal nonetheless included all of the domestic initiatives in the early years of the Cold War. Truman intended his program to pick up where the liberal New Deal of Franklin Roosevelt left off, but it never really fulfilled its promise or achieved its goals. There were some accomplishments, to be sure, yet on balance there often seemed to be more failure than success. Truman faced considerably more political resistance than Roosevelt had, as the coalition of southern Democrats and Republicans that had begun to form in the 1930s came into its own. Truman was also preoccupied with foreign affairs, especially as an emerging consensus gave Cold War policies bipartisan support. In that climate, despite pressure from disadvantaged groups for reform, domestic aims got short shrift. Though Truman continued to trumpet his goals, even he recognized the unavoidable restraints.

TRUMAN'S FIRST YEAR

Truman quickly established a framework for domestic reform as World War II came to an end, but his program ran into trouble from the start. The new president lacked the confidence of the liberal community, which refused to forget FDR. He also faced immediate problems of reconversion that took precedence over any longer-term goals. His scattershot approach led critics and supporters both to wonder just where his priorities lay. By the end of his first year, Truman was in trouble at home.

The Truman Team

The new president, his government service notwithstanding, was not well known in 1945. "Who the hell is Harry Truman?" Admiral William D. Leahy had asked when informed the year before of the choice of the vice-presidential nominee. Some of those who knew the little man from Missouri were even more disturbed when he became president of the United States. "That Throttlebottom Truman" TVA director David Lilienthal called him as the transition took place, and others said much the same thing.

At the start, Truman found himself surrounded by officials who wondered how anyone could replace Franklin Roosevelt. He was uncomfortable with the strangers he found in positions of authority—the "crackpots and the lunatic fringe" appointed by FDR. Nor did many of them like him. Within several months a number had gone and others were on the way out. Henry A. Wallace and Harold Ickes, two of the most prominent New Dealers, stayed longer than some but then departed in dramatic ways. Ickes, Roosevelt's incorruptible secretary of the interior, protested when Truman's nominee for under secretary of the navy sought important federal concessions in return for campaign support. Ickes thereupon resigned in a huff. Wallace was fired as the 1946 elections approached for proclaiming his more moderate position toward the Soviet Union as the administration was beginning to take a tough line.

Truman lost the liberals who were sympathetic to Fair Deal goals and appointed people of a more conservative bent. Some of those were able men, but others, like John W. Snyder, a St. Louis friend who became secretary of the Treasury in 1946, were of the second rank. And then there was Harry Vaughn, Truman's military aide and poker-playing crony, who became the man to see for favors. The crew was hardly a distinguished one, charged radical journalist I. F. Stone. "The composite impression was of big-bellied, good-natured guys who knew a lot of dirty jokes, spent as little time in their offices as possible, saw Washington as a chance to make 'useful' contacts, and were anxious to get what they could for themselves out of the experience. . . . The Truman era was the era of the moocher. The place was full of Wimpys who could be had for a hamburger." Critics were hardly surprised as scandals surfaced in the second term, but other complaints had surfaced well before then.

Reconversion

Truman's first major difficulties began in the immediate aftermath of World War II. The country had been geared up for war but now needed to return to a peacetime pace. Although administration officials understood the importance of a phased reconversion, there was strong public sentiment for a quick end to the wartime controls. After military victory, the soldiers wanted to come home, and politicians were deluged with messages that said, "No boats, no votes." More pressing were the demands for the material goods that had long been in short supply. Americans had known deprivation during the Depression and then further sacrifice during the war when they had money again but not enough to spend it on. Now they wanted the consumer goods that they had done without for years. They wanted better meat for their meals and tires for their cars. They wanted to enjoy prosperity again.

Truman faced pressures from all sides. Businessmen sought immediate demobilization and an end to price and production controls. Workers demanded the relaxation of wage restrictions and a boost in earnings to make up for the limits of the war years. Consumers insisted that rationing cease, though they still wanted to keep inflation in check.

In the face of those pressures, the administration's record was mixed at best. The servicemen did return quickly; the number abroad dropped from a total of 12 million in 1945 to 3 million in mid-1946 to 1.6 million in mid-1947. The influx of ex-servicemen into the economy caused competition in the housing and employment markets that made the transition difficult for some. Yet other problems were even more severe.

Inflation was a major source of concern. Americans had gone along with the rationing program of the Office of Price Administration (OPA) for the duration of the war, but now they demanded that it come to an end. The goods they wanted, however, were often in short supply, and with controls suddenly lifted a rapid rise in prices would be the inevitable result. The real question was what would happen until supply caught up with demand. Truman was in an impossible position, but his handling of the situation only made things worse. OPA director Chester Bowles urged him to stand firm and hold the line on prices; John Snyder, reconversion director, advised flexibility where the pressures were greatest, and Truman initially took that route. Bowles was furious, but there was little he could do.

Meanwhile, the increasingly conservative Congress got into the act too. Just before Christmas in 1945, it extended OPA's authority for six months and then took up the issue again in early 1946. Truman now pressed for a yearlong extension to allow for the regulation of prices and rationing of scarce items, with the pledge that he would ease controls as the situation changed. Business groups, such as the Chamber of Commerce and the National Association of Manufacturers, protested vigorously as they denounced OPA. One week before the agency's authority was due to lapse, Congress produced a bill that would have extended OPA's authority for another year but stripped it of the powers of enforcement. Truman responded with a protest veto that left the country with no control mechanism at all.

Almost immediately prices began to soar. Within a month the cost-of-living index was up 6 points and consumers had begun to demand action. In Princeton, New Jersey, housewives calling themselves the "militant marketers" moved to boycott stores that charged inflated prices. Though Congress eventually moved to pass a weak bill to stem the tide, the damage was already done. Truman had spoken out, to be sure, but had not been able to move early enough to avoid the confrontation. Chester Bowles, who resigned at the height of the trouble, was disturbed by the president's approach and argued, "The government's stability policy is not what you have stated it to be, but is instead one of improvising on a day-to-day, case-by-case method, as one crisis leads to another—in short . . . there is really no policy at all." A year and a half after the end of the war, the consumer price index was up almost 25 percent, and one critic tartly observed that the OPA name and acronym should be changed to the "Office for Cessation of Rationing and Priorities," OCRAP.

So too did Truman manage to bungle his first dealings with labor. After the wartime years of restraint, labor wanted wage increases regarded as long overdue. When businessmen refused, millions of workers went on strike. The situation was bad at the end of 1945 but became even worse the next year. In 1946, 4.6 million workers were out on strike—more than ever before in the history of the United States. There were strikes in the automobile, steel, and electrical industries, and there was serious trouble with soft-coal miners and railroad workers.

The railroad problem came to a head in the spring of 1946. Union leaders rejected an arbitrated settlement and set a strike date. A concerned Truman told them, "If you think I'm going to sit here and let you tie up this whole country, you're crazy as hell." He also decided to ask Congress for the power to draft strikers into the armed forces if their actions caused a national emergency. Questioned about the constitutionality of his proposal, he said, "We'll draft 'em first and think about the law later." In his own speech, he wrote, "Let's put transportation and production back to work, hang a few traitors and make our country safe for democracy." He toned that down a bit when he went before Congress, yet even though he received word that a settlement had been reached as he spoke, he pressed on with his plan for a strikers' draft. The House of Representatives quickly went along, but in the Senate cooler heads prevailed, and the plan was allowed to die.

Truman, however, had antagonized labor by his actions and did so again in his handling of the coal strike. John L. Lewis, the arrogant and defiant head of the United Mine Workers, led his followers out of the mines on April 1, 1946. A settlement was ultimately reached, but Lewis later backed out of it, and Truman again decided to act. Just after the midterm elections, the administration obtained a court injunction, which Lewis defied. Both leader and union were cited for contempt of court, and after a trial Lewis received a fine of $10,000, the union one of $3.5 million. At that time the workers returned to the mines.

In both episodes the feisty Truman showed the same willingness to take quick action he demonstrated in foreign affairs. But while in some corners he gained prestige for his approach, in others he lost valuable support. He needed the aid of labor; it was a necessary part of his political base. Labor was a major segment of the Democratic coalition Roosevelt had put together, and labor leaders had supported Truman for vice-president in 1945. Now, however, their views began to change.

Fair Deal Aims

As Truman attempted to cope with the immediate problems of reconversion to peace, he also set out his larger priorities for domestic reform. As a senator he

Ex-servicemen picketing coal mines in Panther Valley, Pennsylvania, in early 1946 to try to get their jobs back. (*AP/Wide World*)

had supported the New Deal; now he wanted to consolidate the gains made before the Second World War and move further toward the achievement of related liberal goals.

Truman had a good base on which to build. Roosevelt had retreated from his New Deal during the war as he recognized the need to maintain political support in the struggle to defeat enemies abroad, but as the conflict drew to an end, he sought to revive the earlier aims and to restate them for future use. The "Economic Bill of Rights," announced in 1944, was the result. Roosevelt proclaimed the right of all Americans to fair pay and useful work, to decent living conditions, and to security from the ravages of unemployment, old age, or ill health. Roosevelt knew those were lofty goals, and to avoid trying to do too much at once, he sought as a first step to guarantee the necessary assistance only to the veterans of the war. Still, the larger vision remained.

Truman picked up on Roosevelt's start and showed that he shared his predecessor's view that government in modern America needed to play a positive role. It could and should move in behalf of defined economic and social goals. To that end, as the war ended, Truman called on Congress to pass legislation to stabilize the economy and smooth the transition to peace. He contended that his 21-point program, which included full-employment legislation, a higher minimum wage, greater unemployment compensation, housing assistance, and a host of other items, would produce stability and security in the postwar years. In the course of the next ten weeks he sent further messages to Congress as he added to the basic proposals already made. By early 1946 he had a program that included health insurance and atomic energy legislation as well as the earlier goals.

The Truman program, unfocused and diffuse, was a haphazard compilation of basic liberal goals, yet it provided the only domestic framework for Truman's two terms. The ties to the New Deal were clear. Truman wanted to maintain the gains of the emerging welfare state and to extend those gains to Americans still left out. Nevertheless, important differences from the New Deal became more evident as time went on. Roosevelt had assumed power in the midst of depression, and the New Deal sought to deal with extraordinarily serious economic problems. The Fair Deal, by contrast, unfolded in a period of relative prosperity, and the need for reform consequently seemed less pressing to opponents of change. The liberal aims remained, but political realities made them harder to achieve.

The Employment Act of 1946

Truman's difficulties with his program were foreshadowed by agitation over the Employment Act of 1946. After years of depression, spending—first for defense, then for war—seemed to vindicate the theories of English economist John Maynard Keynes, who had argued that sustained countercyclical measures could move an economy out of a permanently low equilibrium and bring a restoration of prosperity. The influx of money had made a difference. With that lesson in mind, liberals wanted to commit the government to the use of countercyclical tools to head off any future disruptions before they became severe. A bill introduced in Congress in 1945 sought to commit the government to maintain full employment by monitoring the economy and then taking the necessary monetary and fiscal actions in case of decline. These actions could come in the form of tax cuts or spending programs or in other ways that would achieve the same end.

The measure was a firm statement of the view that the government had a definite responsibility to maintain equilibrium at home and to enable its citizens to work. Since the days of the New Deal, liberal forces in America had been working toward that end, and the employment bill was an important first step in committing the government to that goal. Yet there were significant segments of American society that viewed such action as an intrusion into their domain. Business groups took aim at the proposals, and the National Association of Manufacturers and other organizations claimed that it undermined free enterprise and moved the United States one step closer to socialism.

In the end Congress gutted the proposal, and the Employment Act of 1946 that emerged came nowhere near to doing what its sponsors had hoped. As passed, it created a Council of Economic Advisers to make recommendations to the president on the state of the economy, and it directed the president himself to present an annual economic report. It dropped the notion of an annual budget geared toward the maintenance of full employment and hence shelved the use of Keynesian policies. It was nonetheless a symbolic first step, for the economic tools were better understood now, and the nation had begun to consider how they might be used. It had hedged in 1946, but further steps could come in later years.

POLITICS AND POLICIES

The experience with the Employment Act, and with the problems of reconversion, demonstrated the divisions the administration faced. The Democratic party, reflecting the country as a whole, was split into liberal and conservative camps, and Truman was caught in the middle. Unprepared for the presidency, his first efforts to craft a liberal program had failed, and he found his political fortune in jeopardy.

The Troubles of 1946

Truman needed whatever support he could get, but he faced significant opposition even within his own party. The Democratic party had been split into northern and southern wings for some time, and the southern Democrats had allied themselves informally with the Republicans in a coalition that had begun to emerge when Franklin Roosevelt sought to pack the Supreme Court a decade before. In the House of Representatives, Republican leaders Joseph Martin and Charles Halleck often worked with Democrat Howard Smith, while in the Senate, Republican Robert Taft frequently found himself on the same side as Democrats Harry Byrd and Richard Russell. The conservative coalition dominated Congress both during and after the Second World War and made it difficult for more liberal elements to pursue their goals.

As the midterm elections of 1946 approached, Truman and his supporters were in sad shape. Liberals still pined for FDR, and when they questioned what Roosevelt would have done had he been alive, the standard retort was, "I wonder what Truman would do if he were alive." Truman's heavy-handedness with striking unions alienated labor, and his haphazard inflation policies hurt consumers. Other groups were similarly discouraged about the leadership of the administration. Truman often seemed like a petty, bungling administrator who could not do anything right, and he became the butt of countless political jokes. Some people went around saying, "You just sort of forget about Harry until he makes another mistake." In another story, the question of why the president had been late to a press conference was raised. The answer: On getting up in the morning, he was a little stiff in the joints and had difficulty putting his foot into his mouth. Truman's level of support dropped from 87 percent after he assumed the presidency to 32 percent in November 1946. Gleeful Republicans said that "to err is Truman" as they asked the voters, "Had Enough?"

The results of the election mirrored the popular mood. Republicans won majorities in both houses of Congress—51 to 45 in the Senate and 245 to 188 in the House—and emerged with a majority of the governorships, too. In Atlantic City, New Jersey, a Republican candidate for justice of the peace who had died a week before was victorious in the sweep. If Truman had known trouble in his first year and a half as president, the next two promised to be even worse.

Truman and the 80th Congress

The lines of opposition were clearly drawn after the congressional elections of 1946. The Republicans were in charge, and when their votes were buttressed by those of conservative Democrats, the Truman program had little chance of success. There was still a liberal group in the administration that wanted to push beyond the start the New Deal had made, and indeed, Truman's own instincts ran along those lines, as his early programs and proposals made clear. Yet within his Cabinet a more conservative view prevailed; many members of his top staff argued that the time for liberal experiment had passed and time for consolidation had come. They were willing to safeguard the gains of the New Deal but hesitant to move any further.

The real resistance, however, came from the 80th Congress of the United States. Republicans generally supported the Democrats on foreign affairs, and a bipartisan spirit prevailed. The real split came on domestic issues, where the Republicans, after years of Democratic rule, were determined to reassert their power. They wanted to see Congress reestablish its authority and cut the executive branch back to size. In direct contrast to Truman, they also wanted less government intervention in the business world and in private life.

Spearheading the Republican cause was Senator Robert A. Taft of Ohio. Son of former president William Howard Taft, he was knowledgeable, articulate, and self-assured, and he had ambitions of his own. Elected to the Senate in 1938, he had established himself as a political and intellectual leader of the GOP. In the 80th Congress he hoped to create a record that could lead him to the White House in due time. Taft knew what he wanted to do and had the ability to move in those directions. According to his critics, he had the best mind in Washington—until he made it up. Now, for him, the direction was clear. He argued that the Republicans had a mandate to take stock and reverse direction where the New Deal had gone too far. The government, he asserted, should not try to dictate to responsible adults who could work out their destinies on their own. Just before the 80th Congress met, Taft declared that the recent election had revolved around the question of freedom and had underscored the need to eliminate or reduce interference by government in family and business affairs.

In addition to tempering government authority, Taft and the Republicans had to deal with other major areas of concern. They wanted to reduce taxes, and they wanted to cut back on the privileged position they felt labor had come to enjoy.

When the Congress met, it sought to achieve those goals. One measure undertook to limit any future president to two terms. Enacted as a constitutional amendment, it was ratified in 1951. Republicans who had bridled through four Roosevelt elections, even though he did not survive the fourth term, had finally found a way to get back at FDR. They justified their support

Senator Robert A. Taft, Republican leader, running unsuccessfully for president. (*AP/Wide World*)

for the amendment by claiming it was the only way to ensure that a dictator would not arise. Democrats countered by charging a lack of faith in popular rule and by arguing that it might limit future response if and when a crisis should occur. But the symbol was important, and the measure became law.

In the area of taxation, the Republicans also fought back. Government, they charged, was interfering too much in the lives of its citizens. It was time to cut federal spending and, by so doing, to ease the tax burden, which had grown too great. Taft believed that cuts of $5 to $6 billion could be made to bring the federal budget down to a $30 billion level. Congress moved in that direction and in 1947 passed tax-cut measures twice. Both times Truman vetoed them, but in 1948, an election year, Congress overrode another veto and the cut became law.

The heaviest fire, however, was directed at labor policies first formulated during the New Deal. The union movement had been in serious trouble during the Depression until Section 7a of the National Industrial Recovery Act of 1933 helped it revive. That provision protected the right of unions to organize; though it kept employers from interfering with the right of workers to join unions, it stopped short of guaranteeing the right to bargain collectively. Many employers established company unions and even then did not always bargain in good faith. When the Supreme Court declared the National Recovery Administration unconstitutional in 1935 and Section 7a went by the boards, the Wagner Act filled the void. Passed in the same year, it established a National Labor Relations Board to oversee union elections and also prohibited employers from engaging in practices aimed at circumscribing employee rights. Labor revived overnight and gave its political support to FDR. He was, one North Carolina mill worker declared, "the only man we ever had in the White House who would understand that my boss is a sonofabitch." Labor became an integral part of the Roosevelt coalition that formed in 1936. But now the Republicans argued that labor had gone too far.

Taft and his supporters had already begun to try to keep labor in check. In an earlier session a bill had sought to require notice for strikes, then a cooling-off period if a strike occurred, and other restrictions as well. Though Truman had successfully vetoed that measure, after 1946 the Republicans had more votes.

Some sort of labor legislation seemed a sure thing. Business had been seeking restrictions for some time, and with the labor turbulence and unrest at the end of World War II, employers were even more eager to regain control. Union leaders on occasion seemed to exercise arbitrary rule and were not always willing to engage in the process of reform from within. Now the public, inconvenienced by the postwar strikes, appeared amenable to some sort of movement for control. In 1947 legislatures in more than 20 states passed laws to restrict the activities of unions in at least some way. Truman himself, as if to try to head off further action, endorsed some mild labor restrictions.

But the real initiative came from the 80th Congress in the Taft-Hartley Act of 1947. It spelled out unfair labor practices and ruled illegal the closed shop in which an employee had to join a union before he could get a job. The act allowed the president to call for an 80-day cooling-off period, during which time workers engaging in strikes affecting national safety or health had to return to work, and it required union officials to sign non-Communist oaths in order to be able to use the National Labor Relations Board.

Response was bitter. Unions called it a "slave-labor law," and Truman claimed that it was unworkable and unfair. Asserting that it would hinder, not help, labor-management relations, he vetoed the bill. He said it would "conflict with important principles of our democratic society" and went on nationwide radio to seek public support for his stand. He may have regained the political support of labor by that move, but in Congress it made no difference at all. The Taft-Hartley measure passed over the veto and became law.

The Taft-Hartley Act aroused labor's ire, but it did not really check the union movement. Both union leaders and Truman proved themselves able to live with the measure in later years, even though they made political capital out of it whenever they could.

All in all, the 80th Congress tore Truman's program to shreds. In addition to the tax and labor measures, the Congress turned down programs to aid education and provide public housing, even though they had Taft's support. So too the Congress rejected an administration plan for universal military training. It did not abolish established welfare programs that had by now been accepted as facts of life, but it did move toward contraction, with a clear conservative bent.

The Election of 1948

As his term dragged on, Truman occasionally became discouraged by the troubles he faced. He seemed stymied at every turn, unable to lead in the direction he wanted to go. In the fall of 1947 he even sent a member of his staff to talk to Dwight D. Eisenhower, then army chief of staff, to see if Ike was interested in the Democratic nomination for president in 1948. In strict confidence Truman offered his help, but Eisenhower turned him down. Gutsy fighter that he was, Truman decided to seek reelection himself, even though he knew that his influence was at an unprecedented low. Looking ahead to the convention, columnists Joseph and Stewart Alsop declared that if nominated, Truman would "be forced to wage the loneliest campaign in history."

Not everyone in the administration agreed. Clark Clifford, one of Truman's advisers, argued that the president should select issues of interest to voters and hammer them home. Specifically, he should turn to the left on domestic questions and stress his leadership in foreign policy. Clifford knew that Truman stood little chance of legislative success, but he could at least build a record against the 80th Congress that he could use in the coming campaign. Truman therefore called again, almost defiantly, for all of his liberal goals. He sought to attract farmers and workers and blacks—all elements of the old New Deal coalition that he hoped to re-create. In his State of the Union message and in other addresses, Truman began the long, slow process of drumming up support.

By the summer of 1948, the Democrats were discouraged. A boom for Eisenhower began—with slogans like "Ike, You're A-1 With Us, Be 1-A in the Draft"—but it proved short-lived and fizzled. At the convention, Truman ended up with what most people thought was a worthless nomination. Not only was Truman's popularity down; the Democratic party itself seemed to be falling apart.

Splinter groups were forming on both the left and the right. At the convention there had been serious trouble over the civil rights plank in the platform. The issue was becoming more intense, but Truman hoped to waffle, at least until after the election, so as not to alienate the South. He favored a moderate proposal, just like the plank in the platform of 1944, saying that Congress should exert its constitutional powers to see that racial and religious minorities enjoyed conditions of equality. It met defeat at the hands of liberals who pressed for something more. Hubert Humphrey, mayor of Minneapolis, declared, "The time has arrived for the Democratic Party to get out of the shadow of states' rights and walk forthrightly into the bright sunshine of human rights." At that, all delegates from Mississippi and half of those from Alabama did some walking of their own and left the convention. The renegade southerners later formed their own States' Rights or Dixiecrat party, and at their convention delegates from 13 states nominated Governor J. Strom Thurmond of South Carolina as their candidate for president of the United States. They stood for "the segregation of the races" and wanted no interference with race relations as they were. The southern defection seemed to undermine any remaining Democratic hopes for success. The South had long been a Democratic source of strength, but now it was gone.

That was not all. The Democratic party was threatened from the left as well. Henry Wallace, Roosevelt's vice-president during the third term and secretary of commerce after that, had been fired from the Cabinet by Truman for his more temperate stand on the Russian threat. On leaving the administration,

Wallace's differences with Truman became even sharper. He claimed that Truman's hard-line stance was provoking the Soviet Union and intensifying the Cold War. Arguing that "we are whipping up another holy war against Russia," he became the presidential candidate of the Progressive party. Wallace initially attracted widespread liberal support, but as Communists and fellow travelers appeared active in his organization, other followers dropped off. Nonetheless, his candidacy drew away at least some of Truman's support.

In that fragmented state, Truman and his segment of the Democratic party faced the Republicans, who were itching for the presidency after two decades of being outside. Once again they nominated Thomas E. Dewey, the governor of New York. Dewey, somewhat stiff and egocentric, looked to Alice Roosevelt Longworth like the bridegroom on a wedding cake. Once, in a story critics told, a photographer asked Dewey to smile; "I thought I was," he replied. Other critics said he was a man "who could strut sitting down." Dewey had lost one election to the Democrats in 1944 and was determined not to lose again. He had taken the offensive with a series of shrill attacks on FDR the last time, and that approach had not worked. In 1948 he seemed to have victory firmly in hand. All the polls picked the Republicans to win, and Dewey therefore saw little value in brawling with his Democratic opponent. He decided to take a quieter approach, spoke in platitudes and generalities, and conducted his campaign, according to one commentator, "with the humorless calculation of a Certified Public Accountant in pursuit of the Holy Grail."

Truman had little to lose and so came on strong. Immediately on receiving the Democratic nomination, the president struck the first blow. In his acceptance speech, he declared that the Republicans in their platform seemed to favor many of his goals—medical, housing, and education programs. Since they had stymied those very measures in Congress, he intended to test their sincerity and give them a second chance. "I am going to call that Congress back in session," Truman said, "and I am going to ask them to pass some of these laws they say they are for in their platform." Truman knew full well that the Congress would do nothing at all. But his challenge was a bold political stroke that set the tone for the campaign ahead.

Truman appealed for labor's help and used his veto of the Taft-Hartley Act as part of his quest for that support. He also seized on the farm issue. This was a problem for which both Republicans and Democrats were to blame, but he exploited it for partisan ends. In the farm price-support program, farmers used the Commodity Credit Corporation to borrow money and store surplus crops until the market could better absorb them. Not long before, the 80th Congress had failed to provide additional storage bins, and with a good harvest and increasing surplus, farmers found they had nowhere to store the crops to wait for a better price. Truman jumped on the mistake: "The Republican Congress has already stuck a pitchfork in the farmers' backs. . . . When you have to sell your grain below the support price because you have no place to store it, you can thank this same Republican Congress."

Truman began to change his speaking style, with visible results. Talking from a prepared text, his delivery was stiff and dull. Now he discarded the

speeches and began to talk off the cuff in the stump style he had always preferred. In the campaign he believed that everyone was against him but the
people, so he decided to address the people in terms they could understand. In
an ostensibly nonpolitical trip west just before his renomination, he began to
blame Congress for all troubles. He blamed the people, too, for staying home in
1946. He preached the message again and again: "If you send another Republican Congress to Washington, you're a bigger bunch of suckers than I think
you are."

Over and over Truman excoriated the "do-nothing" 80th Congress. He
called the Republicans "gluttons of privilege." They were "bloodsuckers with
offices on Wall Street." They were "just a bunch of old mossbacks" all set to do
the New Deal in. Truman sought to tie Dewey to the 80th Congress, and even
though the connection was slim, he persisted in viewing the Republicans as all
part of the same cloth, cut from the Hoover bolt. In whistle-stops around the
country he covered 32,000 miles by train, made several hundred speeches, and
saw millions of people. Speaking without a text in his choppy, aggressive style,
he warmed to the crowds and they warmed to him. "Give 'em hell, Harry," they
yelled. "Pour it on." And he did.

Truman approached the election still an underdog, according to the polls.
Life magazine referred to Dewey as the next president. In mid-October, 50
political experts polled by *Newsweek* unanimously picked Dewey to win. Poll-
sters ended the interviewing process before the very end of the campaign on the
assumption that the election was all but wrapped up.

They were wrong. On election day, despite the bold headline DEWEY
DEFEATS TRUMAN in the Chicago *Tribune,* the president scored one of the great
political upsets of all time. He received 24.2 million popular votes to Dewey's
22 million and won by a 303 to 189 margin in the electoral count. Democrats

Harry Truman scoring an upset victory in 1948. (*UPI/Bettmann Newsphotos*)

also regained control of Congress with a 54 to 42 margin in the Senate and a 263 to 171 margin in the House.

Why did Truman win? Republican overconfidence helped. So did Truman's courageous stance in the face of overwhelming odds. Voters who had been undecided for much of the campaign finally ignored the polls and decided the president was all right after all. Yet in the end Truman won primarily because he was able to re-create major elements of the Democratic coalition Franklin Roosevelt had put together more than a decade before. After the rocky days of 1946, Truman regained labor support; he won in the farm belt, where he seemed to have a better grasp of farmers' needs; and he drew the votes of blacks, who found his civil rights stance preferable to any of the alternatives. The fragmentation of the Democratic party, which had threatened to hurt severely, ended up helping instead. The States' Rights and Progressive parties siphoned off some votes, to be sure, but they also allowed Truman to make a more direct appeal to the center, and that ultimately accounted for his success. Now Truman was president in his own right and could once again attempt to push ahead.

The Fair Deal: Failure or Success?

After reelection, in his 1949 state-of-the-union message, Truman declared that all Americans had "a right to expect from our Government a fair deal." That statement provided the name for the domestic program he had been proposing for the past three years. In office in his own right, Truman proved more effective than he had been before, particularly in the area of civil rights, but even so, his program was only a mixed success.

Some parts of the Fair Deal worked; others did not. In the area of housing, initial setbacks in the chaotic reconversion period were finally overcome and some modest gains achieved. There was a desperate housing shortage as the soldiers began to come home at the end of World War II. The building trade had suffered during the Depression, and the crowding in industrial centers only became worse during World War II. People of all races and ethnic groups poured into hastily constructed developments near the factories that often seemed little more than slums. The administration after the war sought larger appropriations for public housing, without success. Despite Robert Taft's support for a housing program, rural interests blocked all measures. A few years later, in 1949, a National Housing Act, sponsored by both liberal and conservative forces, called for federally funded construction of hundreds of thousands of inexpensive units over the next several years. There as elsewhere, Truman pushed a policy the New Deal had begun but was unable to go as far as need demanded.

Other efforts fared even less well. Secretary of Agriculture Charles Brannan proposed a major reform of the farm program. The New Deal had sought to assist farmers by supporting prices, and though that effort had made a difference in Depression days, it was expensive to both the government and the public. It also seemed to favor large producers over small and to encourage overproduction. Under the Brannan Plan, the administration proposed to end price supports and to let prices respond to the open market. The government would, however, provide income support through a basic income floor. The complex plan, Brannan hoped, would help farmers, particularly small ones, as well as the government, but it soon ran into trouble when larger farmers voiced irritation at the limitations on payments they foresaw and the American Farm Bureau Federation came out against the proposal. With that kind of pressure, it died in Congress.

The Fair Deal raised the minimum wage from 40 to 75 cents an hour, expanded the social security program to include almost 10 million more people, extended public power production efforts, and saw some action on soil conservation and flood control. On other major measures, however, the record was less good. The American Medical Association came out four-square against the program for a national health insurance plan. Although doctors could choose not to participate if they wished, the medical lobby contended that it was socialized medicine and violated the canons of American life. In the face of such resistance, particularly when the nation was paying more attention to the Communist issue and foreign affairs than to domestic programs, the program stood little chance. Congress also rejected a measure designed to provide federal aid to education. The issue of assistance to parochial schools intruded, and the $300 million bill got bogged down in a House committee and never emerged.

On the home front, Truman started off with grandiose plans that inevitably fell short. He was a liberal in the New Deal mold, but the eclectic approach that had survived contradictions in the 1930s worked less well in the decade that followed. Truman seemed to ask for too much in a scattershot approach, without always sorting out his goals. As the *New Republic* reported, "Truman would ask Congress for about 120 percent more than he expected. Congress, with a great show of indignation, would slash it to 75 percent. Truman would smile his little-man smile and bounce back with something else. It's a funny way to run a country." Less skillful than FDR, Truman never enjoyed the domestic success of his predecessor.

AMERICAN SOCIETY IN THE POSTWAR YEARS

In the years after 1945, Americans sought to re-create the prosperity they remembered from before the Depression and the war. After the dislocations of the reconversion period, middle-class Americans began to enjoy the fruits of the greatest industrial power the world had ever known. Yet not all citizens enjoyed either prosperity or privileges to which they were entitled. Blacks in particular, but Hispanics and Native Americans as well, began to lay claim to their rights in a long, slow struggle that had barely begun.

Black Gains

During Truman's administration the issue of civil rights became a national concern. Blacks had made strides during World War II as they pushed for an end to discrimination wherever they could. Through the actions of the Fair

Employment Practices Committee, they had moved to better jobs and, where permitted, had fought valiantly in the war itself. With some momentum generated during the struggle, they were determined to persevere. Court cases moved quietly through legal channels in the Truman years, as the NAACP sought to overturn the judicial justification for segregation. The racial question became more visible in 1947, when Branch Rickey, general manager of the Brooklyn Dodgers, broke the baseball color line by signing Jackie Robinson to his National League team. Blacks, formerly confined to the old Negro leagues, now started to move into the major leagues. On a larger stage, the United States found its racial problems intertwining with those of the Cold War. As leader of the free world, it sought to appeal for support in Africa and Asia, where its discriminatory policies appeared in an unfavorable light. There was now a larger reason to confront the problem of change at home.

Truman was in a position of authority as the civil rights issue came to a head, and in a somewhat halting way he helped move it along. His first involvement with the civil rights movement came more for political than for moral reasons. He was a humane man, moderate on questions of race, but he came from a border state and had Confederate ancestors in his past. His uncle had fought with the southern army in the Civil War, and his mother retained strong sympathies for the Confederate cause. Yet Truman understood the strength of the black vote, first in Kansas City, then in Missouri, and finally in the United States as a whole. He saw that black interests needed protection and realized that, especially in urban areas, black support could make the difference between victory and defeat. During World War II he had supported the Fair Employment Practices Committee, and as chairman of an investigating committee, he had agreed to look into instances of racial discrimination. But always his quest was for justice, not for equality in the social sphere. In 1940 he said in a speech to a black audience, "I am not appealing for social equality of the Negro. The Negro himself knows better than that. . . . Negroes want justice, not social relations."

Jackie Robinson of the Brooklyn Dodgers stealing home. (*AP/Wide World*)

Truman's first formal efforts as president did not bring much success. The future of the FEPC, a wartime agency, was a matter of concern, and the question was whether it would be allowed to continue in some form after the hostilities came to an end. Truman called for a permanent FEPC, which had almost no chance of being established, yet in the chaotic transition to peace he made but a half-hearted effort to perpetuate the wartime organization. As the conservative Congress cut funds, he made gestures in the direction of FEPC support but was unwilling to expend much effort when other issues were at stake. In June 1946, after a period of decline, the agency finally expired, with no prospects for a permanent body in sight.

Truman did better on other fronts. In September 1946 he listened to the National Emergency Committee Against Mob Violence tell of lynchings and other brutalities still occurring in the South. Disturbed by the account and determined to seek an end to such terror, he agreed to pursue the matter further. After the midterm elections, he appointed a distinguished Committee on Civil Rights to investigate the problem and recommend what should be done. The report, "To Secure These Rights," was released in October 1947 and provided evidence of the magnitude of the problem that still existed in the United States. Blacks remained second-class citizens in all areas of American life. They received unequal treatment in education, housing, medical care, and countless other categories. They were segregated by law and discriminated against in violation of traditional ideals the nation professed to follow. It was time, the committee asserted in strong terms, for the federal government to secure the rights of all.

Truman responded cautiously at first. As with his Fair Deal program as a whole, he called for legislative action with little hope of success. Now up against the 80th Congress, he knew his hands were tied. He did ask Congress to set up machinery to monitor progress in civil rights and to outlaw the most violent crimes, but he stopped short of moving against segregation itself.

Then the political situation changed and pushed Truman along. When the southern wing of the Democratic party departed in 1948, the way was clear for the president to be more aggressive in his political approach. He was clearly going to lose a part of the South, but he now had to be sure to hold the urban vote elsewhere in the land. At the same time he felt the pressure from Henry Wallace's left-wing challenge, and that too pushed him toward a more liberal stand.

Truman acted where he had the power to do so. By executive order in July 1948 he barred discrimination in the federal establishment. This was a start toward chipping away at segregation in the government bureaucracy, begun in the time of Woodrow Wilson. Truman also took the first steps to bring an end to segregation in the military forces. There should be, another executive order stated, "equality of treatment and opportunity for all persons in the armed services without regard to race, color, religion or national origin," and the president created a committee to pursue the matter further.

The military question was a major one. Military service had long been seen as evidence of loyalty to the nation and cause for enjoyment of full rights.

Yet with charges of inherent racial inferiority, the military establishment sought to limit that chance to fight and thereby limited the subsequent opportunity to enjoy the broader privileges of citizenship as well. The issue was real, as blacks demonstrated by their pressure to participate in World War II, but it had symbolic importance as well.

Issuing an executive order was one thing; implementation was another. The committee investigated the problem for two years, then recommended following through. The effort brought success in the navy, air force, and marine corps but encountered resistance from the army. Though the army had more blacks, for it relied on the draft to fill its ranks, it kept them in segregated units. Earlier, Army Chief of Staff Omar Bradley had complained that the army was not an agency of social reform, and Truman had rebuked him, making clear that he wanted progress on the matter. Nonetheless, the president allowed the army to move slowly and even agreed to allow it to restore a limiting quota if the process of liberalization brought in too many blacks. Segregation persisted in the army until the Korean War, when that struggle finally brought about the change. The army needed manpower and proved willing to set blacks next to whites in combat as long as the results were good. The war indeed turned out to be a proving ground. Blacks fought better in integrated than in segregated units, and army officials discovered that the new arrangements in fact cut down on prejudice and conflict. The new policy worked; it was Truman's greatest civil rights success.

In other areas there were small gains. The Justice Department became active in the battle against segregation and filed briefs challenging the constitutionality of restrictions in housing, education, and interstate transportation. Those "friends of the court" briefs resulted from growing national pressures and helped move the Supreme Court toward tackling the racial issue more directly. A 1948 decision prohibited enforcement of restrictive housing covenants, which kept blacks or other minority members from buying property in white areas. Another decision in 1950 determined that segregated dining facilities on southern railroads violated the commerce clause of the Constitution, and a number of rulings in education cases foreshadowed the landmark decisions that came during the Eisenhower years.

In the legislative sphere, however, the record was weak. Again and again, Truman called for congressional action for political effect, with little expectation of seeing results. In October 1949 he asked for national legislation that would make lynching a federal crime, forbid use of the poll tax to restrict the right to vote, and establish a new FEPC. As in other areas, it was an aggressive program that barely got off the ground. One civil rights supporter observed that Truman seemed "to start with a bold measure and then temporize to pick up the right-wing forces. Simply stated, backtrack after the bang." In Congress, southern Democrats who held important committee posts as a result of long tenure in the single-party South quickly demonstrated their unwillingness to follow the president's lead. Mississippi senators John Stennis and James Eastland headed two significant subcommittees responsible for considering the items the White House had proposed. If that first line of defense failed, they could always mobilize to filibuster any liberal measure to death. Watering down Truman's request, political opponents proposed instead a compromise that would have been meaningless at best. They would have set up, among other things, an FEPC with no powers of enforcement. Truman understandably refused to go along.

Truman's record in civil rights was mixed. He spoke out throughout his tenure in the presidency. Early in his administration he revealed his moral support for the issue and made blacks aware of his sympathies. Later, particularly when political benefit beckoned, he moved still further along, and the legislative stalemate notwithstanding, achievements were visible by the end of his second term. If he sometimes seemed to speak out but then hesitated to act, he eventually came around and ended up compiling a record better than that of any of his presidential predecessors in the twentieth century. He was definitely a moderate who was wary of going too far, yet while he may have been hesitant at first to lead the crusade for legal equality, in time he became genuinely active in the quest. Aggressive fighter that he was, he ended up playing a major role in moving the question of civil rights to center stage in American life.

Hispanics and Native Americans

In the years after World War II, Spanish-speaking groups in the United States suffered from many of the same problems as blacks. Undocumented workers coming to work in the fields encountered difficulties in the best of times. When the economy faltered, they faced efforts on the part of immigration officials to return them to their countries of origin. Unskilled and illiterate, many of them gravitated to the cities, where they often lived in depressing conditions from which there seemed no escape.

Chicanos throughout the country endured the same troubles faced by other members of the working class. Those active in factories and firms suffered from the conservative attacks on the labor movement as the Taft-Hartley Act became law.

Equally troubling were the political attacks in the dark days of the Red Scare. Chicanos active in radical causes now faced serious trouble. Men like Agapito Gómez, who had lived in the United States for 25 years and had an American wife, now had difficulties that were unimaginable before. In the 1930s he had been part of a depression relief organization and had joined the CIO. Later, when he refused to divulge the names of people with whom he had worked, immigration officials took away his alien card.

Others besides field hands and laborers felt oppressed. Chicanos in all areas experienced the contradictions of American life. They encountered discrimination in the schools, uncertain access to public facilities, and exclusion from the governing process.

Like blacks, they protested such restrictions and occasionally met with success. In mid-1946, the Tempe (Arizona) Chamber of Commerce allowed Chicanos entrance to the city's swimming pool as a result of pressure from a Chicano veterans' group. Elsewhere they moved to take political action. A concerted effort to register new voters in Los Angeles led to the election of Edward Roybal to the city council in 1949. He was the first person of Mexican descent to serve there since 1881.

Yet those small gains hardly compensated for the problems still faced. Hispanics remained troubled by frequent episodes of police brutality, particularly in the cities. Los Angeles, with a large Chicano population, was the scene of numerous episodes. In mid-1951, on receiving a complaint about a loud record player, officers raided a baptismal gathering without a warrant and assaulted members of the party. At the end of the year, in the "Bloody Christmas" case, police removed seven Chicanos from jail cells and beat them. Chicanos protested such episodes. Sometimes they achieved recourse; sometimes they did not. Many considered the situation hopeless. Real change had to wait for another day.

Native Americans had an even harder time. In the post–World War II years, they had to fight the forces of cultural change that were eroding tribal tradition. As power lines reached the reservations, televisions, refrigerators, washing machines, and other appliances found their way into Indian life. Automobiles were in greater supply. In the face of those new machines, old patterns changed. Many Indians gravitated to the cities, where they often had difficulty adjusting to urban life.

Native Americans also encountered trouble during the Red Scare. Navajos in the United States, facing starvation in the bitter winter of 1947–1948, were denied government relief because of charges that their communal way of life was communistic and therefore un-American.

For Indians, as for other minorities, the need to struggle for equal treatment became clear in the postwar years. But like other groups, Indians were not yet organized. Only when mobilization occurred could they look forward to improvement in their lot.

Women in the Postwar Years

Women faced real changes in the years immediately following World War II. The war had caused earlier patterns to shift as male servicemen went overseas and women began to take their jobs. Later, however, men who had relinquished their positions when the war called expected them to be waiting on their return. After 1945 there was a period of adjustment that led to the reemergence of more traditional patterns.

Women were not always comfortable with the transition. Many had enjoyed working during the war and were reluctant to retreat to the home. In 1947, *Life* magazine ran a long story on the "American Woman's Dilemma" and argued that women were torn between the traditional expectation that they stay home and the possibility of working outside. A 1946 *Fortune* poll likewise reflected the sense of discontent some women felt. When asked whether they would prefer to be born again as men or women, 25 percent of the female respondents said they would prefer to be men. Opportunities were greater in the male sphere.

By the 1950s, doubts and questions had been suppressed. Women continued to work, to be sure, but the more common pattern was to marry and have a family rather than pursue a career. Women could find comfort in Benjamin Spock's enormously popular book *Baby and Child Care,* first published in 1946 and ultimately responsible for the child-rearing patterns of the postwar years. In it he advised mothers to stay at home with their children and not to work if they wanted to raise stable and secure children. Many women did.

THE TRUMAN YEARS IN PERSPECTIVE

In the years following World War II, the United States sought to re-create a stable balance at home. The society seemed healthy, though there were groups left out of the benefits of American life who began to make their voices heard. Harry Truman recognized the need for reform but found himself stymied at every turn. He faced terrific resistance from a conservative coalition in Congress that had its own priorities. He also found himself preoccupied with the programs of the Cold War.

Despite his pronouncements about the need for a fair deal for all, Truman often seemed more concerned with foreign policy, particularly as he strove to secure bipartisan support. It took the major share of his attention and required the expenditure of what limited political capital he had. Committed to an aggressive stance in the face of a perceived Soviet threat, something had to give, and the domestic program suffered as a result. As defense expenditures began to mount, there was correspondingly less money for projects at home, and political and financial stalemate therefore occurred. The Korean War also distracted policymakers from affairs at home, leading government officials to deal with military and diplomatic measures first, with the domestic pieces to be picked up later if there was time.

The Fair Deal did produce some results at home. On balance, however, Truman's program was but a limited continuation of the New Deal approach. Americans were better off than before, and the postwar prosperity sometimes made further change less pressing than it might otherwise have been. Real reform was not in the cards in the immediate postwar years. Constrained by the culture and limited by his own approach, Truman left a mixed legacy as his term came to an end.

SUGGESTIONS FOR FURTHER READING

There are a number of good accounts of the Truman administration. Robert J. Donovan, *Conflict and Crisis: The Presidency of Harry S Truman, 1945–1948* (1977) is a detailed overview of Truman's first term. Robert J. Donovan, *Tumultuous Years: The Presidency of Harry S Truman, 1949–1953* (1982) carries the story through the second term. Cabell Phillips, *The Truman Presidency: The History of a Triumphant Succession* (1966) remains a useful narrative treatment of the Truman years. Other pertinent narratives include Alfred Steinberg, *The Man from Missouri: The Life and Times of Harry S. Truman* (1962) and Bert Cochran, *Harry Truman and the Crisis Presidency* (1973). A useful short biography is Robert H. Ferrell, *Harry S. Truman and the Modern American*

Presidency (1983). Barton J. Bernstein and Allen J. Matusow, *The Truman Administration: A Documentary History* (1966) is an excellent collection of documents on various facets of policy in Truman's two terms.

Harry S. Truman, *Memoirs,* 2 vols. (1955, 1956) is Truman's own account of his years at the top. Margaret Truman, *Harry S. Truman* (1972) is his daughter's assessment of his presidency.

A number of other books approach the Truman years from different perspectives. Alonzo L. Hamby, *Beyond the New Deal: Harry S. Truman and American Liberalism* (1973) is the best treatment of the successes and failures of the Fair Deal. Barton J. Bernstein, ed., *Politics and Policies of the Truman Administration* (1970) is a useful collection of revisionist essays. I. F. Stone, *The Truman Era* (1953) is a sharply critical collection of contemporary pieces about the president. Merle Miller, *Plain Speaking: An Oral Biography of Harry S. Truman* (1973) is an engaging collection of Truman's reminiscences and Miller's related observations.

Joseph C. Goulden, *The Best Years, 1945–1950* (1976) is a brisk account of social developments in the immediate postwar period.

On the black struggle for equality, see William Berman, *The Politics of Civil Rights in the Truman Administration* (1970).

For a lively overview of the 1948 election, see Irwin Ross, *The Loneliest Campaign* (1968). For the failed challenge mounted by Henry Wallace, see Norman D. Markowitz, *The Rise and Fall of the People's Century: Henry A. Wallace and American Liberalism, 1941–1948* (1973).

chapter 4

The Fifties: The Age of Ike

In the 1950s Americans found the peace and prosperity they had sought through years of depression and war. The country had survived the troubles and was now doing very well indeed. There was a sense of security about the world beyond, and while the Cold War continued and the Korean conflict lingered on, the fundamental orientation was one of peace. The economy was similarly stable, booming in a way that promised never to cease. There were occasional downturns, to be sure, but those could be overcome and never threatened to cause a devastating crash. There were also Americans who were less fortunate than others, yet in a self-confident age of consensus, the culture paid them little heed. For this was the Age of Ike, and Dwight D. Eisenhower, war hero in the past, now president of the United States, seemed to reflect the faith that all was well and would so remain in future years. Ike was a symbol of what Americans wanted and needed at that time. His famous grin and easy way persuaded people that the nation was in good hands. The United States had seemingly reached a plateau of prosperity from which it need never retreat.

THE PROSPERITY OF THE FIFTIES

The United States in the 1950s seemed healthy and comfortable with its lot. It had weathered both the disruptions of war and the difficulties of the Truman years. Now there was a satisfying sense that the American way, materialistic as never before, reigned supreme, within the land's borders and beyond.

Economic Growth

In economic terms, the nation was stronger in the 1950s than it had ever been. Simple figures told a part of the story. During the war years, gross national product (GNP) jumped from just over $200 billion in 1940 to more than $300 billion in 1950. By 1960 it had climbed to over $500 billion. Per capita income rose too, from $2100 in 1950 to $2435 in 1960.

Workers seemed comfortable. Union members seemed secure. In 1955 the AFL and CIO merged and as a single organization worked toward a common goal. Union membership remained relatively constant, but more and more unionized blue-collar workers found themselves entering the middle class as wages and benefits improved. In 1948, General Motors and the United Automobile Workers had agreed on automatic cost-of-living adjustments in wages, and that agreement provided a pattern that was implemented in other industries. As he took office in 1955, AFL-CIO president George Meany declared, "American labor has never had it so good."

Average Americans had the wherewithal to buy the new products they seemed unable to resist. By the end of the decade, most homes had an automobile, a refrigerator, a washing machine, a television, and a vacuum cleaner, as well as countless other new gadgets that became part of the American way of life. Electrical magic flooded the land, and there were now all kinds of devices, some less necessary than others, available to all.

EARNINGS OF PRODUCTION WORKERS IN MANUFACTURING, 1950–1960

Year	Average Weekly Earnings
1950	$58.32
1951	63.34
1952	67.16
1953	70.47
1954	70.49
1955	75.70
1956	78.78
1957	81.59
1958	82.71
1959	88.26
1960	89.72

Source: Historical Statistics of the United States, Colonial Times to 1970.

Technological developments helped provide a framework for the prosperity. Computers began to fulfill their creators' dreams. Inventors in Europe and America had devised electromagnetic mechanisms even before World War II, but those were large and clumsy machines. The Electronic Numerical Integrator and Calculator, built in 1946, contained 18,000 tubes and could perform only one type of task at a time. Then came the development of the transistor. John Bardeen, Walter Houser Brattain, and William Bradford Shockley, scientists at Bell Laboratories, created small, solid-state components that ended reliance on tubes. First devised in 1948, transistors became more common in the 1950s.

In time the computer changed the nature of American society. It allowed for sophisticated forms of space exploration. It had commercial uses of all sorts. Airlines, hotels, and other businesses eventually turned to computers for daily tasks. The changeover did not occur overnight, but it began in the 1950s and accelerated in the years that followed.

Television also made a difference in American life. A relatively new phenomenon, television swept the nation in the 1950s. As of 1946 there were fewer than 17,000 sets; by 1949, 250,000 a month were being installed; and by 1953 two-thirds of all American families had sets of their own. Television provided entertainment as radio had done, but it became even more important as an advertising medium used to persuade viewers to buy. Switched on in most homes for several hours each day, TV provided constant exposure to the luxury items ostensibly needed for the good life. There was a veritable bombardment of advertising images. The print media did the same thing, of course, but television did it better, and there was no escape. As one critic observed, "It could

The ENIAC computer, a large electronic digital computer developed in 1946. (*Smithsonian Institution*)

almost be argued that the articles in magazines and programs on television are simply a device to keep the advertisements and commercials from bumping loudly together. The message of the media is the commercial." Advertising executives understood the financial possibilities of the new force at hand and worked hard to sell their wares. Some commercials were genuinely "artful," *Newsweek* later commented, "which is more than can be said for many of the tasteless, saccharine, and irritating programs supported by the sponsors."

American spending, spurred on by TV, encouraged business growth, and private investment rose significantly to meet demand. Technological advances offered new opportunities to entrepreneurs. But large-scale defense spending also played a major part in the prosperous growth. The development of a military-industrial complex, which had its roots in World War II, led to substantial financial outlays. The rapid increase during the Korean War pumped a good deal of money into the economy, and military budgets even after the conflict had come to an end remained much higher than before. That spending created jobs and channeled wages to the masses of Americans, who then had the ability to go out and buy the gadgets they had come to demand.

The United States in the 1950s became, as economist John Kenneth Galbraith observed in the title of his popular book, "the affluent society." It had weathered the problems of poverty and want. Now it faced instead the problems of abundance, which were different from those of past days. The materialistic values of the 1920s, chastened in the 1930s and renascent in the 1940s, revived in full bloom in the 1950s as the nation moved ahead. Americans enjoyed their prosperity as if it was their due, and in their own self-indulgent ways they sometimes neglected to look beyond the immediate objects of their desire. The decade, journalist William Shannon wrote, was one of "flabbiness and self-satisfaction and gross materialism. . . . The loudest sound in the land has been the oink and grunt of private hoggishness. . . . It has been the age of the slob."

Population Growth and Mobility

As America prospered, it grew. The birthrate in the United States had dropped during the Depression as people delayed marriage or parenthood or both in the face of hard times. The rate rose again during World War II, then soared in the postwar years. The "baby boom," which peaked in 1957, marked a phenomenal period of growth. The population spurt of 19 million in the 1940s, which was over twice the rise of the decade before, paled against the increase in the 1950s, which totaled 29 million. The rising birthrate made the major difference, but the death rate was declining, too. Miracle drugs played a large part in curing illnesses attacking all ages, and life expectancy rose. In the middle of the decade, the average for whites was 70 years, for blacks 64.

As the nation grew, it showed real movement. Population in the Pacific states rose far more rapidly than in other parts of the country, with California leading the way. Some cities there and in the Southwest grew significantly. Houston, Albuquerque, Tucson, and Phoenix experienced phenomenal growth;

the population of Phoenix, for example, soared from 65,000 in 1940 to 439,000 in 1960. In the 1950s Los Angeles pulled ahead of Philadelphia as the third-largest city in the United States, and by 1963 California had moved past New York as the nation's most populous state.

Suburbanization

The most significant pattern of mobility in the 1950s was the movement to the suburbs. White middle-class Americans fled from inner-city homes to the fringes of urban areas. In the decade, 14 of the 15 largest cities in the United States lost population; New York, Boston, Chicago, Philadelphia, and Detroit were among those that declined. Nonwhites often moved into the void, and while that took up some of the slack, it also created urban and racial problems that the nation never successfully resolved. But the suburbs were on the move. By the end of the decade, as many Americans resided in suburbs as in cities. If the 1920s had known a rural-to-urban shift, the 1950s saw a reverse shift to the quieter suburbs only accessible by car.

Americans moved to the suburbs to be able to buy their own homes. The houses built by developers like William Levitt—who mass-produced dwellings

One of the Levittowns, typical of many of the suburban developments built after World War II. (*Bettmann Archive*)

in Levittowns in New York, New Jersey, and Pennsylvania—were often cheap, fragile, and overpriced. Yet they provided at least the appearance of comfort and space and the chance to have a place of one's own. Folksinger Malvina Reynolds understood what was going on as she described the standardized squares built in leveled regions, where it was cheaper to remove all trees than work around them:

Little boxes on the hillside
Little boxes made of ticky-tacky
Little boxes on the hillside
Little boxes all the same.
There's a green one and a pink one
And a blue one and a yellow one
And they're all made out of ticky-tacky
And they all look just the same.

Americans could afford their tacky homes with two-car garages and manicured lawns, for lending agencies like the Federal Housing Administration and the Veterans Administration were willing to finance purchases on easy terms and so helped transform ownership patterns in the United States. The automobile was likewise a factor without which suburban development could not have occurred. The auto industry expanded after the war; there were 2 million cars made in 1946, 8 million in 1955. As production boomed, the government began work on a massive interstate highway system to link all parts of the nation. Justified in part on the grounds that it would make evacuation quicker in the event of nuclear war, the highway system eventually provided over 40,000 miles of federal road. Now Americans could transport themselves with ease and could afford to live where they chose.

Consequences of Suburbanization

Meanwhile, businesses began moving out to the suburbs to take advantage of growing demand. There had been a few shopping centers earlier—eight at the end of World War II—but in the 1950s the number multiplied astronomically. Within a single three-month period in 1957, 17 new centers opened; by 1960 there were 3840 in the United States. They were all over: Eastland in Detroit, Mayfair in Milwaukee, Big Town in Dallas, Penn Square in Oklahoma City. Every suburban region had one or more, and they changed shopping habits throughout the country. Suburban dwellers could remain out of the cities altogether if they wished and still have whatever they needed.

Other industries catered to a more mobile clientele too. Ray Kroc, an ambitious salesman, bought the right to franchise a fast-food establishment run by Richard and Maurice McDonald. In 1955 he opened his first McDonald's in Des Plaines, a suburb of Chicago, then another in Fresno, California, and was on his way. Scouting out new locations, almost always on highway "strips," Kroc persuaded people to put up the capital and provided them with specifications guaranteed to ensure future success. For his efforts, he received a percentage of the gross take.

McDonald's, of course, was a tremendous success. In 1962, total sales were over $76 million. In 1964, before the company had been in operation ten years, it reported that it had sold over 400 million hamburgers and 120 million pounds of french fries, with the numbers rising all the time. Kroc's vision of a business catering to an automobile clientele sparked other entrepreneurs to follow his lead. The franchise system became a prominent pattern in the land.

Not everyone applauded the changes that were taking place. City planner Victor Gruen charged that the automobile was raping American cities and helping destroy whatever national beauty was left. Billboards, ever-present along American roads, led to "the planned deterioration of America's landscape," according to author and photographer Peter Blake. Author John Keats referred to the suburbs as "developments conceived in error, nurtured by greed, corroding everything they touch." Even so, Americans enjoyed what they had. After the deprivations of the past, they craved the packaged world they found in the suburbs and were determined to enjoy what they could at prices they could afford.

CONSENSUS IN THE UNITED STATES

That craving reflected a shared consensus about the nature and quality of American life. Most Americans believed that the new affluence was here to stay. They clung to the optimistic idea that social problems could be solved as easily as industrial problems, that ever-increasing economic growth would make it possible to meet the needs of all the people and thereby abolish social conflict and class distinctions at the same time.

Intellectual Justification

Intellectuals, politicians, and citizens at large were in general agreement about the possibilities of fruitful existence in the United States. Historian David Potter noted in *People of Plenty,* published in 1954, that "in every aspect of material plenty America possesses unprecedented riches" and argued that those were spread throughout the land. David Lilienthal, active in government for many years, observed the same thing: "One finds the physical benefits of our society distributed widely, to almost everyone, with scant regard to status, class, or origin of the individual." Some people clearly had more than others, but the prevailing assumption was that income or wealth would "trickle down" the economic ladder so that all had enough in the end.

At the same time there was the sense that Americans from all walks of life had certain common goals that gave the society a basic unity that could be maintained. Sociologist Daniel Bell made perhaps the most pointed statement in his 1960 volume *The End of Ideology.* "There is today," he wrote, "a rough consensus among intellectuals on political issues: the acceptance of a Welfare State; the desirability of decentralized power; a system of mixed economy and of political pluralism. In that sense, too, the ideological age has ended." American society, he argued, seemed flexible, yet stable at the same time. Different groups struggled for position, but conflict could be averted by compromise, with certain assumptions shared across the board.

The Culture of Conformity

On the surface, at least, the culture reflected that consensus. This was the great age of conformity, when Americans seemed to want to emulate those around them rather than strike out on their own. Corporations grew into ever-larger organizations that became even more impersonal than before. The bureaucratic style emerged supreme, with corporate employees seemingly dressing, thinking, and acting all the same. One and all they appeared as "the man in the gray flannel suit," in the title of a popular novel by Sloan Wilson. The corporations preached that teamwork was far more important than individuality and went out of their way to indoctrinate employees and convey to them the appropriate standards of conduct they were to meet. "Personal views can cause a lot of trouble," an oil company recruiting pamphlet noted and went on to suggest that business favored moderate, conservative ideas that would not threaten the system. William H. Whyte, in *The Organization Man,* described young executives who believed in "belongingness" as their ultimate goal. C. Wright Mills observed the same thing in *White Collar* when he wrote, "When white-collar people get jobs, they sell not only their time and energy but their personalities as well."

The urge to conform spread beyond the corporations to the rest of society. Even children could not escape the homogenizing influences of the culture in those years. Sociologist David Riesman, in *The Lonely Crowd* in 1950, argued that the nation was moving from an inner-directed orientation where parental influence helped people develop individual goals to an other-directed framework where peer-pressure became all-important. In the old nursery rhyme "This little pig went to market," Riesman wrote, each pig went his own way. "Today, however, all little pigs go to market; none stay home; all have roast beef, if any do; and all say 'we-we.'" To emphasize his point further in his influential work, he cited the story of *Tootle the Engine* in the popular Little Golden Books series. It was, he observed, "a cautionary tale." Tootle was a young engine learning the tricks of his trade who found that it was more fun playing in the flowers in the field than staying on the tracks. To break him of his bad habit, the citizens of Engineville all turned up with red flags whenever he began to stray and showed him a green flag only when he stayed on the track. Tootle finally learned the lesson: "always stay on the track no matter what." The story, Riesman concluded, was "an appropriate one for bringing up children in an other-directed mode of conformity," for showing them the way to success in modern life.

In the colleges and universities the "silent generation" held sway. Students were cautious and prudent and sought above all to be secure. They joined fraternities and sororities, engaged in panty raids and other pranks, but took little interest in larger issues in the world beyond. "I observe," Yale president

A. Whitney Griswold told a graduating class in 1950, "that you share the prevailing mood of the hour, which in your case consists of bargains privately struck with fate—on fate's terms." Here as elsewhere it was a case, in one critic's words, of "the bland leading the bland."

Standards of acceptability seemed to govern all spheres of American life. In the 1950s the people of the United States returned to their churches in record numbers. In part their church attendance reflected a desire to challenge godless communism at the height of the Cold War; in part it was a result of the power of suggestion that led Americans to do what others were doing at the same time. Whatever the cause, religion became an even more important part of American life. Evangelist Billy Graham preached to millions in his revivals and used radio, television, and film to spread his message. By the end of the 1950s, 95 percent of all Americans identified with some denomination. In 1954 Congress added the words "under God" to the pledge to the flag, and the next year voted to require the phrase "In God We Trust" on all pieces of American currency. Religion became commercial, too. Those in need could turn to Dial-A-Prayer or take comfort from advertisements reminding them that "the family that prays together stays together."

Sex Roles and Patterns of Conformity

There were also definite standards defining men's and women's roles in the 1950s. Men were expected to go to school and then find jobs that would allow them to support the families they hoped to raise. As earlier in the American past, they viewed themselves as the primary breadwinners and prepared themselves for that role. Women, despite their experience working in World War II, were expected to remain at home, redecorating houses and gardens and transporting children to and from activities and schools.

American women in the 1950s subscribed to the values that defined their place at home. They married young and had children early, and in the stereotype that held sway, supported their husbands' careers. Betty Friedan, who challenged the system in 1963 with an explosive critique, *The Feminine Mystique,* wrote that women "could desire no greater destiny than to glory in their own femininity. . . . All they had to do was to devote their lives from earliest girlhood to finding a husband and bearing children." And always, even if that proved difficult, they had to adjust. "It was unquestioned gospel," Friedan wrote "that women could identify with *nothing* beyond the home—not politics, not art, not science, not events large or small, war or peace, in the United States or the world, unless it could be approached through female experience as a wife or mother or translated into domestic detail! "

In 1956, when *Life* magazine produced a special issue on women, it profiled Marjorie Sutton and praised the "Busy Wife's Achievements" as "Home Manager, Mother, Hostess, and Useful Civic Worker." Married at 16, she was now busy with the PTA, Campfire Girls, and charity causes. She cooked and sewed for her family, which included four children, supported her husband by entertaining 1500 guests a year, and worked out on the trampoline "to keep her size 12 figure."

Adlai Stevenson, the Democratic presidential candidate in 1952 and 1956, transformed that model into political terms when he told a group that "the assignment for you, as wives and mothers, you can do in the living room with a baby in your lap or in the kitchen with a can opener in your hand." A woman was to "influence man and boy" in the "humble role of housewife."

Movies and movie magazines seized on sex symbols like Marilyn Monroe or saccharine heroines like Doris Day. They became the models for other women to emulate. Fashions stressed femininity at the expense of practicality. Everywhere feminism was held in disrepute. In *Modern Woman: The Lost Sex,* historian Ferdinand Lundberg and sociologist Marynia Farnham called feminism a "deep illness." The Women's Bureau of the government argued that but a small group showed resentment with women's lot. Always there was pressure to conform.

For all the pressure, women did continue to enter the labor force in the 1950s. By 1960 approximately 40 percent of all American women worked, either full or part time. Yet the impetus was income rather than satisfaction, and the pressures to sidestep a career remained strong.

Outsiders

There were, in the 1950s, occasional challenges to the system. There were individuals who felt alienated from the culture and rebellious against the shared

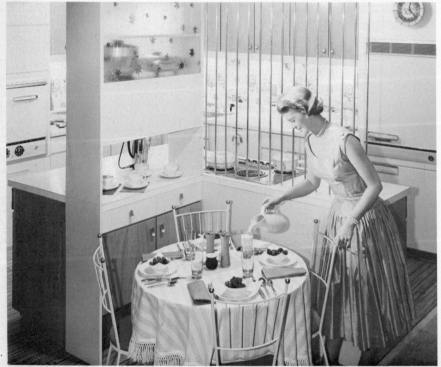

The ideal homemaker in her dream kitchen, as advertised in the 1950s. (*Bettmann Archive*)

values they saw. Even as adolescents and young adults of college age struggled to meet the standards of their peers, they were intrigued by Holden Caulfield, the main figure in J. D. Salinger's 1951 novel *The Catcher in the Rye.* Holden, a sensitive student at boarding school, was disturbed by the hypocrisy he saw in the world outside. Both in school and out he felt himself surrounded by "phonies" who threatened whatever individuality remained. In the enormously popular novel, Holden made a sad and ill-fated effort to preserve his own integrity in the face of pressures to conform. It was a brave attempt, even if the system seemed to win out in the end.

Another fictitional figure protesting the institutional conformity of the period was Randle Patrick McMurphy, hero of Ken Kesey's boisterous novel *One Flew Over the Cuckoo's Nest.* Published early in the 1960s, before upheaval had begun, the novel was really a pointed critique of the 1950s patterns of life. McMurphy, confined to a mental hospital, refused to accept the system as it was. The hospital was a microcosm of the world beyond, a world where conformity and compulsion held sway. But McMurphy's individuality could not be contained. He challenged the dictatorial control of the Big Nurse time and again, with the system triumphing only by resorting to lobotomy. McMurphy, too, had lost, but not without a good fight.

Other figures made a different kind of challenge to the system. Members of the "beat generation"—writers for the most part—espoused values very different from those of the culture at large in the poems and stories they wrote and in the "happenings" they staged. They confronted the apathy and conformity of American culture head-on. Instead they stressed spontaneity and spirituality. Intuition became more important than reason, Eastern mysticism more valuable than Western faith. The beats went out of their way to challenge the norms of respectability. They threw off materialistic values, behaved with overt promiscuity designed to shock, and helped popularize marijuana as a shortcut to the good life.

Their literary work reflected their general approach. Critical of conventional academic forms, which they found sterile and artificial, they branched out in new directions. Jack Kerouac typed his best-selling novel *On the Road* on a 250-foot roll of paper. Lacking conventional punctuation and paragraph structure, it showed the restlessness and confusion of the subculture of the time. Poet Allen Ginsberg, a Columbia University deserter like Kerouac, became equally well known for his poem "Howl." That effort made a scathing critique of the modern, mechanized culture and its effects. The poem began:

> I saw the best minds of my generation destroyed by madness, starving
> hysterical naked,
> dragging themselves through the negro streets at dawn looking for an
> angry fix,
> angelheaded hipsters burning for the ancient heavenly connection to the
> starry dynamo in the machinery of night,
> who poverty and tatters and hollow-eyed and high sat up smoking in the
> supernatural darkness of cold-water flats floating across the tops of
> cities contemplating jazz, . . .

Poet Allen Ginsberg reading in New York. (*AP/Wide World*)

The poem continued with its relentless attack on groups in America, such as those

> who were burned alive in their innocent flannel suits on Madison Avenue
> amid blasts of leaden verse & the tanked-up clatter of the iron
> regiments of fashion & the nitroglycerine shrieks of the fairies of
> advertising & the mustard gas of sinister intelligent editors, or were
> run down by the drunken taxicabs of Absolute Reality, . . .

Ginsberg became something of a celebrity when "Howl" appeared in 1956. It quickly became a cult piece, but then the police seized it and arrested poet Lawrence Ferlinghetti, owner of the City Lights bookstore in San Francisco, who had published and sold the work. The authorities charged that "Howl" was lewd and obscene and took the matter to court. National acclaim soon followed for Ginsberg and his work, as he and the other beats provided a model for rebellion for a later generation in the decade ahead.

If some Americans challenged the system head-on, others found it hard to accept common values because they lived at a poverty level with few of the benefits of the packaged world outside. America in the 1950s was prosperous indeed, but there were Americans who were left out. Economic growth favored the upper and upper middle classes and, trickle-down theory notwithstanding, did little for those at the bottom of the ladder. According to the Federal Bureau of Labor Statistics in 1960, $3000 was a minimum yearly income for a family of four, $4000 for a family of six. There were, the Bureau reported, 40 million people below those levels, and almost that many only marginally above the line. Michael Harrington's *The Other America* shocked Americans in 1962 as it exposed the conditions known by blacks in urban slums or lower-class workers in coalfields or decaying mill towns. Two million migrant workers enjoyed few government benefits and labored long hours for a wage on which they could barely survive. Yet many people living in more permanent dwellings were not much better off. According to the 1960 census, 27 percent of the residential units in the United States were substandard, and even acceptable buildings were often hopelessly overcrowded in some slums. This side of the 1950s was less pleasant to see, but it was easy to ignore as more fortunate middle-class Americans pursued their own materialistic ends.

THE EISENHOWER YEARS

The best political symbol of the age was Dwight D. Eisenhower, president for most of the decade. Serene and secure, he reflected the times and seemed to encourage a confidence that everything was going to turn out all right. As Americans sought to enjoy the fruits of their labor, Ike conveyed the sense that the nation was in good hands.

Ike at the Polls

Eisenhower and the Republicans swept into power in 1952. Harry Truman had scored an upset victory in 1948, but now the country was more than ready for

Ike accepting the Republican presidential nomination in 1952. (*UPI/Bettmann Newsphotos*)

a change. Truman had the support of only 23 percent of the American people, and all indicators pointed to a political shift. The Democrats nominated Adlai Stevenson, the governor of Illinois, who took a liberal approach to national problems. The Republicans turned to Ike, the war hero Americans loved.

Stevenson made a concerted effort to approach issues in intellectual terms. "Let's talk sense to the American people," he said. "Let's tell them the truth." While that effort gained him the firm backing of liberals like Max Lerner, who called him the "first figure of major stature to have emerged since Roosevelt," even Stevenson realized that his thrust fell short. In the campaign, when told that he would get the vote of every thinking person, he observed that it was not enough; he needed a majority. How, he wondered, could a man named Adlai beat a soldier called Ike?

Stevenson understood the political realities of the day. The Republicans were hungry and were determined to win. Eisenhower represented the old American values and virtues and kept them visible for all to see. Everywhere the Republican slogan echoed: "I like Ike." The GOP took a $K_1 C_2$ approach. The acronym singled out their major issues—Korea, communism, and corruption. The Republicans called the Democrats soft on communism; vice-presidential candidate Richard Nixon referred to "Adlai the Appeaser" who was a "Ph.D. graduate of Dean Acheson's cowardly College of Communist Containment." The Republicans criticized assorted scandals surrounding Truman's cronies and friends. They also promised to end the Korean War. Just 11 days before the election, Eisenhower declared that "an early and honorable" peace required a personal effort and stated, "I shall go to Korea." What he intended to do there was not clear, but he seemed prepared to do something. Eisenhower himself struck a grandfatherly pose, unified the various wings in his party, and won a massive victory at the polls. He received 55 percent of the vote and carried 41 states. He moved into office with a Republican Congress as well.

In 1956, the same two candidates squared off again. While Stevenson anticipated doing better the second time, the results proved that Ike was even more popular than before. Though Eisenhower had been seriously ill during his first term, the public wanted him back for another. He received 57.6 percent of the vote this time and won by an even larger electoral margin. The Republicans were less lucky in congressional races after 1952 as the Democrats gained control. Yet the president still served as a symbol of the nation's mood.

Eisenhower as President

Eisenhower, raised on the Kansas prairie, had an easy, natural manner. His twinkling eyes and "leaping and effortless smile," in reporter Robert Donovan's phrase, reflected the sense that all was well. Privately he had a real temper, but that was something the public never saw. Ike conveyed a sense of honesty and strength that translated into a magnetic appeal. On occasion his answers to questions in press conferences or other public gatherings were convoluted and imprecise and seemed inarticulate at best. Yet appearances could be deceiving, for behind the surface smile was a real shrewdness. At one point, as he prepared for a session with newsmen and his aides briefed him on a delicate matter, he said, "Don't worry, . . . If that question comes up, I'll just confuse them." His syntax may have left something to be desired, but in the eight years he spent in office, he made not one major verbal blunder.

Eisenhower had not taken the typical political route to the presidency. He had in fact had very little formal political experience at all. He was first and foremost a military man whose career peaked during World War II, after which he served as army chief of staff, president of Columbia University, and then head of NATO. Political inexperience notwithstanding, he did have an ability to get people to compromise and to work together, and his leadership in the European theater of war had been instrumental in keeping the Grand Alliance intact. But his limited involvement with everyday American politics conditioned his sense of the presidential role.

Ike took a passive approach to the presidency. It was no "bully pulpit" for him as it had been for Theodore Roosevelt or even for FDR. Eisenhower believed that his office had become too strong, and he was interested in seeing a restoration of what he considered the delicate constitutional balance. "I am not one of those desk-pounding types that likes to stick out his jaw and look like he is bossing the show," he said. He told his Cabinet members that he would "stay out of your hair" and in the same way was reluctant to use the patronage power to further his own ends; he preferred a less aggressive approach. He wanted to be, according to critical journalist I. F. Stone, "a president in absentia, with a sort of political vacuum in the White House which other men will struggle among themselves to fill."

More experienced politicians understood the liabilities of that stance. Truman observed, "He'll sit there, and he'll say, 'Do this! Do that!' And nothing will happen. Poor Ike—it won't be a bit like the army." And Sam Rayburn, Speaker of the House, once reportedly commented about Eisenhower, "Nope, won't do. Good man. Wrong business." Comics jibed about the limited leadership at the top. One observed that Ike demonstrated that the country didn't "need" a president. Another spoke of the Eisenhower doll—you wound it up and it did nothing at all. Comedian Mort Sahl, in the 1960 campaign, told people to vote "no" for president—to keep the White House empty for another eight years.

Aware of the criticisms of his approach, Ike came to his own defense: "Now, look, I happen to *know* a little about leadership. I've had to work with a lot of nations, for that matter, at odds with each other. And I tell you this: you do not *lead* by hitting people over the head. Any damn fool can do that, but it's usually called 'assault'—not 'leadership.' . . . I'll tell you what leadership is. It's *persuasion*—and *conciliation*—and *education*—and *patience*. It's long, slow, tough work. That's the only kind of leadership I know or believe in—or will practice." That approach, however, did not always work.

Organizing his office, Eisenhower fashioned a centralized system based on a military line of command. Roosevelt had surrounded himself with people of conflicting views who could report directly to him and in that way preserved the power of decision in his own hands. Eisenhower worked differently. Everything moved through channels, and the president himself dealt mostly with Sherman Adams, his somewhat abrasive chief of staff, and other immediate assistants at the top. That insulated him to a degree and may have foreclosed certain options before a fuller hearing could be had.

His Cabinet also provided a measure of insulation from the outside world. It included mostly successful businessmen, plus a union leader who was head of a plumbers' and steamfitters' organization, which prompted critics to declare that the Cabinet consisted of "eight millionaires and a plumber." Three of the Cabinet appointees came from the automobile industry, and that led Adlai Stevenson to remark that the New Dealers had given way to the car dealers. Quips aside, the Cabinet reflected Eisenhower's attitudes and approach. It also reflected the business orientation of the day.

Bases of Foreign Policy

The Cabinet also reflected strong Republican views about the Cold War. Eisenhower and other leaders of his party accepted basic American assumptions about the persisting conflict between East and West and basically agreed with the broad outlines of American foreign policy since 1945. While Republican rhetoric was often critical of the Democratic approach, the underlying perception of the struggle was the same. Eisenhower, like Truman, felt that the Kremlin in Moscow was orchestrating subversive activity around the globe. He believed in the notion of a monolithic Communist force struggling for supremacy in all parts of the world. In his 1953 inaugural address he declared, "Forces of good and evil are massed and armed and opposed as rarely before in history. Freedom is pitted against slavery, lightness against dark."

To help formulate foreign policy to meet that threat, Eisenhower chose John Foster Dulles to head the Department of State. Dulles was a dedicated anti-Communist whose views sometimes seemed more uncompromising than those of Ike himself. Grandson of one secretary of state and nephew of another, he had attended the 1919 Peace Conference at Versailles and had in later decades become the major Republican spokesman on foreign affairs. An able lawyer, he was also a devout Presbyterian who hated atheistic communism and was rigidly moralistic in his approach to foreign affairs. Eisenhower viewed him as "a patriarch out of the Old Testament," and there was a ring of truth to the characterization. Dulles's speeches sounded like sermons, and his convictions proved difficult to change. Humorless in his stance, critics sometimes called him "Dull, Duller, Dulles."

Dulles was responsible for the foreign policy plank in the Republican platform of 1952, and it accurately reflected his view. It condemned containment as a policy that was "negative, futile, and immoral." The Democratic effort lost "countless human beings to a despotism and Godless terrorism." A spiritual offensive was necessary. Instead of advocating containment, the United States should make it "publicly known that it wants and expects liberation to occur."

The language was extreme, but in practice the aggressive posture was harder to maintain. A basic agreement notwithstanding, Eisenhower was more conciliatory than Dulles, and he kept his secretary of state in check. Comparing himself to Dulles, Ike once said, "There's only one man I know who has seen more of the world and talked with more people and knows more . . . and that's me." He understood that there were limits to the possibilities of liberation, and when the chance to test the policy arose, he was unwilling to translate rhetoric into action. When in 1953 there were anti-Soviet protests in East Germany, the United States maintained its distance and did not move in. So too in 1956, when freedom fighters in Hungary arose against Russian domination, the United States stood back as Soviet forces quelled the uprising and maintained their hold on that land. Western action might well have precipitated a more general war, and Eisenhower was unwilling to go that far. In the final analysis, the notion of liberation came to nothing; the commitment to containment remained intact.

Although they maintained the commitment to containment, the Republicans shifted their military approach. On entering office, Eisenhower found sizable force levels that were both expensive and, he felt, poorly used. The defense effort was fragmented and simply cost too much. Concerned with bringing the budget under control, Eisenhower was reluctant to expand military structures still further to meet all contingencies at all times. Instead, the Republicans chose to rely on atomic weaponry as the key element of American response. Rather than counting on conventional forces to meet aggression when it occurred, the United States would depend on its nuclear arsenal. Drawing on theorists like Henry Kissinger of Harvard University, who argued that atomic weapons could be used in conventional struggles, Dulles believed that the new approach would allow for instant response, "by means and at places of our own choosing," whenever Communist aggression occurred. Troop levels could therefore be cut back and saved in the "new look," or policy of "massive retaliation," which gave "more bang for the buck."

The new approach took hold, even though there were certain problems that were never resolved. "Massive retaliation" dictated an all-or-nothing scenario; there was no middle course. It provided no real alternatives between those of nuclear war or passive response. Still, it was wholly consonant with the secretary of state's willingness to use the most extreme threats to assert the American way. The threat of direct retaliation, properly used, he felt, could deter Soviet intrusion around the world. "The ability to get to the verge without getting into war is the necessary art," Dulles declared. "If you cannot master it you inevitably get into war." Critics called the policy "brinkmanship" and wondered what would happen if the line was crossed.

Dulles, meanwhile, devoted himself to winning friends for the American camp. He sought allies around the world and tried to tie them to the Western side. Aware of the ferment in less advanced areas of the world, he saw that "to oppose nationalism is counterproductive." Nonetheless, he regarded national strivings within the context of the Cold War and demanded that nations everywhere make a choice. Neutralism, he declared, was "immoral." He therefore set up alliances, like the Southeast Asia Treaty Organization (SEATO) in Asia and the Central Treaty Organization (CENTO) in the Middle East. Similar to NATO in structure, they were less binding than the Atlantic alliance but did bring countries together for common purposes. By the time Dulles was done, the United States was tied to 43 other nations around the world.

Foreign Policy in Action

In its quest for diplomatic stability, the United States had to deal with crises in all parts of the globe but never did become embroiled in a major foreign war. American forces landed in trouble spots from time to time and sought to pursue national interests, yet they avoided becoming hopelessly bogged down in a struggle that could not be won. Eisenhower's impeccable military credentials allowed him to use troops as he saw fit but also enabled him to restrain the military when necessary at no cost to his own reputation. Recognizing the unavoidable stalemate in Korea, he rejected all talk of a military victory and, with the threat of nuclear weapons, brought the conflict to an end. The Republican administration managed to obtain an armistice where the Democratic government had not, and after three years of war brought peace at last.

Elsewhere in Asia, the United States maintained its stubborn stance against the Communist Chinese. Firmly entrenched on the mainland, the People's Republic remained unrecognized by the new administration. Instead, in 1954, the United States committed itself to defend Formosa, where Jiang Jieshi and the Nationalists had set up their own government in the aftermath of the civil war. When Communist China began firing on Quemoy and Matsu, two islands close to the mainland still in Nationalist hands, the president asked for and received from Congress the authority to use force in the face of any crisis near Formosa if he alone felt it necessary. Presidential power, enhanced during the Korean War, grew still further by the blanket grant Ike received, despite his own desire for a limited role.

In Southeast Asia, where Vietnamese nationalists were struggling against a French colonial regime, the United States supported its Western ally. The liberation movement, led by Communist and nationalist Ho Chi Minh, had been going on since the start of the Second World War, when the Japanese had superseded the French, and continued after that struggle when the French returned. The United States had not been much interested at first. To gain French support for the containment policy in Europe, however, Truman began, in his second term, to offer aid to France. When France suffered a major Indo-Chinese defeat at Dien Bien Phu in 1954, the Eisenhower administration was faced with the decision of whether or not to intervene. Ike indicated that the United States would become involved only if Congress voted the necessary support and other European allies went along. He believed in the domino theory, in the argument that "you have a row of dominos set up, and you knock over the first one, and what will happen to the last one is the certainty that it will go over very quickly." By that notion, if one nation fell to communism, others were sure to follow. But he also sensed the potentially troublesome implications of involvement, and in the end the United States stayed out. The country was partitioned, with Ho Chi Minh in charge in the north, an American-supported, non-Communist government taking over after France's withdrawal in the south.

The Republican administration was active in the Middle East too. In Iran in 1953, the Central Intelligence Agency helped the local army place the shah of Iran securely on the Peacock Throne. That entailed overthrowing the nationalist government of Mohammed Mossadegh, which had seized oil wells formerly under British control. With the coup, British and American companies regained command of the wells, and whatever the consequences in Iran, private enterprise flourished once more.

A far more serious episode unfolded in Egypt several years later. General Gamal Abdel Nasser's nationalistic government had forced Great Britain to remove forces from the Suez Canal. Nasser then turned his attention to building the great Aswan Dam on the Nile River to produce electricity for Egypt. Dulles offered financial support, but when Nasser began to deal with the Soviet Union, the secretary of state withdrew his earlier offer. Nasser's response was to seize the Suez Canal in July 1956, to use the tolls to finance the dam. At the same time he closed the canal to Israeli ships. In October, Great Britain, France, and Israel moved in with military force. The United States was furious with its allies. It had supported Israel since its origin in 1948 but now feared a massive conflagration and sponsored a UN resolution condemning the nations that had attacked. The United States also cut off oil from England and France and finally persuaded them to pull back. Eisenhower, on the eve of reelection, had again managed to avoid war, but not without some cost to the unity of the West. In the Middle East as elsewhere, American aims came into conflict with those of other powers.

Two years later, the United States again intervened in the area. In 1958, still concerned about stability in the region, Eisenhower authorized the landing of 14,000 soldiers in Lebanon to prop up a right-wing government challenged from within. He acted along the lines of a congressional resolution passed the year before that committed the United States to stop Communist aggression in the Middle East. With oil at stake throughout the region, the United States was concerned with any external threat, but even if the problem was purely internal, as in Lebanon, America was still willing to step in.

For similar reasons the United States became involved in Latin America as well. Not long after taking office, Dulles began to fear Communist activity in Guatemala and so moved to support a coup aimed at overthrowing the government of reform-minded Colonel Jacobo Arbenz Guzmán. The right-wing movement succeeded, restored property seized earlier from the United Fruit Company, and demonstrated again the American commitment to stability and private enterprise, regardless of the internal issues or ultimate cost.

That effort caused ill feeling throughout Latin America, for it was but one more example of the interference of the powerful neighbor to the north. Dulles denied the existence of hostile sentiment, but when Vice-President Nixon traveled to Venezuela in 1958 he encountered rabid crowds that stoned his car and almost tipped it over. He escaped, but the episode shook the administration and led it to reassess the policies followed until then. When Fidel Castro overturned a dictatorial regime in Cuba the next year, the shortsightedness of American policy became even clearer. Nationalism was on the rise and could not be contained, nor could liberation movements of the masses be squelched. Milton Eisenhower, Ike's brother and adviser, understood what was going on: "Revolution is inevitable in Latin America. The people are angry. They are shackled to the past with bonds of ignorance, injustice, and poverty. And they no longer accept as universal or inevitable the oppressive prevailing order."

On balance, in foreign affairs Eisenhower followed Truman's lead even as the world began to change. Despite sharper rhetoric, the basic position remained the same. Containment continued to be the policy of the United States. Eisenhower, like his predecessor, saw the Communist threat in monolithic terms, yet the liberation movements springing up around the globe were hardly all orchestrated from Moscow and could not effectively be treated as such. Neither Dulles nor Ike ever really understood the shift that was taking place and were consequently unprepared to alter course. Stalin's death in 1953 might have provided an opportunity for better relations with the Soviet Union, but the tensions remained. Part of that was due to Russian intransigence, of course, as in the U-2 episode of 1959 when the Soviets downed an American spy plane and used the incident to torpedo a summit conference between Russian and American leaders before it began. But part was due, too, to a stubborn American Cold War stance.

Still, for all the troubles, Eisenhower kept the nation at peace. He knew how to assess the arguments for military action and how to resist moving when the odds or opportunities were too slim. He understood the value of keeping military expenditures under control and warned in his farewell address of a growing military-industrial complex whose influence could easily become difficult to check. He made efforts at arms control, even if a treaty eluded his grasp. In foreign affairs Ike seemed to be what the United States wanted and needed at the time. He voiced American values as he faced the Communist threat, but he did not want to divert all resources to the quest in a way that could threaten the good life.

Republican Policy at Home

Eisenhower took office in 1953 with a clear sense of what he hoped to do on the domestic front. He was eager to restore a measure of balance in government, to cut back on the role of the federal establishment in public affairs. While doing so, however, he hoped to avoid eliminating gains of the last 20 years that even the Republicans had come to accept. The American experience in the Great Depression and thereafter had demonstrated the need for a governmental role that could not be denied. Eisenhower sometimes termed his approach "dynamic conservatism." More often it carried the name "modern Republicanism," which, he explained, meant "conservative when it comes to money, liberal when it comes to human beings." Adlai Stevenson responded that Ike appeared to be arguing that he would "strongly recommend the building of a great many schools . . . but not provide the money."

Financial concerns dominated the Eisenhower years. The president and his chief aides wanted desperately to preserve the value of the dollar, pare down levels of funding, cut taxes, and balance the budget after years of deficit spending. Sherman Adams once remarked of Ike that "if he was able to do nothing as President except balance the budget he would feel that his time in the White House had been well spent." To that end he appointed George Humphrey, a man of conservative fiscal views, as secretary of the Treasury. Humphrey hung in his office a picture of Andrew Mellon, Calvin Coolidge's conservative Treasury head, and declared; "We have to cut one-third of the budget and you can't do that just by eliminating waste. This means, whenever necessary, using a meat axe."

But the process caused real political trouble. In time some deficits were accepted as necessary, though the administration's priorities were not always clear. The greatest problems arose with the budget for fiscal year 1958. In keeping with "modern Republicanism," the budget Eisenhower presented included allotments for assorted welfare programs. Even as the president released the figures, Humphrey pressed for further cuts. In a press conference the Treasury secretary said that if the government did not reduce the tax burden in the United States, "you will have a depression that will curl your hair." More trimming was necessary to cut taxes. Thereupon everyone tried to get into the act, and Ike, who took a subdued view of his office to begin with, lost control. There was a cut here, a cut there, in an effort to see that no one was hurt more than others. The upshot was that with the cuts the economy began to slump, tax revenues dropped, and the final deficit was even greater than the administration had predicted. Even worse, Eisenhower's credibility and leadership were undermined.

That episode reflected the general approach of the Eisenhower team to economic affairs. With business interests in mind, Republican leaders argued that preservation of the dollar's value and contraction of the government's role took precedence over all else. Such activity would encourage the business system best of all. Defense Secretary Charles E. Wilson, former president of General Motors, stated priorities clearly when at his confirmation hearings he declared that "what was good for our country was good for General Motors, and vice versa." Within the administration the prevailing view was that in tough times, the government should stand back and risk unemployment if necessary to keep inflation under control. In 1954 Wilson again put his foot in his mouth when he went to Detroit where thousands of workers were out of jobs. Talking about the virtue of independent initiative, he said, "I've got a lot of sympathy for people where a sudden change catches them, but I've always liked bird dogs better than kennel-fed dogs myself. You know, one who'll get out and hunt for food rather than sit on his fanny and yell."

With that attitude, and with the reluctance to stimulate the economy too much, the rate of economic growth declined from 4.3 percent between 1947 and 1952 to 2.5 percent between 1953 and 1960. Growth continued, but not as fast as before. Worse, the country suffered three recessions in Eisenhower's years. In 1953–1954, 1957–1958, and 1960–1961 the economy slumped and brought hard times. Liberal economists might argue that Keynesian tools were available to avert such troubles, but they had to be used to do any good.

The business orientation guided the Republican administration in other ways too. After support from oil interests in the campaign, Congress, with a strong endorsement from Ike, passed the Submerged Lands Act in 1953. The measure transferred control from the federal government to the states of about $40 billion worth of oil lands. It was, the *New York Times* said, "one of the greatest and surely the most unjustified give-away programs in all the history of the United States."

With regard to the generation of power, the administration's position was the same. Again Ike sought to reduce federal activity whenever he could. He favored corporate rather than public development of power if possible. Privately he said of the Tennessee Valley Authority, that extensive public power and development project of the New Deal, "I'd like to see us *sell* the whole thing, but I suppose we can't go that far." He did oppose a TVA proposal to expand to provide power to the Atomic Energy Commission and instead authorized a private group, the Dixon-Yates syndicate, to build a plant in Arkansas to meet the need. Later, when charges of scandal arose, the administration had to cancel the agreement, but the basic preference for private development remained.

In the farm sector the record was similar. The problem, in the 1950s as before, lay with rising output and surpluses that exceeded demand. The government had two decades earlier become involved in a price-support system that was becoming more expensive all the time. Secretary of Agriculture Ezra Taft Benson, another economic conservative, wanted a free-market situation to prevail, with the government out of the support business altogether. The supports, he contended, only encouraged more production. Yet the administration never succeeded in its goals. Soil-bank programs and surplus-removal schemes were tried, but output continued to rise and prices continued to fall. In the end, the federal government spent more on agriculture than ever before, while the basic course of farm policy remained unchanged.

MINORITIES IN THE FIFTIES

Though middle-class Americans were comfortable in the 1950s, not all citizens shared in the benefits of the American dream. Minorities in particular found themselves treated as second-class citizens and began to struggle for an equality that had long been denied. Blacks were most successful as the civil rights movement came into its own. It provided a model for Hispanics, Native Americans, and other groups in the years ahead.

Blacks and School Desegregation

In the 1950s, the movement for black equality progressed with a momentum of its own and could not be contained. Ever since World War II, the National Association for the Advancement of Colored People had been working through the courts to overturn the judicial justification for the policy of segregation. In 1896, in the case of *Plessy* v. *Ferguson,* the Supreme Court had determined that segregation of the black and white races was constitutional if the facilities used by each were "separate but equal." Facilities were seldom if ever equal, to be sure, but the Court's decree was used nonetheless to sanction the rigid patterns of segregation that took root. Now, following the lead of Thurgood Marshall, later to be the first black justice on the Supreme Court, the NAACP won a series of victories that slowly but surely eroded the doctrine handed down by the High Court more than 50 years before. Several education cases in 1950 declared that separate facilities denied blacks equal protection under the law and prepared the way for an even more important decision.

The *Brown* v. *Board of Education* case was one of the landmark cases heard by the Court. It began in 1951 when the parents of fourth grader Linda Brown sued the school board in Topeka, Kansas, to allow their daughter to attend a school for white children she passed as she walked to the bus stop on her way to a black school farther away. Appeals brought the case to the Supreme Court. Justices there were well aware of the importance of the case. Schools in 21 states and the District of Columbia were segregated at the time, and all could be affected by the ruling handed down. Adding other school segregation cases to the one before it, the Court took the matter on.

The Supreme Court in the early 1950s was hard to predict. Led by Earl Warren, an Eisenhower appointee who had formerly been governor of California, its new direction had not yet become clear. The Court heard arguments in the *Brown* case a number of times and drew on psychological and sociological evidence. Finally, on May 17, 1954, it handed down the bombshell ruling. Unanimously the Court decred that "separate facilities are inherently unequal" and concluded that the "separate but equal" doctrine had no place in public education. Warren was largely responsible for the clear signal issued by the Court. The justices had been divided when he joined their ranks, but he persuaded some that the racial theory of half a century before should no longer govern American life and convinced others that unanimity on the Court was necessary for peaceful change. After the first decision, the Court turned to the question of implementation and, in 1955, declared that local school boards, acting with the guidance of lower courts, should move "with all deliberate speed." The approach defined was a gradual one, for the Court sensed the problems that lay ahead.

Charged with the ultimate responsibility for executing the law, Dwight Eisenhower found himself in an uncomfortable position, for he doubted that simple legal changes could improve race relations. On one occasion he observed, "I don't believe you can change the hearts of men with laws or decisions." If values were to shift, he told the daughter of early twentieth-century black leader Booker T. Washington, "we cannot do it by cold law-making, but must make these changes by appealing to reason, by prayer, and by constantly working at it through our own efforts." Privately commenting on the *Brown* ruling, he said, "I personally think the decision was wrong." But he understood, too, that "it makes no difference whether or not I endorse it." According to the Constitution it was his duty to see that it was carried out.

Eisenhower moved quickly to that end. Even while urging sympathy for the South in its transition, he acted immediately to desegregate the Washington, D.C., schools to provide a model for the rest of the country. He urged an end to continuing discrimination in other areas, too, as he mandated desegregation in navy yards and veterans' hospitals.

But there was resistance nonetheless. While the Court's decision was clear, so too was the bitterness it sparked. Some politicians swore they would defy the ruling. In Virginia, Senator Harry Byrd and members of the state administration called for a policy of massive resistance to desegregation, and that call was written into law. In 1956, 101 senators and representatives from the 11 states that had formed the Confederacy almost a century before signed the Southern Manifesto. It called the Supreme Court's decision "unwarranted," termed it a "clear abuse of judicial power," and ended with a pledge "to use all lawful means to bring about a reversal of this decision which is contrary to the Constitution."

The Southern Manifesto provided a direct challenge to the decision. Worse, it helped make defiance acceptable and encouraged action to try to change the result. In some areas southerners applied economic sanctions to harass blacks or sympathetic whites who worked for equality. In other places they took even more aggressive action to achieve their own ends.

The crucial confrontation came in Little Rock, Arkansas, in the fall of 1957. A desegregation plan, to begin with the token admission of a few black children to Central High School, was ready to be implemented. Then, just before the school year was to begin, Governor Orval Faubus declared on television that it would not be possible to maintain order if integration took place as planned. National Guardsmen, posted by the governor to keep peace and armed with bayonets, turned away nine black students when they tried to enter the school. Quickly the Federal Bureau of Investigation began looking into the matter, but not until three weeks later did a federal court order the troops to leave. The school opened, the black children entered, but the white students, spurred on by the example of their elders, became riotous and belligerent and began to chant such slogans as "Two, four, six, eight, we ain't gonna integrate." In the face of the growing mob, the blacks were taken from the school.

The lines were drawn, and all attention focused on the moderate man in the White House. Earlier, as the crisis began, Ike had repeated his view that laws alone could not make people change and had compounded that by observing that southerners "see a picture of mongrelization of the race, they call it."

Vacationing in Newport, Rhode Island, Eisenhower had met with Faubus while the Guardsmen were still at the school and had taken a cautious stand in the hope that the crisis in Little Rock would dissolve of its own accord. Now,

Confrontation at Central High School in Little Rock, Arkansas, in 1957. (*AP/Wide World*)

however, he faced a situation in which there was clear defiance of the law. An old military man, Ike knew that such resistance could continue no longer. He denounced the "disgraceful occurrence," urged those obstructing the law to "cease and desist," and finally had to take the one action he had earlier called unthinkable. For the first time since the end of Reconstruction, an American president called out federal troops to protect the rights of the blacks. Paratroopers entered Little Rock, and National Guardsmen were placed under federal command. The black children entered the school and attended classes with the military protecting their right. Under those circumstances, desegregation was achieved.

The crisis was not yet over. In 1958 the school board sought to delay the integration plan, and when permission was denied, the governor ordered all high schools closed for the next school year. An effort to call them all private institutions failed, and in 1959 they opened again. The Little Rock episode was over at last.

The Black Bus Boycott

Meanwhile, American blacks themselves were drawing on the examples of the World War II years as they began to engage in activities that were to have an equally profound impact on the development of the civil rights movement. The peaceful protests against the Jim Crow system of segregation that had been relatively isolated episodes in the war period generated a new momentum starting with events in Montgomery, Alabama, at the end of 1955. On December 1, Rosa Parks, a 43-year-old black seamstress, sat down in the front of a city bus in a section reserved by custom for whites. When told to move back, she refused and was subsequently arrested and ordered to stand trial for violating the rigid segregation laws. The next evening resistance began. Fifty black leaders met to discuss the case and decided to organize a massive boycott of the bus system. Martin Luther King, Jr., the 27-year-old minister of the Baptist church in which the meeting was held, soon emerged as the most prominent spokesman of the protest. Eloquently he declared, "There comes a time when people get tired . . . of being kicked about by the brutal feet of oppression." It was time to be more assertive, to cease being "patient with anything less than freedom and justice." King was arrested, as he was to be time and again, but the movement continued as the 50,000 blacks in Montgomery walked or formed car pools to avoid the transit system. Their actions cut gross income by 65 percent on city buses. Eventually, almost a year later, the Supreme Court ruled that bus segregation, like school segregation, violated the Constitution, and the boycott came to an end. But the mood it fostered continued to develop, and peaceful protest became a way of life.

Blacks and Voting Rights

At the same time a movement to guarantee blacks voting rights began. The provisions of the Fourteenth Amendment notwithstanding, many states managed to circumvent the law. Some required a poll tax; others instituted literacy tests. Still others required answers to questions such as "How many bubbles are in a bar of soap?" No civil rights act had been passed since Reconstruction days, but as the pressures for reform grew, the time seemed ripe.

Eisenhower believed in the right to vote, yet still had reservations. At a press conference he declared, "I personally believe if you try to go too far too fast in this delicate field that has involved the emotions of so many millions of Americans, you are making a mistake." As a bill worked its way through the legislative process, Ike himself was not always much help. At another press conference he was asked about provisions and responded, "Well, I would not want to answer . . . in detail because I was reading part of the bill this morning, and I—there were certain phrases I didn't completely understand."

Owing less to the aid of Ike and more to the legislative genius of Lyndon B. Johnson of Texas, the civil rights bill moved along. Johnson, the Senate majority leader, had his eye on the presidency and wanted to establish his credentials as a man who could look beyond the narrow interests of the South. He pared the bill down to the provisions he felt could pass and pushed the measure through. The Civil Rights Act of 1957 created a Civil Rights Commission and empowered the Justice Department to go to court in cases in which blacks were denied the right to vote. The bill was a compromise measure, to be sure, but as the first successful effort in 82 years it was nonetheless a start. With loopholes evident and limited enforcement, it was soon clear that something else had to be done. Again Johnson took the lead, and after beating back a filibuster, he helped secure the Civil Rights Act of 1960. It set stiffer punishments for people who interfered with the right to vote but again stopped short of authorizing federal registrars themselves to register blacks to vote.

The civil rights movement came a long way during the Eisenhower years. Not much of the progress came about as a result of Ike's actions, but the efforts of blacks themselves and the rulings of the courts both brought significant change. The period had been a turbulent one, and the movement had only begun.

Hispanics and Native Americans in the Fifties

Other groups faced problems as serious as those encountered by blacks in the 1950s. But they were less well organized, and their movements for equality took longer to get off the ground.

Chicanos who had come up from Mexico for the past decade to assist with American crops never enjoyed an easy life but faced even greater difficulties in hard times. During the 1953–1954 recession, with Operation Wetback, the Eisenhower administration embarked on a move to send illegal entrants home. Large-scale deportations occurred—875,000 in fiscal 1953, 1,035,282 in 1954. As immigration officials warmed to their task, all Chicanos found themselves vulnerable. They complained bitterly about the violations of their rights, but their complaints did no good.

Throughout the 1950s, Hispanics faced the same discrimination and exclusion they had known in past years. They began to protest the abuse they met through such organizations as the *Asociación Nacional México-Americana*, founded early in the decade in New Mexico to protect the human rights of Mexican-Americans facing trouble on assorted fronts. Sometimes they achieved recourse; sometimes they did not. For most of the decade, Hispanic activism seemed without direction. Many Hispanics considered the situation hopeless. Real progress had to wait.

Native Americans were equally troubled about the approach of the Eisenhower administration. The government, aware that past policies had not worked, was determined to cut back on federal activity wherever possible and stabilize the relationship with the Indians once and for all. It proposed settling all outstanding claims, wiping out trust funds, and eliminating reservations as legitimate political entities.

The new "termination" policy victimized the Indians. A number of tribes suffered serious disruption. With their lands no longer protected by the government and their members without treaty rights, they had a difficult time. Though the Indians were told that they now had the rights of any citizen to dispose of their resources as they chose, they were often unwitting victims of people who wanted to seize their land. The harsh and abrupt policy caused undue disruption and was eventually discontinued.

Resistance to termination brought a sense of pride. A Seminole petition to the president of the United States in 1954 summed up a growing view: "We do not say that we are superior or inferior to the White Man and we do not say that the White Man is superior or inferior to us. We do say that we are not White Men but Indians, do not wish to become White Men but wish to remain Indians, and have an outlook on all things different from the outlook of the White Man." It was one thing to state that view; it was another to gain acceptance for it in the 1950s.

THE FIFTIES IN PERSPECTIVE

In the 1950s the United States suffered from occasional economic problems. It began to become aware of those groups who never knew the comfortable patterns others enjoyed. On balance, however, the nation seemed stable and secure. For the most part, business boomed, and even when recession intervened, the cycle seemed to right itself before too long. There was a continuing confidence, perhaps misplaced, that all problems could be overcome.

Yet occasional doubts and anxieties could not be ignored. In 1957, the Soviet Union launched the first artificial satellite to orbit the earth. Every 96 minutes the 184-pound *Sputnik,* going "beep-beep," went around the globe at a speed of 18,000 miles an hour. The next month the Russians put an even larger *Sputnik* into orbit. That one weighed 1120 pounds and carried a live dog. The United States, which had long hailed its own scientific accomplishments, suffered a serious blow to national pride. It became even worse when an American rocket launched at Cape Canaveral rose only a foot before crashing to the ground. When the nation finally managed to launch a satellite of its own, it weighed but 2½ pounds.

Now some Americans, still preoccupied with the Cold War, began to criticize the materialistic orientation that had left the nation behind. Had the United States become flabby and weak while the Soviet Union grew strong? There were serious examinations of the national purpose of the land. Just what did the United States want to achieve? How could Americans get where they wanted to go?

Critics questioning their own approach became increasingly aware of the inequities in American life. They became frustrated with the political stalemate that hampered the process of reform in the Eisenhower years. Ike remained overwhelmingly popular, but he faced Democrats in control of both houses of Congress for much of his tenure. That meant there was often a standoff, and progress was possible only through interparty cooperation.

The nation remained optimistic but had to confront problems in American society that could not be ignored. Less visible and less vocal in the 1950s than they later became, groups struggling for their own rights became louder as Eisenhower stepped down after two terms. The country still seemed secure as he left office, but observant Americans could already see the first stirrings of the difficulties that came to haunt the United States in the decade ahead.

SUGGESTIONS FOR FURTHER READING

There are a number of good books that describe domestic developments in the 1950s. Richard Polenberg, *One Nation Divisible: Class, Race, and Ethnicity in the United States Since 1938* (1980) is a useful survey of recent America that describes different groups and the changes they experienced. William E. Leuchtenburg, *A Troubled Feast: American Society Since 1945* (1983) is a perceptive assessment that focuses on the consumer culture that came into prominence after World War II. John Kenneth Galbraith, *The Affluent Society* (1958) is a contemporary account of the implications of growing prosperity in America. Sloan Wilson, *The Man in the Gray Flannel Suit* (1955) is a novel that gives a good sense of the materialistic values of the 1950s. David Riesman, *The Lonely Crowd: A Study of the Changing American Character* (1950) remains a perceptive sociological analysis of developments in the United States.

On the Eisenhower administration, Charles C. Alexander, *Holding the Line: The Eisenhower Era, 1952–1961* (1975) provides a good general introduction to mood and policy during Ike's years as president. Herbert S. Parmet, *Eisenhower and the American Crusades* (1972) is a detailed account of domestic policy. See Peter Lyon, *Eisenhower: Portrait of the Hero* (1974) for another view of Ike. Fred Greenstein, *The Hidden Hand Presidency* (1982) suggests that Eisenhower was more active than commonly thought. Gary W. Reichard, *The Reaffirmation of Republicanism: Eisenhower and the 83rd Congress* (1975) is a useful assessment of political and policy questions under Ike. Dwight D. Eisenhower, *Mandate for Change, 1953–1956* (1963) is the first volume of Ike's memoirs of his years in office. Dwight D. Eisenhower, *Waging Peace* (1965) is the concluding volume of his own personal account. See Emmet John Hughes, *The Ordeal of Power* (1963) for an insider's view of the Eisenhower years.

For a good assessment of one of the major Republican leaders of the time, see James T. Patterson, *Mr. Republican: A Biography of Robert A. Taft* (1972).

On foreign policy, Townsend Hoopes, *The Devil and John Foster Dulles* (1973) is a searching examination of the secretary of state. Robert A. Divine, *Eisenhower and the Cold War* (1981) is a brief and sympathetic account of the president's diplomatic efforts.

On women in the 1950s, William H. Chafe, *The American Woman: Her Changing Social, Economic, and Political Roles, 1920–1970* (1972) is an outstanding survey that has particularly pertinent observations on the postwar years. Betty Friedan, *The Feminine Mystique* (1963) is an angry book describing the stereotypical role of women in the 1950s as they focused on being housewives and mothers.

Regarding civil rights, Harvard Sitkoff, *The Struggle for Black Equality, 1954–1980* (1981) is a readable account of the movement since the 1950s. Richard Kluger, *Simple Justice* (1975) tells the full story of the *Brown* v. *Board of Education* decision and its implications. See also Martin Luther King, Jr., *Stride Toward Freedom* (1958) for a personal view of where the struggle was going.

Several other recent books provide good background on the efforts of other minorities to gain equality in America. Rodolfo Acuña, *Occupied America: A History of Chicanos* (1981) gives a good sense of the Chicano struggle in the years after World War II. Alvin M. Josephy, Jr., *Now That the Buffalo's Gone* (1982) describes Indian struggles in the past several decades.

chapter 5

Kennedy and Camelot

In the early 1960s, America's confidence in its destiny and its design grew stronger than ever before. The years of the decade just past had been good ones, for middle-class Americans at least, and despite a growing awareness of inequity in the society, a basic sense of security remained. A new leader following eight years of Ike promised to give more vigorous leadership to the United States. John F. Kennedy seized upon the notion of national purpose that had troubled Americans as the 1950s came to an end and reaffirmed the dedication of the nation to deal aggressively with its problems in the years ahead.

Energetic and articulate, Kennedy was able to voice his aims in terms the rest of the country could understand. He made it clear from the start that the United States would hold its own in foreign affairs, and he seemed to convey the sense that the country was ready to address nagging social concerns at home. There was a new spirit evident, both in Washington and in the nation at large. For a brief time there was the feeling that anything was possible in the United States.

THE KENNEDY ADMINISTRATION

Kennedy's style gave a new stamp to the age. He was far younger than his predecessor; at 43, he was the youngest man ever elected to the office of president. Eager to make his mark, he was determined that his administration provide a contrast to the one it succeeded. In the campaign he demonstrated the power of television on the electoral process. In office he surrounded himself with people of talent and promised an activist approach.

The Road to the White House

John Kennedy had pointed toward the presidency for a number of years. A member of an Irish Catholic family from Massachusetts, he was pushed by his father, a wealthy businessman who sought social acceptance in Protestant America. Somewhat frail as a youth, Kennedy became stronger as he grew up, but throughout his life suffered from a variety of physical ailments. He graduated from Harvard University and went on to serve heroically in the navy during World War II. When his brother was killed during the war, he inherited the family's political hopes. His first electoral victory came when he was elected to the House of Representatives in 1946. After three terms he was elected to the Senate in 1952 and reelected in 1958 by the largest majority in the history of his state. At no time was Kennedy a particularly effective member of Congress. He had a reputation as a playboy of sorts, and colleagues sometimes wondered whether he shared their own legislative concerns. Yet at the same time Kennedy grew in each office he held and seemed able to handle the successive responsibilities he assumed.

John F. Kennedy and his young son with military leaders at Arlington National Cemetery. (*UPI/Bettmann Newsphotos*)

The Election of 1960

In 1960 he aimed for the top. He had unsuccessfully sought the vice-presidential nomination in 1956; now he went after the Democratic presidential nomination itself. The Catholic issue was the first hurdle he had to overcome, for no Catholic had ever been elected president of the United States. Al Smith had failed in his 1928 bid, and the conventional wisdom held that no Catholic could attain the office. All kinds of pointed stories circulated during the campaign. One critic charged that JFK was collecting bowling balls to make a string of rosary beads for the Statue of Liberty—which could then be called Our Lady of the Harbor. Another advised voters to join the church of their choice—while there was still time. Those attacks notwithstanding, Kennedy managed to defuse the issue in the primary campaign. His victory in Protestant West Virginia, where opponent Hubert Humphrey had long been a friend of labor interests there, showed that a Catholic could win.

Kennedy pushed hard and used his advantages as well. His own personal wealth made a major difference. His family assisted, both in active campaigning and in the organizational work that was even more important. The Kennedy team played politics with precision. A tenacious concern with detail characterized the organization, and a passion for victory helped attain that goal.

Kennedy insisted it was time to get the country moving again. Pursuing the issues of the Cold War, he charged that the Eisenhower administration was being too soft in its resistance to the Communist threat, and he pledged an even stronger approach. In his speech accepting the Democratic nomination he noted "uncharted areas of science and space, unsolved problems of peace and war, unconquered pockets of ignorance and prejudice, unanswered questions of poverty and surplus." Those could not be avoided, for "the New Frontier is here whether we seek it or not." That phrase provided Kennedy's administration with a name. Over and over he countered the Republican claim that Americans never had it so good with the contention that the country could do better.

Richard Nixon, Eisenhower's two-term vice-president, had a number of problems in the campaign. An economic recession hurt the Republicans, and Eisenhower's lukewarm support hardly helped. The two men had never been personally close, but Ike made things worse when he was asked in a press conference what decisions Nixon had helped make and he responded, "If you give me a week, I might think of one." Even so, Nixon had a distinct advantage as the campaign began. Better known than Kennedy on the basis of national experience alone, he seemed to be a favorite in the race.

That all changed in the first televised debates ever held. Television, increasingly important in American life, came to play a major role in the political process as well. Both candidates were articulate, and if debating scores had been kept, Nixon might have won. But Kennedy came across as more polished and relaxed, and largely because of the image he projected, he managed to gain the upper hand. Nixon appeared tired on TV. He had been hospitalized for a staph infection some weeks before and had not yet fully recovered his strength,

Richard Nixon and John Kennedy in one of their televised debates during the 1960 campaign. (*AP/Wide World*)

even though he had been campaigning actively as the debates drew near. He looked haggard and drawn; the weight he had lost was visible in the fit of the collar of his shirt. Worst of all, he was poorly made up for the first, and probably most crucial, debate. His beard was covered only by a light coating of "Lazy Shave" rather than a more substantial makeup that would have hidden the dark stubble at the end of the day. On camera and under hot lights, the powder streaked even as it exaggerated the beard growth it was supposed to hide.

In the first debate the candidates expressed agreement on ends, disagreement on means. Nixon took issue with points his opponent made, but Kennedy looked beyond Nixon and seemed to be addressing the American people. His self-possession paid off, for the public was impressed with the appearance he conveyed, and the momentum shifted his way. Television, growing more important all the time, was now a significant part of the political process as well.

In the end, Kennedy won an extraordinarily close victory. The electoral tally of 303 to 219 masked the narrowness of the popular margin. Kennedy won by barely 120,000 of 34.2 million popular votes, a margin of approximately one-tenth of one percent. If but a few thousand people had voted differently in Illinois, where there were allegations of irregularities, the result would have been reversed. Kennedy won because he carried traditionally Democratic areas. He did well in the cities, with black and ethnic support. The Catholic issue did hurt to some degree, but largely in areas, such as the South, where he could withstand the loss of some votes. The debates also had an important impact on the final result. In a survey for CBS, pollster Elmo Roper estimated that 57 percent of the people who voted felt that the debates had affected their choice.

Another 6 percent said their final decision resulted from the debates alone. As Kennedy himself concluded after his narrow victory, "It was TV more than anything else that turned the tide."

The Kennedy Style

The Kennedy inaugural of 1961 helped establish in striking terms the new start the administration intended to make. Well aware of how Franklin Roosevelt had given the nation a lift in 1933, the new president sought to do the same thing. Black singer Marian Anderson sang the national anthem. Poet Robert Frost recited from his work. Kennedy himself sparked the nation with his own stirring address. "The torch has been passed," he said, "to a new generation of Americans—born in this century, tempered by war, disciplined by a hard and bitter peace, proud of our ancient heritage." It was time to reaffirm American values and to move ahead together, he concluded: "And so, my fellow Americans: Ask not what your country can do for you—ask what you can do for your country."

The new administration was buoyant in the extreme. Youth seemed to prevail, and glamour, too. Kennedy and his wife Jacqueline conducted themselves with charm and grace. Intellectuals frequented the White House; Nobel Prize winners were guests at a special dinner. Artists and musicians like Pablo Casals performed before invited guests. The Kennedys and their friends played touch football on the grass and showed an energy and exuberance that was amplified by the press. The administration seemed like the Camelot of King Arthur's day, and the image stuck, even when performance failed to match promise.

Kennedy himself helped generate a sense of confidence. He relished characterizations like "tough-minded" and "hard-nosed," for, unlike Ike, he wanted to be a strong president. Well before his election, in a speech before the National Press Club, he declared that the next chief executive "must be prepared to exercise the fullest powers of his office—all that are specified and some that are not," and he clung to that notion throughout his term. The president, he believed, "must serve as a catalyst, an energizer," who would perform "in the very thick of the fight." He favored, in reporter Joseph Kraft's phrase, a "bang-bang" style where it sometimes seemed action was important for its own sake. A student of history, Kennedy sought to follow not Ike's but FDR's example, where the president kept power in his own hands and worked through problems himself. Yet he wanted to avoid the feuding Roosevelt had tolerated, even encouraged, among subordinates, and he surrounded himself with able people who nonetheless saw the world in his terms.

On his staff he had 15 Rhodes scholars and numerous authors of note. Yet his assistants were also tough administrators who were prepared to assert themselves and lead. The secretary of state was Dean Rusk, a former member of the State Department who had then become president of the Rockefeller Foundation. The secretary of defense was Republican Robert S. McNamara, successful president of the Ford Motor Company, who had gained a reputation for brilliance through the use of computer analysis and quantitative assessment. For secretary of the Treasury, Kennedy chose Republican C. Douglas Dillon, a Wall Street executive who had been under secretary of state under Eisenhower. Kennedy's brother Robert, after running the victorious campaign, assumed the post of attorney general. When complaints arose that Bobby was too young for such a position, Kennedy quipped that his brother might as well get some experience before beginning to practice law. With a characteristic sense of humor, when asked how he would announce such a controversial choice, he said, "Well, I think I'll open the front door of the Georgetown house some morning about 2:00 A.M., look up and down the street, and, if there's no one there, I'll whisper, 'It's Bobby.'" Harvard was well represented in the new administration. McGeorge Bundy, the former dean of the college, became national security adviser, and noted historian Arthur M. Schlesinger, Jr., was a top aide.

Those appointees were all able men who contributed to the dazzling reputation of the Kennedy team. Yet few of them had experience with the political realities they would face in Washington. Vice-President Lyndon Johnson, uncomfortable with the top staff, once spoke of the brilliance to Sam Rayburn, Speaker of the House. Rayburn responded, "Well, Lyndon, you might be right and they may be every bit as intelligent as you say, but I'd feel a whole lot better about them if just one of them had run for sheriff once." Rayburn understood the limitations of the Kennedy staff. His assessment showed an understanding of how style could sometimes outweigh substance in the public view.

KENNEDY AND FOREIGN AFFAIRS

For all its promise, the Kennedy administration often blundered at home and abroad and never attained the goals it had proclaimed. That was most true in the domestic sphere, yet held as well in the field of foreign affairs. Kennedy promised action and delivered on his promise, but with results that were sometimes questionable.

Kennedy's View

Kennedy himself was most interested in the foreign field. He felt that domestic issues were potentially more divisive but also less pressing than overseas concerns. He once remarked that the country would be hurt by a domestic failure but devastated by a foreign one. He wanted to lead in that area, and by relying on his National Security Council, he often tended to disregard his own Department of State.

Kennedy, as much as Truman and Ike, saw the world in Cold War terms. He too perceived a threat mounted by Communists abroad, and his rhetoric was every bit as sharp as that of John Foster Dulles the decade before. During the campaign, at the Mormon Tabernacle in Salt Lake City, he declared, "The enemy is the communist system itself—implacable, insatiable, unceasing in its drive for world domination. For this is not a struggle for the supremacy of arms alone—it is also a struggle for supremacy between two conflicting ideologies: Freedom under God versus ruthless, godless tyranny." He proclaimed the same theme even more dramatically in his inaugural address, when he asserted, "In the long history of the world, only a few generations have been granted the role of defending freedom in its hour of maximum danger. I do not shrink from this responsibility. I welcome it."

The president was intent not merely on buttressing nations facing a direct Communist threat but on maintaining a more general stability in vulnerable regions as a whole. Indeed, by using power to preserve peace, he seemed to hope to reshape the world to American specifications. Despite a real dedication to the cause of peace, he was insistent on standing firm even at the risk of war. His rhetoric asked for sacrifice—as in his inaugural address's description of the mission of the United States: The nation would "pay any price, bear any burden, meet any hardship, support any friend, oppose any foe, to assure the survival and the success of liberty."

The Bay of Pigs

Kennedy's first effort in that direction came at the Bay of Pigs. Cuba had been a problem for the United States ever since Fidel Castro had seized power in early 1959. The revolutionary leader expropriated private property and moved increasingly close to the Soviet Union. Kennedy spoke during the campaign of the danger of revolution spreading elsewhere in Latin America, and he even suggested that the United States arm Cuban exiles to prepare them to retake their land. After the election but before the transition took place, the United States broke diplomatic relations with the Castro regime. Kennedy meanwhile learned that the CIA was already covertly training anti-Castro exiles in Guatemala to storm the Cuban coast at the Bay of Pigs.

When Kennedy became president, the CIA sought to press on with its plan. The agency wanted the United States to give logistic support to an exile invasion, and the Joint Chiefs of Staff went along. There was, however, some resistance to the scheme. Senator J. William Fulbright, chairman of the Foreign Relations Committee, declared on learning of the plan that "to give this activity even covert support is of a piece with the hypocrisy and cynicism for which the United States is constantly denouncing the Soviet Union." The situation was not a desperate one: "The Castro regime is a thorn in the flesh; but it is not a dagger in the heart." Marine Commandant David Shoup took another tack. He argued that Cuba was larger than commonly thought and that it would not be taken with ease. Better to reckon the consequences before a commitment was made. Nonetheless, the administration moved ahead. The plan was a bold one that would look even better if it succeeded. There was an element of risk, to be sure, but the top aides were still eager to push on.

The invasion of April 17, 1961, was an unmitigated disaster. When an early air strike failed to destroy Cuban air power, Castro was able to hold off the troops coming ashore. Urged to use American planes for air cover, Kennedy drew the line, for by that time failure was all too clear. Rather than supporting the exiles, the Cubans had followed Castro instead. Kennedy quickly mopped up and brought the affair to a close.

For the United States the whole invasion was a dismal failure. The nation had broken agreements not to interfere in others' hemispheric concerns. It had intervened in a clumsy and incompetent way that showed no sense of restraint or understanding of revolution elsewhere in the world. European leaders, who had high hopes for the new president, were troubled by the incident. For Kennedy, who took personal responsibility for the fiasco, the episode was a painful one indeed, but one that left him intent on asserting authority and demonstrating competence in other ways.

The Berlin Crisis

Chastened by the experience at the Bay of Pigs, Kennedy was more determined than ever to deal sternly with the Communist threat. Inexperienced and young, he was afraid that the appearance of weakness would hurt the United States. When he met Soviet leader Nikita Khrushchev in Vienna in June 1961, he was subjected to bullying and served with another crisis that demanded a response. The situation in Germany had not been formally settled after World War II. Germany had been divided into zones, and in time the Western zones had been amalgamated into one, so that there were in effect two new German states. Tension in 1948 had culminated in the Berlin airlift; further pressure for a resolution of the Berlin issue came in 1958, when the Russians first made demands, then backed off once again. Now, with Kennedy in office, Khrushchev pressed for a peace treaty that reflected the reality of the division that had occurred. He was concerned about the flow of East Germans into West Germany, particularly from East Berlin into West Berlin, for that city was divided too. Abandoning the assumption that Germany was but one land that would someday be reunited, he wanted a settlement soon.

Kennedy was afraid of being cornered and claimed that the Soviets were moving in Germany as a prelude to movement on the continent as a whole. Intent on standing firm, he told the American people a month and a half after his return home that West Berlin was "the great testing place of Western courage and will." The United States would not be pushed around: "We do not want to fight—but we have fought before." He then asked Congress for an increased defense appropriation of more than $3 billion. He asked for more men for the army, navy, and air force and doubled, then tripled draft calls and at the same time called up reserve forces. He also requested $207 million for a civil defense fallout-shelter program, which would not have helped much in the event of nuclear attack but which served to underscore the perceived stakes in the struggle.

The Russian response was to erect a wall in Berlin, which effectively sealed East Berliners in and, in the Soviet view, alleviated the immediate problem. After some tough rhetoric in response, the United States indicated a willingness to negotiate, and the threat of war faded. Ultimately the crisis passed, but only after Kennedy had demonstrated that the United States would not be pushed around.

The Cuban Missile Crisis

On the foreign front, Kennedy's first year had been a tough one. When a reporter indicated that he was considering writing a book about the term so far, Kennedy wondered who would read a book about disasters. The next year Kennedy had a chance to recoup some of his lost prestige, though this time at the risk of war.

Again the stage was Cuba. Irritated about American intentions at the Bay of Pigs, the Russians had pledged to support Cuba in the future. In October 1962, American air photographs revealed that the Soviets were indeed aiding their ally; there were clear shots of offensive missiles being placed on Cuban soil. The Russians may have moved to locate the missiles there for the enhancement of their international standing. Khrushchev may have hoped to buttress his own internal position with a show of toughness to demonstrate that the Russians would not allow the Cubans to be pushed around. Still, the missiles did not really change the strategic balance; the Soviets could wreak untold destruction on American targets from already existing bases elsewhere as easily as they could from Cuba. But the actual balance was less important than public appearance. Kennedy faced a direct challenge, and political realities dictated that he had to respond.

Respond he did. Top administration officials quickly convened and went over the various alternatives. Some members of the Executive Committee of the National Security Council wanted an air strike to knock out the sites, but Robert Kennedy opposed such a move by recalling the Japanese attack on Pearl Harbor in 1941 and declaring that JFK would not be the Tojo of his day. Still, the United States did move to a position of full alert. Bombers and missiles were fueled, armed with nuclear weapons, and readied to go. The fleet prepared to move, and troops prepared to invade if given the word. On October 22, Kennedy went on nationwide TV to tell the American people about the missiles and to demand that they be removed. He declared that the United States would not shrink from the risk of nuclear war and announced a naval blockade around Cuba to prevent Soviet ships from bringing any more missiles in. He called the move a quarantine, for a blockade was an act of war.

Khrushchev condemned the American actions, and for two days, as the opposing powers stood "eyeball to eyeball" on the brink of disaster, the Soviet ships steamed toward the blockade. Then Khrushchev called the ships back, even while work on the missile sites themselves continued. On October 26, Khrushchev backed off still further when he sent Kennedy a long letter in which he pledged to remove the missiles if the United States promised to end the blockade and stay out of Cuba. The next day another letter arrived demanding that the United States remove its missiles from Turkey too. At Robert Kennedy's suggestion, the United States ignored the second letter and responded affirmatively to the first. (In fact, JFK had already ordered the removal of the missiles in Turkey some months before.) The crisis was over. Dean Rusk observed, "We have won a considerable victory. You and I are still alive."

The Cuban missile crisis was the most terrifying confrontation of the Kennedy administration and, indeed, of the entire Cold War. The world was closer to nuclear war at that moment than it had ever been before. Kennedy emerged from the crisis as a hero who had stood firm. He had refused to be cowed by the Soviets and had shown that the United States would not be pushed around. His reputation was enhanced, as was the image of his party in the congressional elections only weeks away. Yet as the relief of the moment began to fade, some critics came to charge that what Kennedy saw as his finest hour was in fact an unnecessary crisis in which the response was too extreme. Kennedy had shown some restraint in not authorizing an invasion, to be sure, but he had not used normal channels of diplomacy to press his case and had seemed willing to move all the way to the brink and beyond. He avoided disaster, as Dean Acheson observed, by "plain dumb luck" and by Khrushchev's eventual decision to pull back from a position that was hard to hold. Were the risks commensurate with the possible gains? What might have happened if Khrushchev had not backed off and brought the crisis to an end?

Southeast Asia

Throughout the Kennedy years, the United States was also involved in Southeast Asia. There had been trouble in the tiny land of Laos for some years. Although Laos was supposed to be neutral under the terms of the Geneva Accords of 1954, neutralist, Communist, and pro-Western elements struggled for control. Eisenhower, who felt that Laos was the key to the whole region, had been unable to bring the conflict to an end. As the CIA and Joint Chiefs of Staff urged him to make a stand, Kennedy decided to try to avoid a confrontation there if he could. He and Khrushchev were able to agree to a cease-fire, and though the coalition they established failed to last, the administration managed to avoid serious trouble, largely because Kennedy's attention was focused elsewhere in the world.

In Vietnam, Kennedy took a stronger stand, and the consequences there lasted far beyond the short life of his administration. Ho Chi Minh's struggle for independence had been going on for years and showed no sign of abating. Vietnam had been partitioned temporarily by the Geneva Accords of 1954, but the anticipated elections to reunify the country had not taken place, and the division into two lands became more firm. Ho Chi Minh held power in the north. Ngo Dinh Diem, a Catholic in a Buddhist country, governed in the south with methods that became increasingly authoritarian and extreme.

The United States saw the war in Vietnam as but a part of the larger Cold War struggle. Ho Chi Minh's version of communism was rigorously nationalistic, but Americans insisted on seeing it as of a piece with the Soviet variety. For that reason Truman had sided with the French as they had attempted to subdue the Vietnamese, Eisenhower had supported Diem when the French left, and now Kennedy decided to make the American commitment even clearer.

In 1956 Kennedy had argued that "Vietnam represents the cornerstone of the Free World in Southeast Asia, the keystone to the arch, the finger in the dike. Burma, Thailand, India, Japan, the Philippines and, obviously, Laos and Cambodia are among those whose security would be threatened if the red tide of Communism overflowed into Vietnam." That position governed his approach when he became president.

Kennedy inherited a deteriorating position in 1961. As Eisenhower stepped down there were 675 American military advisers assisting the South Vietnamese. After the Bay of Pigs disaster and the crisis in Laos, Kennedy decided to increase the number of advisers in Vietnam. He sent Vice-President Lyndon Johnson to Saigon to assess the situation and to underscore the American commitment to the south. Johnson hailed Diem as "the Winston Churchill of Southeast Asia" and reported to Kennedy that a fundamental decision had to be made: "We must decide whether to help these countries to the best of our ability or throw in the towel and pull back our defenses to San Francisco and a 'Fortress America' concept." He recommended further aid. Others in the administration felt the same way. Dean Rusk, with a background in Asian affairs, saw Vietnam as a proving ground and was eager to proceed.

Kennedy therefore began sending more and more advisers to the Asian land. They began going in the first year of his term and continued to the end. The Cuban missile crisis only strengthened the resolve to stand firm. Kennedy felt that a hard line had succeeded once against the Russians and should be followed by a similar stance in other trouble spots in the world. Not simply advisers, however, went to South Vietnam. American troops began to move into the conflict to aid in the struggle. By the end of 1963 almost 17,000 Americans were engaged in the war.

The major problem was Diem's lack of support. Iron-willed and strict, he ruled through members of his family, resisted promised reforms, and became even more rigid as time went on. When he began to insist that Buddhists obey Catholic religious laws, resistance began. In June 1963 a Buddhist monk covered himself with gasoline and then ignited it with a match. Immobile in the flames, he continued his silent protest until he tumbled over dead. Other monks followed suit as opposition to Diem grew. Kennedy and his aides finally decided that Diem had to go, and American officials in Vietnam indicated that they would not object to an internal revolt. With that encouragement, military leaders struck. In early November they removed Diem, then killed him. Upset by the assassination, American officials nonetheless approved of the result.

When the Kennedy administration came to an abrupt end later that month, the situation in Vietnam was in a state of flux. Kennedy had clearly increased the American effort. But just how far was he willing to go? In September he commented, "I don't think that unless a greater effort is made . . . to win popular support that the war can be won out there. In the final analysis it is their war. They are the ones who have to win it or lose it." Yet he showed no inclination to pull out of the struggle. "For us to withdraw from that effort would mean a collapse not only of South Vietnam but [of] Southeast Asia," he declared near the end. "So we are going to stay there." Taking over a difficult situation from his predecessor, Kennedy only exacerbated it, and the United States ended up staying a long time.

Foreign Policy in Perspective

Foreign policy in the Kennedy years moved from crisis to crisis as the administration sought to make good on its rhetorical aims. As Kennedy took office, the world was beginning to change. Independence movements were forcing maps to be redrawn and blurring the patterns of confrontation that had held in the past. No longer did the polarization of the world into two camps always seem as necessary or as extreme as it had before. Kennedy asserted in mid-1963 that it would be helpful to reassess Cold War attitudes, yet for the most part he only helped sustain the tensions of prior years without fully acknowledging the changes that had occurred.

Kennedy stood firm in the crises he seemed to encourage, even when he might have softened his stance. He also moved to extend still further the defenses of the United States. In the campaign of 1960 he argued that the nation suffered from a "missile gap" when compared to the Soviet Union. Evidence after his accession to office revealed that no such gap existed, but he pursued a missile-building program nonetheless. The number of intercontinental ballistic missiles (ICBMs) in 1967 was five times the number in 1960, as the nation built far more than it could ever use. So did the Soviet Union, of course, and a massive arms race was under way.

At the same time, Kennedy moved to diversify the defense forces at his command. He was uncomfortable with the notion prevalent during the Eisenhower years that a nuclear deterrent alone could provide for national defense. The policy of massive retaliation may have helped stabilize the budget, but it left the nation vulnerable in a crisis that was not serious enough for leaders to contemplate nuclear attack. Kennedy therefore sought to increase America's ability to wage conventional war by boosting the number of troops available and the support mechanisms necessary for combat. He also began to prepare for guerrilla war. Having read works by Mao Zedong and other revolutionary leaders, he believed that a counterinsurgency capability was necessary to deal with struggles in developing lands. To that end he authorized the creation of the Special Forces, known as the Green Berets, and personally helped choose the equipment they would use. The United States, the administration contended, would not be caught unprepared.

Balancing those defense measures were a number of ventures for peace. In the aftermath of the Cuban missile crisis, Kennedy and Khrushchev moved to establish a "hot line"—an open telephone connection to allow for handling further episodes in a more rational way. In the summer of 1963 they also signed a nuclear test ban treaty prohibiting testing above the ground. It still permitted underground testing, and indeed led to increased explosive experimentation beneath the surface of the earth. Nonetheless, it helped cut back on accumulating atmospheric radiation and was, as Kennedy said, "an important first step toward peace, a step toward reason, a step away from war."

The Alliance for Progress, aimed at Latin America and developed in Kennedy's first year, sought to promote stability in the Western Hemisphere and to head off future revolutionary disruptions before they occurred. The administration earmarked billions of dollars for social and economic ventures but soon ran into problems that ultimately limited effectiveness. The Bay of Pigs episode cast doubt on American intentions at the start; later, the expanding commitment in Vietnam drew necessary funds away from countries closer to home.

One other effort, limited in scope but unlimited in idealistic aim, involved the formation of the Peace Corps to assist in underdeveloped parts of the globe. The idea quickly caught on, and soon after the agency was established in 1961, thousands of volunteers began serving in various nations abroad. Sometimes criticized as imperialistic tools, the volunteers were free of CIA ties and made modest contributions overseas. They tried to promote goodwill over a two-year term and returned home with a better sense of the problems of underdeveloped lands.

Those ventures helped offset some of the foreign policy difficulties of the Kennedy years. Despite occasional efforts to deal with the world on a more flexible basis, however, the United States, in the early years of the new decade, still hewed to a Cold War line. The nation's efforts to confront crisis in terms of the lessons of the past led to frustration at first and overreaction and overinvolvement in the end.

THE DOMESTIC SPHERE

Kennedy had similar difficulty on the domestic front. Though he espoused liberal goals and spoke as if he intended to promote social justice for all, once in office he proved restrained. The real problem was that he lacked the support to embark on a major program of reform. Political realities could not be ignored.

Early Problems

Kennedy never had the mandate he sought. The election had been painfully close, and he himself had frequently trailed other Democrats in state and local campaigns. His party lost two seats in the Senate and 22 in the House in 1960, and while it still had majorities in both chambers, many of the congressional leaders were conservative southerners who were hardly sympathetic to liberal aims. With men like Wilbur Mills of Arkansas heading the House Ways and Means Committee, Howard W. Smith of Virginia leading the House Rules Committee, and Harry Byrd, also of Virginia, chairing the Senate Finance Committee, the administration could anticipate a tough time.

Further, Kennedy had never gained a solid reputation with congressional colleagues, despite his years in the Senate and the House. They questioned the depth of his concern and sensed his interest in other things. In the White House, the president found it easy to follow his preference for foreign affairs, even as he operated on the mistaken assumption that the fundamental problems at home were close to being solved. To maintain unified support for America's posture abroad, the administration wanted to avoid internal division, particularly since it did not have the necessary congressional votes. As a result, it took a modest approach, for as Kennedy observed, "There is no sense in raising hell and not being successful."

On the domestic front, the administration sought an increase in the minimum wage, federal aid for education, medical care for the elderly, and housing and urban reform. The liberal rhetoric Kennedy used and the sense of purpose he conveyed all helped create the sense that he could bring about the change he sought, but the limitations soon became clear.

The first congressional thrust seemed to be a success. The Kennedy team wanted an expansion of the House Rules Committee, where Howard Smith could sidetrack virtually anything he chose. Speaker of the House Sam Rayburn approved of the proposal to allow him to add two Democrats and one Republican to the committee. Those votes could help offset the chairman's power and ease the way for substantive discussion of the administration's proposals. In a close vote, the reform measure won. After that step, the administration hoped that the way was clear for other action in the months ahead.

The administration's effort to increase the minimum wage demonstrated the resistance it still faced. As a Kennedy proposal began to move through Congress, it encountered opposition from a far weaker measure. Kennedy aides, hoping to avoid a bitter fight, threw their support to a compromise bill but then failed to hold the votes even for that. In the end the House of Representatives followed the path of least resistance, the Senate came closer to meeting Kennedy's aims, and the final measure was much what the president had sought at the start. Nonetheless, the lack of legislative leadership was visible on Capitol Hill. The prevailing view was that while Kennedy had been lucky in his first fray, he was not an aggressive leader who could force his way. Rhetorical promises notwithstanding, the administration was not going to have an easy time achieving its goals.

Aid to Education

The difficulties were even more visible in the struggle for federal aid to education. Soon after taking office, Kennedy proposed a $2.3 billion program of grants to the states over a three-year period to help build schools and raise teachers' salaries. But he soon ran into the same problems that had stymied federal aid for the past 15 years. Was it appropriate to spend large sums of money for social goals? Would federal aid bring federal control? Should assistance go to segregated schools? Should it go to parochial schools? Some of the objections were easily met. Even conservative Robert Taft had earlier come to support the principle of aid, and a good case could be made that the government was the only body able to help. On the racial question, the administration was willing to allow assistance to go to segregated schools. But the Catholic issue proved to be the stumbling block that could not be overcome.

A Catholic himself, Kennedy was aware that he would face charges of favoritism if he supported aid for religious schools. During the campaign he had said repeatedly that he would not allow his religion to influence the actions he took. Even though advisers argued that Catholic votes were necessary for passage, Kennedy cited the constitutional principle of separation of church and state and refused to change his mind. Parochial pressure from the Catholic lobby was intense. Francis Cardinal Spellman of New York called Kennedy's stance "unfair" and "blatantly discriminating" to whose who wanted "a God-connected education" for their children. Eventually the administration accepted the notion that loans for the expansion of scientific or mathematical or language facilities would be all right. Even then the Kennedy staff could not twist enough arms to get its way. In the House Rules Committee, despite the earlier expansion, the measure died. Success hinged on the vote of one northern—and Catholic—Democrat who was dissatisfied with the compromise and joined the opposition. Kennedy had little leverage, and as he watched the bill go down to defeat, members of Congress watched the administration with the sense that they could go their own way and not be called to task.

Kennedy and the Economy

Kennedy had trouble in dealing with broad economic questions, too. He took office concerned about the continuing recession and wanted to work with the business community to restore prosperity. Though he listened to the corporate leaders who held Cabinet posts, he still faced outside resistance from executives who favored Eisenhower's orientation and feared a Democratic approach. Kennedy was clearly irked when they blamed the White House for anything that went wrong. "I understand every day why Roosevelt, who started out such a mild fellow, ended up so ferociously antibusiness," he said. "It's hard as hell to be friendly with people who keep trying to cut your legs off."

The major confrontation came in the spring of 1962, when steel companies sought to raise prices in what the administration felt was an inflationary way. U.S. Steel announced that it was going to charge an additional $6 a ton, and other companies quickly did the same. Concerned with the general state of the economy, Kennedy was even more irate at the action since the White House had recently worked to persuade labor in the industry to accept a modest and noninflationary contract on the assumption that management would show similar forebearance in keeping prices under control. He termed the price increase unreasonable and unjustifiable and charged that it showed "utter contempt for the public interest." Privately he said, "My father always told me that all businessmen were sons-of-bitches, but I never believed it till now." Publicly he used all the tools at his command to force the steel firms to reverse course. The Justice Department and the Federal Trade Commission moved to investigate the possibility of collusion in price agreements. The Defense Department appeared ready to deny contracts to the companies in question and in fact gave a contract to a smaller company that had held the line.

In the face of considerable pressure, the large firms backed down. Two days after the crisis began, U.S. Steel reinstituted the earlier prices. Kennedy had won. Yet he had paid a price for his victory. Business hostility remained intense, and business leaders showed little confidence in the administration's approach. On May 28, a month and a half after the steel crisis, the stock market fell in the greatest drop since the Great Crash of 1929. The president took the blame, as people on Wall Street joked, "When Eisenhower had a heart attack, the market broke . . . if Kennedy would have a heart attack, the market would go up." Kennedy did seek to appease business the next year when he stood back and just watched as steel prices rose selectively, but suspicions remained.

Kennedy also wanted to end the economic slump. Initially cautious in his approach, he favored a balanced budget when he took office. After a year and a half he changed his mind and came to take a modern Keynesian stance. Budget deficits had worked to promote prosperity during World War II. Why could they not work in peacetime too? Spending for defense and for the space program that sought to put a man on the moon had pumped money into the economy, but now the president began to argue for a major effort to spur economic growth. At the Yale University commencement ceremonies in June 1962 he voiced his new reservations about balanced budgets and his awareness that deficits, properly used, might help the economy begin to move.

At the start of 1963 the president called for a $13.5 billion cut in personal and corporate taxes over the next three years. That would bring a large deficit but would also provide capital that would stimulate the economy and bring added tax revenues in the end. There was opposition to the proposal from various sides. Conservatives refused to accept the basic premise that deficits would help. They felt, as Dwight Eisenhower declared, that "no family, no business, no nation can spend itself into prosperity." On the liberal front, Harvard economist John Kenneth Galbraith claimed that a tax cut was "reactionary Keynesianism" that aided those who needed it least and consequently encouraged frivolous spending: "I am not sure what the advantage is in having a few more dollars if the air is too dirty to breathe, the water too polluted to drink, the commuters are losing out on the struggle to get in and out of the cities, the streets are filthy, and the schools are so bad that the young, perhaps wisely, stay away, and hoodlums roll citizens for some of the dollars that they save in taxes." He wanted to see deficits that came from increased public spending, not from cuts in tax levels. Still Kennedy pressed on, but conservatives in Congress proved too strong. Pigeonholed in committee, the measure failed to emerge.

The Kennedy Administration and the Status of Women

The record was somewhat better on social questions, where sufficient pressure could be applied to make the administration respond. Frequently the Kennedy team took a relatively passive approach until forced to react to aggressive outside actions. That pattern followed with respect to administration support of the rights of women and applied even more directly with regard to civil rights.

Though the real wave of vigorous feminism did not begin until after Kennedy's death, pressures for reform were building in the years he held office. In the 1950s, despite the stress on traditional sex roles and the glorification of homemaking as a career, there had been movement for change as the decade came to an end. After *Sputnik,* the introspective assessment of American resources needed to meet the Soviet threat led to an increasing awareness that the talents of women were going unused. More women, particularly married women with children, entered the labor force. Yet significant job discrimination still occurred, and pay differentials for similar work done by women and men remained great.

Kennedy's campaign for the presidency had created expectations that he would dedicate himself to the cause of change, but once in office he did even less than his predecessors. Truman and Eisenhower had appointed women to visible political positions and thereby sought to keep pressures in check. Kennedy's record on that score was weak. Of the first 240 appointments, only 9 were women, none at Cabinet rank. Eleanor Roosevelt, still a force in Democratic party affairs, was one of those shocked by the Kennedy approach, and she and others finally convinced him of the political need to "do something for women."

The creation of the President's Commission on the Status of Women in December 1961 was the result. It consisted of 15 women and 11 men, including five Cabinet members. After two years of work, the commission demanded equal employment opportunities and increased assistance for working mothers to enable them to take jobs. While endorsing equal rights under law, the group withheld support from the proposed Equal Rights Amendment and argued instead that the Fifth and Fourteenth Amendments to the Constitution already gave strong enough guarantees. The commission sought continued governmental support for its goals.

As the commission concluded its work, Kennedy signed an Equal Pay Act, which, while narrowly drawn, was nonetheless the first federal action challenging discrimination by private employers. The act made pay differentials for equal work in firms engaged in interstate commerce illegal. The measure successfully undermined the contention that women were working only for "pin money" and not for family support and marked the start of a stronger federal role on questions of women's rights.

KENNEDY AND MINORITY RIGHTS

So it was with minority rights in the early 1960s. The movement for black equality had been gaining momentum throughout the Eisenhower years, but Kennedy remained a moderate during that time. As president he found himself pressured to act before it was too late. Now other groups began to follow the blacks' example and mobilize as well. Native Americans and Hispanics became more articulate in advancing their own cause and bringing about change.

The New Frontier and the Movement for Black Rights

Kennedy was aware of the shifting mood in the country and of the political realities he faced. In Congress he had quietly voted for black equality but had never actively embraced the cause. In the campaign of 1960 he knew he needed to hold black votes, for after the *Brown* v. *Board of Education* decision blacks had begun to drift away from the Democratic party. At the same time he wanted to maintain strength among white southern Democrats.

Kennedy's rhetoric, in the area of civil rights as elsewhere, was bold. In 1960 he proclaimed, "If the President does not himself wage the struggle for equal rights—if he stands above the battle—then the battle will inevitably be lost." He also asserted that a "stroke of the pen" could end racial segregation in federally funded housing. The Democratic platform was a strong one, and when, during the campaign, black civil rights leader Martin Luther King, Jr., was arrested for his participation in a protest demonstration, Kennedy telephoned King's wife, and Bobby Kennedy helped arrange King's release from jail. Those gestures made a difference, and in the election blacks gave Kennedy 70 percent of their vote. Particularly in states like Michigan and Illinois, where the tally had been close, their votes swung the election.

Once in office, however, Kennedy was determined to go slow. Well aware of his slender victory margin, he felt that to press hard for civil rights would alienate conservative southerners, whose votes he needed for other measures. There had not even been a civil rights task force in the planning days, and Kennedy quietly chose to defer any request for legislation until after the first year. He did name some blacks to important posts: Robert Weaver became head of the Housing and Home Finance Agency, and Thurgood Marshall accepted an appointment as a United States Circuit Court judge. But on other fronts the president yielded to the pressure of Mississippi senator James Eastland, head of the Judiciary Committee, and appointed a number of segregationists to judgeships on southern courts. His campaign assertion regarding an end to housing discrimination was forgotten despite gifts of numerous pens and bottles of ink. Not until November 1962, after the midterm elections, did he move on the matter, and his executive order was modest and limited. In the early days of the New Frontier, the only real action came from the Justice Department. It pressed to end discrimination in interstate transportation and worked hard to guarantee the right to register and vote in the South. Other than that, the administration was quiet. Integration, Kennedy felt, should come, but with as little disruption as possible. That approach prompted Martin Luther King to respond, "If tokenism were our goal, this Administration has moved us adroitly towards its accomplishment."

Black Pressures

Kennedy's approach was a reactive one, and in time growing pressures forced him to respond. Even before his campaign began, the protest movement had plunged ahead with a momentum of its own. In early 1960 when black college students in Greensboro, North Carolina, were refused service at a Woolworth's lunch counter, they simply stayed in response to the rebuff. Soon the wire services focused on the peaceful protest, and other sit-ins began. Over the course of the next year, thousands of people participated in the movement to bring about reform.

In 1961 the sit-ins gave rise to the "freedom rides," aimed at breaking down segregation in southern transportation facilities. Organized by the Congress of Racial Equality (CORE), the effort involved arranging for groups of blacks and whites together to travel on buses heading south to force the desegregation of terminals along the way. The riders, peaceful themselves, hoped to provoke confrontations that could make the administration come to their defense, and they got the confrontations they sought. Often they stepped down to shouts like "Kill the nigger-loving son of a bitch." Injuries were common as they were attacked with rocks and chains. One bus was first pelted with stones, then burned. Still the movement continued. Arrests were frequent, and background made no difference to authorities in the South. Yale University chaplain William Sloane Coffin, Jr., was but one of many arrested for trying to use facilities in a Montgomery terminal with an integrated group of clergymen. The effort was an expensive one; as the summer of 1961 came to an end, CORE had a $300,000 bill for legal costs alone.

In the next year, other events continued to force Kennedy's hand. James Meredith, a black air force veteran and student at Jackson State College, sought to enroll at the all-white University of Mississippi. Denied admission on racial grounds, he sued to gain entrance and carried his suit to the Supreme Court, where Justice Hugo Black affirmed his claim. Governor Ross Barnet, an adamant racist, asserted that Meredith would not be allowed to enroll, whatever the court decision, and on one occasion personally blocked the way. "We never have trouble with our people," he told Attorney General Robert Kennedy, who was supporting Meredith's claim, "but the NAACP, they want to stir up trouble down here." With the sides clearly drawn, a major riot began. One angry southerner attempted to drive a bulldozer into the administration building, but it stalled. Others burned and destroyed vehicles that brought marshals to the campus. Tear gas covered the university grounds, and eventually the president had to send thousands of federal forces to restore control. At the riot's end, two men were dead and hundreds hurt. But Meredith entered the university with troops on hand to ensure that peace prevailed, and with a tough and gritty effort he remained until he graduated.

An even more visible confrontation began in April 1963, in Birmingham, Alabama. Civil rights leaders decided that the time was right to make a major effort to wipe out more basic patterns of segregation and chose Birmingham as their point of attack. Though 40 percent black, the city was nonetheless rigidly segregated, and the movement aimed, in peaceful ways, to end the customs that had become part of the southern way of life. Activists challenged discriminatory employment practices and separate public facilities that kept the races apart. The protests were nonviolent; the responses were not. City officials declared that protest marches violated city regulations against parading without a license and over a five-week period arrested 2200 blacks, some of them school-children. Worse still were the means used to break up the demonstrations. Police Commissioner Eugene "Bull" Connor used high-pressure fire hoses, electric cattle prods, and trained police dogs to force the protesters back. Newspapers and television cameras recorded the events for people around the world to see, and many who saw were aghast. As newsman Eric Sevareid observed, "A newspaper or television picture of a snarling police dog set upon a human being is recorded in the permanent photo-electric file of every human brain."

In the end, gains were achieved. A compromise, arranged by Assistant Attorney General Burke Marshall, provided for desegregation of municipal facilities, implementation of more equitable hiring practices, and formation of a biracial committee to keep channels of communication open. The mayor, loser in a recent election but active still, branded willing whites "a bunch of quisling, gutless traitors," and Governor George C. Wallace refused to go along. When bombings occurred in the city and riots broke out, the National Guard was federalized once again, and only then did peace and progress come.

Nonviolent Actions and Results

The Birmingham protest, like the broader movement itself, was dominated by a mood of nonviolence. There were occasional moments when it was hard to turn the other cheek, but the pervading mood was one of passive resistance. The movement was integrated; blacks and whites joined together in the interests of bringing about an integrated society in a peaceful way. The dominant figure was clearly Martin Luther King, Jr. Long interested in nonviolent thought, he had talked during the Montgomery bus boycott with a number of pacifists about their approach. In the following years, he had moved toward an even more formal acceptance of the philosophy of Indian pacifist Mohandas Gan-

Police dog attacking a black demonstrator in Birmingham, Alabama, in 1963. (*AP/ Wide World*)

dhi. In 1959 he had traveled to India and met with Prime Minister Jawaharlal Nehru and had returned to the United States persuaded of the rightness of the peaceful approach.

King spearheaded the nonviolent phase of the growing protest movement. Numerous organizations were involved in the massive effort to attain equal rights. CORE and the NAACP were active in the struggle. The Student Nonviolent Coordinating Committee (SNCC) was engaged, as was King's own Southern Christian Leadership Conference (SCLC). But King himself seemed to represent the movement for many blacks and whites alike. An ordained minister and holder of a Ph.D. in philosophy, King was an articulate spokesman who was in the forefront of the cause. Arrested time and again, he became known throughout the United States. *Newsweek,* in July 1963, declared that 95 percent of the civil rights leaders found King the most effective black spokesman, and 88 percent of the black population at large agreed.

King's finest moment came at the March on Washington in August 1963. A. Philip Randolph had a hand in the organization again, and this time, unlike in 1941, the march for jobs and freedom took place. Two hundred thousand people, perhaps even more, were there, wildly enthusiastic at what was almost a festive affair. Celebrities were present: Ralph Bunche, James Baldwin, Sammy Davis, Jr., Harry Belafonte, Jackie Robinson, Lena Horne. The folk-music artists of the early 1960s added their voices as well. Joan Baez, Odetta,

Martin Luther King, Jr., addressing an overflow crowd in Detroit, Michigan, in 1963. (*AP/ Wide World*)

Bob Dylan, and Peter, Paul, and Mary sang songs like "Blowin' in the Wind," "We Shall Overcome," and others that had become associated with the civil rights movement.

But the high point of the day was the address by King. With passion he proclaimed his faith in the decency of his fellow human beings; with all the power of a southern preacher he persuaded his audience to join in his faith. "I have a dream," he said, "that one day this nation will rise up and live out the true meaning of its creed: 'We hold these truths to be self-evident, that all men are created equal.' I have a dream that one day on the red hills of Georgia, the sons of former slaves and the sons of former slave-owners will be able to sit together at the table of brotherhood." It was a fervent appeal, and one to which the crowd responded. Each time King used the refrain "I have a dream," the masses of blacks and whites roared. King concluded by quoting from an old hymn. "When we let freedom ring," he proclaimed, "when we let it ring from every village and every hamlet, from every state and every city, we will be able to speed up that day when all of God's children, black men and white men, Jews and Gentiles, Protestants and Catholics, will be able to join hands and sing in the words of the old Negro spiritual, 'Free at last! Free at last! Thank God almighty, we are free at last!' "

The protest movement, ever gaining strength, was successful in forcing the administration to act. In February 1963, after the James Meredith affair, Kennedy proposed a modest civil rights measure to help affirm the black right to vote and provide funding for schools beginning to integrate. But activists argued that the bill did not go far enough, and after the Birmingham crisis, even Kennedy agreed. On nationwide TV he termed the quest for equal rights "a moral issue," and he asserted, "We preach freedom around the world, and

Demonstrators relaxing near the Lincoln Memorial after the March on Washington parade in August 1963. (*AP/Wide World*)

we mean it, and we cherish our freedom, here at home, but are we to say to the world, and much more importantly, to each other that this is a land of the free except for the Negroes . . .?" Later he asserted that "the time has come for this nation to fulfill its promise." Another bill sent to Congress was far stronger than the earlier one. This time the president sought a measure to prevent segregation in all public places, to prohibit discimination wherever federal money was involved, and to move the process of school integration along. The most comprehensive civil rights bill ever advanced by a president of the United States, it faced tough going on Capitol Hill. Despite large Democratic majorities in Congress, there was still strong southern resistance to the cause of civil rights, and in November 1963 the bill was still bottled up in committee. Not even the March on Washington had moved it along.

The Native American Struggle for Equal Rights

Native Americans continued to experience second-class status as the decade began. They had suffered from the termination policy of the Eisenhower years, which had aimed unsuccessfully at forced assimilation into mainstream American life. In 1961 the United States Commission on Civil Rights observed that for Indians "poverty and deprivation are common. Social acceptance is not the rule. In addition, Indians seem to suffer more than occasional mistreatment by the instruments of law and order on and off the reservations." Indians, in short, faced obstacles like those encountered daily by blacks.

In the early 1960s a new mood of militancy began to grow. Native Americans began to assert the need to protect what was left of their land. For years the federal government had steadily encroached on Indian territory. "Everything is tied to our homeland," D'Arcy McNickle, a Flathead Indian anthropologist told other Indians in 1961, as they started to organize to save what they had.

One such effort occurred on the Seneca Nation's Allegany Reservation in New York State. For more than 30 years the federal government had sought to build the Kinzua Dam there as part of a flood-control project. Though surveys were taken, initially little was done. In 1956 Congress appropriated funds after hearings that did not include the Indians of the region. When court cases brought no recourse, the Senecas finally appealed to President Kennedy in 1961. He simply asserted the government's right to proceed as it saw fit.

In the end the dam was built. Though the government belatedly provided $15 million in reparations to ease the process of relocation, Indians resented the latest incursion on their lands and were more determined than ever to prevent such seizures in the future.

The Hispanic-American Struggle

So too did Hispanic-Americans begin to assert themselves. More and more were in the country: Cubans, Chicanos of Mexican origin, others with different backgrounds. In 1960, nearly 3.5 million people with Spanish surnames lived in the Southwest alone. Their per capita income was half that of whites, and they continued to face social and cultural separation. In the Southwest, as elsewhere, they found themselves mired in poverty, poorly educated, and politically weak.

Like blacks, Chicanos learned the value of pressure politics in a pluralistic society. In the election of 1960 they supported Kennedy, and their support helped him carry Texas. In 1961 Henry B. González was elected to Congress from San Antonio. Several years later, Elizo (Kika) de la Garza of Texas won election to the House and Joseph Montoya of New Mexico went to the Senate. Chicanos were gaining a political voice and could look forward to the day when it could help them improve their lot. But they needed to exert even greater pressure before they were able to bring about significant change.

CAMELOT IN PERSPECTIVE

The record of the Kennedy years was mixed at best. Measures that did emerge from Congress were often limited in scope. The minimum wage act, for example, extended coverage to some workers but excluded millions more. Provisions for medical care for the aged and grants for federal aid to education died in committee, as did legislative attempts to effect a tax cut and advance the cause of civil rights. There was no real effort to redistribute income or deal with the fundamental problems of the poor. The record in foreign policy was also weak. There the administration seemed to move from one crisis to another and often overcommitted the nation with little regard for the ultimate risks involved.

Congress was at least partly to blame for the troubles of the New Frontier. In Kennedy's first two years, according to the liberal Americans for Democratic Action, it produced a record of indifference to national needs. But it was not the fault of Congress alone, for Kennedy himself proved a limited leader at home. From the days of the campaign on, he worked to arouse expectations of progress on the "New Frontier" but then proved unable to follow through. Often he seemed to lack either ability or inclination to take the steps that he led people to expect. He wanted to be a man of action, a president in the tradition of FDR, but Kennedy often could not follow the Roosevelt model. Liberal rhetoric and hope notwithstanding, Kennedy was, as I. F. Stone noted, "a conventional leader, no more than an enlightened conservative, cautious as an old man for all his youth, with a basic distrust of the people." He himself was painfully aware of the state of affairs. After his first spring in office he reportedly declared to Senator Barry Goldwater, "What a lousy, fouled-up job this has turned out to be." He became increasingly aware of the "gap between what he would like and what is possible" that every president had to endure.

His critics who expected more were not always kind. Adviser Arthur Schlesinger recorded some of the stories that circulated in troubled times. Business leaders in Texas, he noted, handed out cards saying, "I MISS IKE. Hell, I even miss Harry." The Kennedy cocktail came to be called "stocks on the rocks," and the rocking chair Kennedy favored for his sore back became a symbol of the New Frontier—"you get the feeling of moving but you don't go anywhere." Some people declared, "Truman showed that anyone can be President, Ike that no one could be President, Kennedy that it can be dangerous to have a President."

Despite the criticisms, Kennedy was determined to press on. In November 1963 he traveled to Texas, where he hoped to pull the Democratic party together with an eye toward carrying again the state he had won three years before. Dallas in particular had a reputation as a site less than cordial to the administration; four weeks earlier Adlai Stevenson had encountered trouble there from a conservative mob. Now, on November 22, Kennedy had a chance to see for himself. Riding downtown in an open car, the president encountered friendly crowds, when suddenly shots echoed and brought him down. Desperately wounded, he soon died.

For a time, Kennedy's death enhanced the Kennedy myth. The record was forgotten as Americans imagined what might have been. Even those opposed to him earlier flocked to his side. While he had been elected in 1960 with only 49.7 percent of the vote, after the assassination the National Opinion Research Center found that 65 percent of those surveyed said they had voted for him. The Kennedy spirit seemed to live on as Americans remembered the heady days of the New Frontier. Kennedy, from beginning to end, appealed to the consensus in America that had formed after World War II. He argued that the United States could act responsibly in the world and solve its problems at home. He seemed to herald, as Robert Frost wrote in lines for the inauguration, an age "of poetry and power." With his untimely death, it appeared as though that age had come.

Slowly the myth began to fade. The limitations of the record could not be ignored, and even the stylish veneer began to tarnish with rumors of Kennedy's extramarital affairs. More important, the sense that all was well in America began to disappear in the turbulent years that followed. The United States had serious unsolved—and even unconfronted—problems that loomed larger after 1963, and Kennedy's death became a harbinger of things to come as the age of consensus he represented began to break down.

SUGGESTIONS FOR FURTHER READING

For a good introduction to the basic foreign and domestic policies of the Kennedy years, see Jim F. Heath, *Decade of Disillusionment: The Kennedy-Johnson Years* (1975). Herbert S. Parmet, *JFK: The Presidency of John F. Kennedy* (1983) is a comprehensive account of Kennedy's White House years. Theodore H. White, *The Making of the President* (1961) is a vivid description of the election of 1960. Arthur M. Schlesinger, Jr., *A Thousand Days: John F. Kennedy in the White House* (1965) and Theodore C. Sorensen, *Kennedy* (1965) are two highly sympathetic portraits of Kennedy by insiders at the White House. Bruce Miroff, *Pragmatic Illusions: The Presidential Politics of John F. Kennedy* (1976); Henry Fairlie, *The Kennedy Promise: The Politics of Expectation* (1972); and Garry Wills, *The Kennedy Imprisonment* (1981) are far more critical.

On foreign policy, see David Halberstam, *The Best and the Brightest* (1969) for a sharp assessment of the assumptions of the administration. Richard Walton, *Cold War and Counterrevolution* (1972) is similarly critical. Peter Wyden, *The Bay of Pigs* (1979) describes one of the early disasters of the Kennedy years. On the Cuban missile crisis, see Graham Allison, *Essence of Decision: Explaining the Cuban Missile Crisis* (1971); Robert A. Divine, ed., *The Cuban Missile Crisis* (1971); and Robert F. Kennedy, *Thirteen Days* (1968).

On domestic questions, James L. Sundquist, *Politics and Policy: The Eisenhower, Kennedy, and Johnson Years* (1968) is a useful description of public policy developments. Jim Heath, *Kennedy and the Business Community* (1969) is similarly helpful.

For a sympathetic treatment of Kennedy's approach to civil rights, see Carl Brauer, *John F. Kennedy and the Second Reconstruction* (1977). Victory Navasky, *Kennedy Justice* (1971) is more critical of the administration's approach.

chapter 6

The Trials of the Sixties

The 1960s brought real upheaval in American life. The period after John Kennedy's death was a turning point when old values and old assumptions gave way to new. Earlier, Americans approached their nation and their world with the optimistic sense that all problems could be solved on their own terms. There were foreign and domestic troubles, to be sure, but the view prevailed nonetheless that the United States could cope with those and ensure the survival of the good life. Americans, nourished on the prosperity of the postwar years, believed that growth could continue forever, that social conflict could be minimized at home, and that their aims and aspirations could provide a model for progress abroad. That consensus, however, was already under attack before Kennedy died. The strains could be ignored at first, as the new president, Lyndon B. Johnson, devoted his considerable political talents to securing the most progressive legislative record of the preceding 40 years. Then, as the Vietnam War escalated and challenges mounted on all fronts, the consensus fell apart. Struggling to define new patterns and new goals, the United States of the 1960s was more volatile than it had ever been.

LYNDON JOHNSON AND THE GREAT SOCIETY

Lyndon Johnson, chief executive for five years, was largely responsible for the triumphs of the mid-1960s. Succeeding a popular leader cut down in his prime, Johnson moved to implement his own vision of reform. The Great Society he crafted built on the example of the Franklin Roosevelt's New Deal as it addressed existing inequities and needs in the United States. But before that

campaign. Pitted against Republican candidate Barry Goldwater, a senator from Arizona, Johnson had a field day. Goldwater, a personable man with deep conservative convictions, had opposed virtually all liberal social legislation of recent years. Now he spoke of selling the TVA among those it aided and criticized social security in enclaves of the old. His supporters could claim that he provided a "choice not an echo" as they asserted "In Your Heart You Know He's Right," but more Americans preferred the assistance Johnson seemed prepared to give. They also saw him as the man of peace, particularly when contrasted to Goldwater, who spoke casually about the use of "nukes." The final results were overwhelming. Johnson won 61 percent of the popular vote, carried the electoral college by a margin of 486 to 52, and swept into office with sizable majorities in both houses of Congress.

Johnson now had the mandate to continue what he had begun when he first assumed command. Astutely, he had capitalized on the wave of emotion following Kennedy's death to act quickly to attain legislative ends. After his own election he pushed ever harder to achieve his goals. "Hurry, boys, hurry," he told his aides. "Get that legislation up to the Hill and out. Eighteen months from now ol' Landslide Lyndon will be Lame-Duck Lyndon." He knew that he had but a limited amount of time until his mandate began to fade. Before then, he told aides, "I want to see a whole bunch of coonskins on the wall."

Johnson sensed that the time was right for action. There was an underlying confidence in the United States that the economy would continue to grow and provide enough for all inhabitants. At the same time there was a growing awareness of poverty in the nation and a realization that an effort was needed to allow all to share in the American dream. Confident of his own ability and eager to assure his own place in history, Johnson was prepared to act.

Act he did. In his first several years in the White House, he orchestrated an effort that produced the strongest legislative program since the New Deal of FDR. Johnson worked closely with Congress in all aspects of the process. He appointed task forces that included legislators to help define means and ends. He worked with them to draft bills that met his expectations but could still secure the necessary support on Capitol Hill. He maintained close contact at all stages of the legislative process, as a sophisticated liaison staff came into its own. Not since the 1930s had there been such a coordinated effort to make the government move.

Johnson's vision assumed that expansion could continue forever but accepted the Keynesian notion that a nudge might be necessary from time to time. John Kennedy had eventually endorsed that view, but the tax cut he had proposed to stimulate the economy had not yet become law. Already through the House by the time LBJ assumed the presidency, it still had to clear the upper chamber. Now Johnson defined passage as one of his primary goals and dedicated himself to that task.

Liberals favored the measure, but conservatives had to be persuaded to go along. To that end Johnson determined to hold spending down. Though advisers pressed for a budget of $108 billion, he demanded that it be reduced until it finally reached a $97.9 billion level. That satisfied Harry Byrd, chairman of the Senate Finance Committee, and in time the measure reached the Senate floor. There Johnson was even more active behind the scenes. At one point Senator Hubert Humphrey, later to be Johnson's vice-president, proposed an amendment to provide a tax credit to families with children in college. Johnson, who wanted no changes in the bill, applied such pressure that Humphrey ended up voting against his own amendment.

Several months after Johnson took office, the measure became law. It endorsed the view advanced by John Maynard Keynes 30 years before and moved the administration closer to the role envisioned in the Employment Act of 1946, before it was shredded to pieces by congressional dissent. For the first time the government was about to embark on the aggressive use of fiscal policy to keep the economy buoyant, for a healthy and expansive economy was the base on which all other reforms lay.

With the tax cut in hand, Johnson pressed for the poverty program Kennedy had begun to plan. Johnson met with groups of all sorts to persuade them that an effort had to come, and he declared to Congress in his 1964 State of the Union message, "This administration today, here and now, declares unconditional war on poverty in America." His focus became the Economic Opportunity Act, passed in August 1964. That measure established an Office of Economic Opportunity, which aimed at providing education and training for unskilled young people unable to manage on their own. It created VISTA—Volunteers in Service to America—a domestic Peace Corps of Americans willing to work with the poor at home. It also included various "community action programs" that gave the poor themselves a voice in setting up efforts on the housing, health, and education fronts in their own neighborhoods. They were to have "maximum feasible participation" in planning and implementing their own goals.

With a start made by the time he won the election of 1964, Johnson pushed even harder in the two years that followed. Aware of the ever-escalating costs of medical care that affected all Americans, he embraced a medical assistance plan. Years before, Harry Truman had proposed such a measure, but like most other items on his Fair Deal list, it had never gotten off the ground. The Kennedy administration had introduced a bill, but it too had become bogged down on Capitol Hill. Now Johnson wanted the bill passed.

There were, however, a number of obstacles in its path. The American Medical Association condemned any approach different from traditional practice as "socialized medicine." Wilbur Mills, head of the House Ways and Means Committee, which had earlier sat on the measure, had to be persuaded that the time was ripe for reform. Again Johnson applied the necessary leadership and control. The administration ended up tying the health plan to the social security system to head off conservative attacks, and it limited the program to the elderly and poor who could not provide for themselves but were not covered by existing plans. Once more the administration met with success, and Johnson proudly went out to Independence, Missouri, to sign the bill with Harry Truman standing by.

The administration was similarly successful in pushing through a measure to aid elementary and secondary schools. Kennedy, who had wanted such a bill, had been defeated on the question of assistance to parochial schools. His own Catholicism had become an issue that helped bring about defeat. Johnson, a Protestant, was freer to move as he saw fit. The administration endorsed a measure that gave money to the states based on the numbers of children from low-income families. Those funds were then to be distributed to public as well as private schools, to benefit all children according to need. With White House pressure, the bill sailed through, and, again with a flair for the dramatic, LBJ went off to Texas to sign it in the small building where he had first gone to school.

The Great Society consisted of other programs, too. In Johnson's expansive vision there was something for everyone, so that all could share in the promise of American life. Under the leadership of the White House, Congress passed a new housing act to provide rent supplements to the poor and created a Housing and Urban Development Department. It reformed the restrictive immigration policy that for decades had rested on racial or national quotas. It went further in funding education, including colleges and universities in its financial grants. It also provided assistance to artists and intellectuals through new National Endowments for the Arts and Humanities. Not since the New Deal's Works Progress Administration had such groups been granted government aid.

The Great Society and Civil Rights

Most important of all, though, was the expanding commitment in the area of civil rights. Action on that front was a necessary part of the broad program the president had in mind. LBJ had been instrumental in securing passage of the Civil Rights Acts of 1957 and 1960 from his leadership post in the Senate, but even he now was ready to acknowledge that they did not go far enough. The movement had continued to push forward every year, but Kennedy's proposed civil rights measure was sidetracked in Congress when he died.

Johnson seized the opportunity he had. Several days after he assumed office, he told Congress and the nation, "No memorial oration or eulogy could more eloquently honor President Kennedy's memory than the earliest possible passage of the civil rights bill." After his audience roared approval, he went on, "We have talked long enough in this country about equal rights. . . . It is now time to write the next chapter . . . into the books of law." LBJ made good on his commitment and became his best publicist for the cause. He told black leaders he would push for the civil rights bill "with every energy I possessed," and he spoke out aggressively wherever he could.

Johnson also threw this political weight behind the bill and indicated that he would accept no compromises. It passed in the House of Representatives, but as a lengthy filibuster unfolded in the Senate, Johnson threatened to sacrifice all other legislation until this bill was passed and, if necessary, to call Congress back into session after the 1964 political conventions and keep it in

GREAT SOCIETY PROGRAMS

1964	Twenty-fourth Amendment (banned poll tax in federal elections)
	Tax Reduction Act
	Civil Rights Act
	Urban Mass Transportation Act
	Economic Opportunity Act
	Wilderness Preservation Act
1965	Elementary and Secondary School Act
	Medicare
	Voting Rights Act
	Omnibus Housing Act
	Department of Housing and Urban Development established
	National Foundations of the Arts and Humanities established
	Water Quality Act
	Immigration laws revised (new quotas set)
	Air Quality Act
	Higher Education Act
1966	National Traffic and Motor Vehicle Safety Act
	Highway Safety Act
	Minimum wage raised and coverage extended
	Department of Transportation established
	Model Cities

Washington until it chose to act. He also went to work on Minority Leader Everett Dirksen to get his help in bringing the matter to a vote. Finally, not wanting to be saddled with responsibility for defeat of a measure that had extensive public support, Dirkson began to work for cloture, a two-thirds vote to cut off debate, which came in June 1964. Passage soon followed, and in early July Johnson signed the bill into law.

The Civil Rights Act of 1964 outlawed racial discrimination in public accommodations and authorized the Justice Department to proceed with greater authority in school and voting matters. An equal-opportunity provision prohibited discriminatory hiring on the basis of race, sex, religion, or national origin in firms of more than 25 employees.

Johnson was prepared to stop there, but the civil rights movement continued with a momentum of its own. It became clear that despite the voting rights measures of 1957 and 1960, blacks still found it difficult to cast ballots in large areas of the South. A student-sponsored Summer Freedom Project in Mississippi in 1964 brought attention to the recurring problems. Martin Luther King, Jr., leading another march from Selma to Montgomery, Alabama, in 1965, served notice that there was still work to be done.

Just a few days before the march, Johnson addressed a joint session of Congress before a national television audience. The speech showed Johnson at his best. Pleading for a voting bill that would close the loopholes of the previous two, he began by saying, "I speak tonight for the dignity of man and the destiny of democracy. . . . It is wrong . . . to deny any of your fellow Americans the right to vote." At one point he stopped and, raising his arms, repeated the words from the old hymn that had become the marching song of the movement: "And . . . we . . . shall . . . overcome." The audience thundered its approval. Again Johnson used all of his gifts to gain votes for the proposed act, and despite another filibuster, that measure too passed into law.

The Voting Rights Act of 1965 finally authorized the attorney general to appoint federal examiners to register voters where discrimination lingered and local officials were not doing the job. No longer were long court battles necessary after episodes of refusal; now federal officers were available to respond. The act affected the South in particular because six states and parts of another did not meet the test of having 50 percent of the voting-age residents registered in 1964. In the following year over 400,000 blacks registered to vote in the Deep South; by 1968 the number reached a million.

In the mid-1960s the civil rights movement began to change. Initially it had been an integrated, peaceful, nonviolent crusade. But now black-white tensions began to appear, and the nonviolent phase seemed to draw to an end. More militant spokesmen began to make their voices heard as they played on a long-suppressed rage that, despite the advances—perhaps because of the advances—forced its way to the top. Malcolm X, an articulate and militant black nationalist, termed the March on Washington the "Farce on Washington." Arguing in favor of black separation from the white race, he declared that he had no use for "all of this non-violent, begging-the-white-man kind of dying . . . all of this sitting-in, sliding-in, wading-in, eating-in, diving-in, and all the rest." Stokely Carmichael, head of the now aggressive Student Nonviolent Coordinating Committee (SNCC), began to talk about "black power" in June 1966, and the new slogan drowned out the older cry for "freedom now." Meanwhile, there were calls for drastic action. Huey Newton of the Black Panthers, another

Black Muslim leader Malcolm X speaking at a black nationalist gathering in 1963. (*AP/Wide World*)

militant organization founded in 1966, argued that "political power comes through the barrel of a gun," while H. Rap Brown declared that "violence is as American as cherry pie."

Violence was visible for all to see. Watts, in Los Angeles, erupted in the summer of 1965. An area that seemed peaceful on the surface, it had an unemployment rate far higher than average and tensions between community members and police. The riot, which lasted five days and left 34 dead, took 14,000 National Guardsmen to end. There were other racial riots in other cities in 1966, and again in 1967. Now cries of "Get Whitey" and "Burn, baby, burn" replaced the gentler verses of the civil rights movement in its earlier days. Martin Luther King, Jr., was himself a victim of the violence that could not be contained. He died at the hands of an assassin in 1968. Lyndon Johnson was shocked and hurt over the urban eruptions and could not understand the aggressive black response. "How is it possible," he asked, "after all we've accomplished? How could it be? Is the world topsy-turvy?" But it was not his fault at all. The movement had simply moved beyond its first stage and was demonstrating clearly that the progress that had occurred was not enough.

Contributions of the Supreme Court

Complementing the legislative actions of the Great Society were a number of important decisions by the Supreme Court. The Court in the 1960s moved into new areas and served as a major stimulus for social change. The *Brown* v. *Board of Education* decision of the Warren Court in 1954 presaged further action, and the Court came to play a far more active role than it had before.

A number of decisions reaffirmed the Court's support of black rights. Having disposed of the issue of school segregation, the Court moved against Jim Crow practices in other public establishments. Providing quick support for the Civil Rights Acts of 1964 and 1965, the justices gave notice that discriminatory customs could no longer continue as they had for decades in the past.

The Court supported civil liberties as well as civil rights. After affirming restrictions on Communists and members of other such groups in the 1950s, the Court now began to pull back and protect the rights of individuals to follow their own bent. So too did the Court seek to protect accused suspects from the police. In *Gideon* v. *Wainwright* (1963) the Justices ruled that poor suspects had the right to free legal assistance. In *Escobedo* v. *Illinois* (1964) they decided that an offender had to be given access to an attorney during interrogation, and in *Miranda* v. *Arizona* (1966) they ruled that a suspect had to be warned that statements extracted could be used against him and that he could remain silent if he chose.

Other decisions also broke new ground. The *Baker* v. *Carr* (1962) case opened the way to reapportionment of legislative bodies on the basis, in Justice William O. Douglas's words, of "one person, one vote." Subsequent rulings followed through on the same course. Meanwhile, the Court ruled that prayer in the public schools was unconstitutional and could no longer be permitted and that obscenity laws could no longer restrict the flow of allegedly porno-graphic material that might have some "redeeming social value."

The Court's decisions were often controversial. Conservatives in particu-lar charged that the Court had overstepped its bounds and began a long fight to restrict the impact of the decisions handed down. Seldom successful at first, their criticisms continued, as did the important changes the decisions had brought.

The Great Society: Failure or Success?

Just as the Supreme Court attracted criticism, so did the entire Great Society come under attack as the components fell into place. Conservatives in the country were critical from the very start. They were uneasy at the centralization of authority as the government took over more and more responsibility for defining the national welfare. They also objected to the notion of involving the poor themselves in community action programs, for they claimed that recipi-ents of aid lacked the broader vision of the needs of all groups in the United States.

Equally sharp were the criticisms from the left. Radicals claimed, with some justification, that the methods of the Great Society were all too similar to the efforts of the earlier New Deal. The same middle-class orientation remained and seemed only to provide the poor with the middle-class values necessary to make it in America. Those tactics had not worked well in the 1930s and were not working well in the 1960s, they charged, for as young critic Tom Hayden saw the situation, "The welfare state is more machinery than substance." There was no effort, opponents observed, to redistribute income in any meaningful way; in the classic liberal faith to which Johnson subscribed, endless growth alone would bring increased benefits for all. Challenging that notion, journalist I. F. Stone remarked that "a little for the poor makes it easier to go on giving a lot to the rich." Even some of those who commended the Great Society's assumptions complained that it did not go far enough. When Michael Harring-ton, whose book *The Other America* had helped catalyze the poverty crusade, called the administration's appropriation request "nickels and dimes," Sargent Shriver, head of the program, responded, "Well, I don't know about you, Mr. Harrington, but this will be my first experience at spending a billion dollars, and I'm quite excited about it." But Harrington had a point. Though a couple of billion dollars were spent in the first few years, that could not adequately meet the needs of 30 or 40 million people. As Harrington concluded, "What was supposed to be a social war turned out to be a skirmish and, in any case, poverty won."

Still, before the war in Vietnam drew off resources and devastated econ-omy and society both, Johnson's program did make a difference in American life. The tax cut worked just as intended. After passage, GNP went steadily up, 7.1 percent in 1964, 8.1 percent in 1965, and 9.5 percent in 1966, while the deficit dropped at the same time. Unemployment fell, and inflation was kept firmly in control. Health needs were met, as Medicare had a real impact on the old. The education establishment flourished as never before, and violence notwithstanding, there was significant progress in the area of civil rights.

By the end of the decade, however, the consensus for change had begun to unravel, and the Great Society encountered hard times. Even without the foreign war, though, the program could only go so far. Johnson, as always, wanted too much too soon. In his passion to do everything at once, his rhetoric promised gains that in fact took a long time to occur. He created expectations that neither he nor Congress could fulfill, and when faced with significant challenges, the Great Society fell short. Even so, for a time it provided a spark of hope for the disadvantaged of the United States.

FOREIGN AFFAIRS

LBJ had expansive dreams, and he came close to achieving them in the domestic realm. When he tried to perform in the same way in the field of foreign affairs, he showed less sensitivity and less skill. The talents responsible for his political success at home were less relevant in the international sphere, and in the end his incursions in foreign affairs brought him down.

Johnson's Approach

Johnson approached foreign policy far differently than his predecessor had. Kennedy was passionately interested in the world outside; Johnson, by contrast, was more concerned with national affairs. Johnson had dealt with international questions in his senatorial years, and he understood the interplay between internal and external policy, but he preferred to concern himself primarily with the political situation at home. Nonetheless, he was a tremendously confident man, and just as he left his imprint on national policy, so he was sure he could cajole and manipulate the world beyond.

Johnson sought to deal with the rest of the world as if it were an extension of the Senate, where he had held sway. He favored personal diplomacy, for he was secure in his ability to handle one-on-one confrontations. As in the domestic realm, he was determined to get his own way.

Johnson's early ventures met with mixed success. Rebuffed by Charles de Gaulle, who was taking France on a course of its own, he enjoyed better relations with German Chancellor Ludwig Erhard, but after a year or so he became somewhat more wary of the personal approach. Nonetheless, he continued to seek such ties whenever he could.

Crisis and Response

Meanwhile, he moved to ensure that the United States was not pushed around. He faced a modest crisis in Panama when that nation sought a renegotiation of the 1903 treaty that had guaranteed Americans access to the Canal Zone. The question of which flag—the American or the Panamanian—should fly in the zone became a symbolic and emotional one and led to a riot in 1964 in which 4 American soldiers and 24 Panamanians were killed. Determined not to appear weak, Johnson immediately got on the phone with his counterpart to the south and warned that "we cannot negotiate under pressure of violence." Eventually the situation cooled, and in time Johnson authorized discussions that led to a new treaty in 1978.

The United States reacted even more forcefully in April 1965 to an unsettled situation in the Dominican Republic. There, in 1961, the dictatorial Rafael Trujillo had been assassinated, and after some jockeying for position, the army had assumed control. But the army regime itself faced resistance from more moderate elements and therefore appealed for help to maintain its own position. Using the unfounded argument that Communist elements were trying to take over, the American embassy supported the army cause and claimed that American lives were in danger. Johnson responded by sending troops to the Central American state, and before long there were over 22,000 marines on hand to eliminate the perceived threat. Eventually stability returned as an anti-Communist regime acceptable to the United States consolidated its strength.

Johnson showed a tendency to see a crisis where none need have existed and then to mislead the public about its nature and its cause. He also showed little hesitation about intervening in a large-scale and impetuous way. He was lucky, for the Dominican affair never got out of hand. That was not the case in Southeast Asia.

Vietnam

Johnson's administration came to catastrophe in Vietnam. The roots of the war stretched far back into the past, though not until the Kennedy years had the United States become deeply involved. Still, despite a growing American presence, the situation was in a state of flux when Kennedy died.

South Vietnam, supported by the United States, was in trouble after the assassination of Ngo Dinh Diem. Guerrillas in the south, known as Viet Cong, challenged the regime, sometimes covertly, sometimes through the National Liberation Front, their political arm. The insurgent elements, eager for reunification with the north, were indigenous in the south but were aided by Ho Chi Minh and the North Vietnamese, and slowly they were gaining ground.

Johnson took the war and made it his own. He came to a fundamental decision as he assumed the presidency. Meeting with Henry Cabot Lodge, American ambassador to South Vietnam, who had returned to report to JFK, he was told that if he wanted to save Vietnam, he faced some tough decisions. Johnson was ready to proceed. "I am not going to lose Vietnam," he said. "I am not going to be the President who saw Southeast Asia go the way China went."

Johnson responded as he did because, like his predecessors, he operated on the basis of his understanding of the lessons of the past. Aggression before World War II had gone unchecked, with tragic results. Johnson was convinced that to refuse to respond to aggression now would lead to World War III. Aggressors had to be stopped, he felt, for "if you let a bully come into your front yard one day, the next day he'll be up on your porch and the day after that he'll rape your wife in your own bed." Furthermore, Johnson was sure he could control matters himself. Frustrated by what he called those "piddly little piss-ant" countries, including North Vietnam, he felt that by behaving abroad as he did at home he could avoid being pushed around. But he misunderstood Ho Chi Minh, the Vietnamese, North and South, and the struggle for independence in which they were engaged.

In the presidential campaign of 1964, Johnson posed as the man of peace. "We don't want our American boys to do the fighting for Asian boys," he declared. "We are not going to send American boys nine or ten thousand miles away from home to do what Asian boys ought to be doing for themselves." He criticized those who suggested using American bombs.

All the while, however, planning for war was under way. As the campaign unfolded, Johnson managed to gain the authorization for war he wanted, even though he refrained from using it until the electoral victory was secure. In August 1964 Johnson announced that North Vietnamese torpedo boats had, without provocation, attacked American destroyers in the international waters of the Gulf of Tonkin, 30 miles from North Vietnam. Only later did the truth emerge. The American ships had been engaged in surveillance in combat zones close to shore, in support of South Vietnamese commando raids. Though the details of the attack remained unclear, Johnson used the episode to his own advantage. He asked Congress for a resolution giving him authority to "take all necessary measures to repel any armed attack against the forces of the United States and to prevent further aggression." Not aware that Johnson had been carrying the resolution around for some time, Congress passed it by votes of 416 to 0 in the House and 88 to 2 in the Senate. It moved the nation a step further toward concentrating power in the president's hands and gave Johnson all the leverage he wanted, for, as he noted, it was "like grandma's nightshirt—it covered everything."

Real escalation began in February 1965 after Viet Cong forces killed 7 Americans and wounded 109 in an attack on an American base at Pleiku. In response Johnson authorized retaliatory bombing of North Vietnam. The effort was intended to cut off the flow of supplies from the north and to persuade the Vietnamese there to cease trying to exert pressure in the south. When it did not achieve the desired aims, the bombing levels increased.

At the same time, Johnson decided to send American ground troops into action. There were 25,000 American soldiers in Vietnam at the start of 1965. By the end of the year there were 184,000, and the number continued to swell until by 1969 there were more than 500,000, and still the war dragged on. The American forces were no longer in Southeast Asia to advise the Vietnamese; they were there to participate directly in the fight to prop up the regime in the south. After a period of instability, the army finally established a government headed by Nguyen Van Thieu and Nguyen Cao Ky, but the level of violence in the far-off land only seemed to increase.

In the north the fearful bombing campaign continued. Fragmentation bombs killed or maimed civilians, while napalm, used extensively, seared human flesh. In the south the same kind of destruction occurred. Despite American firepower, the North Vietnamese were persistent and pressed on even harder than before.

The war did not go well for the United States. In early 1968 the Viet Cong and North Vietnamese launched a major offensive during the holiday of Tet. Striking numerous provincial capitals and other targets, they demonstrated

Southeast Asia During the Vietnam War

their still-strong capacity to fight. Johnson saw his own popularity drop. Between 1964 and 1968 his level of public support fell 36 points. He had never much cared for dissent, and now he kept dissidents even further away. As the criticism mounted, he felt himself "in the position of a jackrabbit in a hailstorm, hunkering up and taking it." Irritated and upset, he lashed out at his critics. But he slowly came to realize that he could not go on. Watching Walter Cronkite of CBS urge withdrawl from Vietnam in 1968, Johnson reportedly said, "Well, if I've lost Cronkite, I've lost Middle America."

In March 1968, facing challenges in political primaries, Johnson declared dramatically in a nationally televised address that he would not run for another term. The consummate politician knew he had lost his base of support and hoped that by ordering a bombing pause and withdrawing from public life he could begin to restore unity to the United States.

Yet even when Johnson left, the war dragged on. The American presence, however, became less visible, less intense, under successor Richard Nixon and finally ended entirely in 1973.

Consequences of the War

Though the United States finally extricated itself, the war took a terrible toll. It was America's longest and least successful war, as diplomat and scholar George F. Kennan observed, "the most disastrous of all America's undertakings over the whole two hundred years of its history." It devastated Vietnam, North and South, as American planes dropped more bombs than had fallen on all Axis powers during World War II. The Vietnamese casualty toll of wounded and dead soldiers ran into the millions, with countless civilian casualties. The struggle left its mark on American society, too.

The war had a powerful economic effect. By 1966 costs ran over $2 billion a month, and the total expense ran to $140 billion. The effort to finance the struggle gave rise to inflation and economic chaos that soon got out of control. LBJ wanted to maintain the Great Society and the war both, and that choice to pursue all things at once had serious results. The economy was already heated up as a result of the tax cut and the spending for social reform. With the rapid increase in the defense budget, the production system in the country could not meet demand. With more dollars chasing limited goods, prices began to rise. Had Johnson cut back spending, he could have kept control. Had he raised taxes, he could similarly have maintained control. Despite the urging of the chairman of the Council of Economic Advisers, Johnson refused to hike taxes, for he wanted to conceal the cost of the war. As inflation got out of hand, Congress finally got into the act and responded by cutting back on Great Society programs, which, in effect, became casualties of the war.

Far worse, however, were the human consequences of the conflict. Some 58,000 American servicemen died in the struggle, and the number of Americans wounded was about 300,000. Many, like Ron Kovic, had dreamed of being heroes as they grew up. Reared on Rootie Kazootie, Howdy Doody, the Lone Ranger, and the Cisco Kid, they also thrilled to John Wayne's exploits in his movie roles. Kovic felt proud to be a marine but finally soured on the war, took a bullet in the spine, and was confined to a wheelchair on his arrival home. "I feel like a big clumsy puppet with all his strings cut," he wrote. "I learn to balance and twist in the chair so no one can tell how much of me does not feel or move anymore." So too was the war a devastating experience for Philip Caputo, another marine who went abroad with the same ideals as Kovic and returned in one piece, but bitter and disturbed by the struggle. He found it difficult to understand what the United States was fighting for and what might constitute victory in the end. Urged to fight as hard as he could, he faced a court martial when he tried to do as asked.

For the soldiers who weathered the ravages of war, the struggle still dragged on when they came home. As psychiatrist Robert Jay Lifton observed, the societal sanction for military killing seemed less secure as the American public came to question the legitimacy of the war. Soldiers who had done what was asked now found themselves less able to rationalize what they had seen or done.

The war not only devastated those who fought overseas, it also shattered the consensus that had guided the nation during and after World War II. It exposed the fallacy that the United States could defend the world from attack anywhere, at any time. American technology and American money were not able to stop the pressures from North Vietnam any more than they could prop up forever the regime in South Vietnam. Ravaged by the war, Americans for the first time since World War II began to question their global mission.

POLITICAL AND SOCIAL UPHEAVAL

The United States in the early 1960s faced challenges on a variety of fronts, and by the end of the decade the more general consensus about the possibility of maintaining peace and prosperity at home was in shreds. The pressures for change grew on all fronts. Folksinger Bob Dylan, politically active himself, captured something of the changing mood with a song in 1963:

> Come mothers and fathers
> Throughout the land
> And don't criticize
> What you can't understand
> Your sons and daughters
> Are beyond your command
> There's a battle
> Outside and it's ragin'
> It'll soon shake your windows
> And rattle your walls . . .
> For the times they are a-changin'.

American society was already beginning to face the effects of rebellion even before the Vietnam War intervened. The war only galvanized the protest, focused it more sharply, and in time provided an organizing principle for the challenges and doubts.

The Roots of Protest

The roots of the protest lay with the dramatic growth of population and with expansion of higher education in America after the Second World War. Between 1946 and 1964 the number of students in college doubled. As of 1968, 50 percent of all 18- and 19-year-olds in the country were in college. College became a training ground for industry, but even more important, it gave students time to experiment and to grow before they had to go out into the real world and make it on their own.

In that situation, some of the more politically sensitive and politically inclined became involved with the struggle for civil rights. Concerned about inequity and injustice, they wanted to play a part in the process of reform. As blacks in the South began to protest and march, white students joined the cause. They had a hand in the mounting effort to bring pressure on the power structure, but they often became discouraged. For a time John Kennedy and the New Frontier seemed to offer hope for a new start, yet gradually the limitations of Kennedy's commitment became clear, and the students came to understand that progress would result only if push came to shove. The assassination caused still further doubts about the possibility of peaceful change.

Against that background, the radical spirit of the New Left began to grow. Civil rights activists were among those who in 1960 organized Students for a Democratic Society (SDS) from the older Student League for Industrial Democracy. In 1962 came its manifesto, the Port Huron Statement, written largely by Tom Hayden of the University of Michigan. "We are the people of this generation, bred in at least modest comfort, housed now in universities, looking uncomfortably to the world we inherit," it began. But loneliness and estrangement pervaded society. In its place, "we seek the establishment of a democracy of individual participation." It pledged SDS to the creation of a New Left.

The Free Speech Movement

The first blow of the growing rebellion came at the University of California at Berkeley. There civil rights activists became involved in a confrontation that soon turned into the Free Speech Movement. In September 1964 the university refused to allow students to distribute protest material outside the main campus gate. The students, many of whom had been involved in the civil rights movement in the South, argued that their tables were off campus and therefore not subject to university restrictions on political activity. Defiantly they committed themselves to fighting back. When police drove up to arrest one of their leaders, students in the growing campaign surrounded the car and kept it from moving all night.

Eventually the administration sought a compromise, and matters might have ended there had not the university regents determined to hold student leaders responsible for their actions in the demonstrations. Mario Savio, one of the leaders, was charged with having bitten a policeman on the thigh, and other accusations were brought, too. Provoked by the charges, which the regents refused to drop, the students took over Sproul Hall, the administration building. Savio called the university an impersonal machine: "There comes a time when the operation of the machine becomes so odious, makes you so sick at heart, that you can't take part, you can't even tacitly take part. And you've got to put your bodies upon the gears and upon the wheels, upon the levers, upon all the apparatus, and you've got to make it stop." Joan Baez sang "We Shall Overcome," the marching song of the civil rights movement, but then police came in and arrested the students in the building. A student strike, with faculty support, took place next and reaffirmed once and for all the right to free speech.

In that first challenge, students aimed their attacks at the university itself. They argued that the university was becoming increasingly impersonal, increasingly bureaucratic as the institution channeled its raw material along. Clark Kerr, chancellor of the University of California, had seemed to hail that development the year before in *The Uses of the University,* in which he spoke admiringly of the "multiversity" with new functions and new connections to the world outside. Students struck back as they argued that their institution had lost sight of its primary purpose, and they demanded that changes occur. Seizing on the instructions on the computer cards that identified and classified students as they moved along, some wore buttons declaring, "I am a U.C. Student. Do not Fold, Bend, or Mutilate."

The Free Speech Movement at Berkeley may have been the opening round of the student revolt, but it was still basically a plea for traditional liberal reform. The students sought only the reaffirmation of a long-standing right and aimed their attacks at the university, not at society as a whole. Later, in other institutions, the attack broadened as the movement surged ahead.

The Antiwar Movement

The ferment at Berkeley spread to other campuses in the spring of 1965 as participants questioned methods of student discipline, attacked outmoded drinking and parietal rules, and sought student involvement in university affairs. Then came the mounting protest against the escalation of the Vietnam War, and that fueled the young movement and gave it a venom it had not had before.

The antiwar movement was initially small, for most Americans supported taking a stand against communism at the start. As escalation began, 82 percent of the people in the United States felt that their troops should stay in Vietnam until the Communist elements backed off. Slowly, however, students in particular began to question the assumptions about the need for American involvement. Some opposed the notion of a distant foreign war for purposes that were unclear. Others questioned America's interests in the struggle. All began to call for withdrawal.

In March 1965 the first teach-in took place at the University of Michigan. Three thousand people attended that meeting, and others soon followed. Even before escalation had gotten out of hand, Senator Wayne Morse, speaking at the University of Oregon, declared that soon "there will be hundreds of thousands of American boys fighting in Southeast Asia—and tens of thousands of them will be coming home in coffins." Both supporters and opponents appeared at the early teach-ins. Then the advocates of resistance began to gain the upper hand.

SDS, at both national and campus levels, embarked on a campaign against the draft and mounted attacks on military officer training (ROTC) units on campus, on recruiters for the CIA, and on firms that produced the tools of destruction in the struggle. "Make love, not war," posters proclaimed as more and more students became involved in the political demonstrations that became common on campuses around the country. Rallies and marches mobilized support for the cause, and marchers chanted such slogans as "Hey, hey, LBJ. How many kids did you kill today?" In 1967, 300,000 opponents of the war marched in New York City, while 100,000 in the Washington, D.C., area tried to close down the Pentagon. Resisters sat in at Selective Service centers and took other steps to sidetrack the draft.

The view of the public at large began to shift. Television played a large part in the growing loss of public support. Images of the war entered American homes nightly on the evening news and showed the brutality in vivid hues. Perhaps the most devastating image of all appeared on NBC on the evening of February 2, 1968, when a film clip showed General Nguyen Ngoc Loan, head of the South Vietnamese National Police, casually firing a pistol point-blank at the head of a Viet Cong suspect and blowing his brains out. With that kind of evidence, public opposition began to grow.

Further Confrontation

By 1968 protest had become a way of life. Between January 1 and June 15 there were 221 major demonstrations at more than 100 educational institutions, and thousands upon thousands of students had become involved. The most dramatic confrontation came on the East Coast, at Columbia University in April 1968, where the issues of civil rights and war were tightly interwoven in a joint attack. A strong SDS chapter sought to get the university to break ties with its Institute of Defense Analysis, which specialized in military research. A black students' organization sought to stop the building of a new Columbia gymnasium, which it claimed encroached on a section of the Harlem ghetto and disrupted the community there. Together they marched on Low Memorial Library and protested at other points. Then the alliance fragmented, as whites occupied one building, blacks another. Finally, the president of the university called in the police, and the uprising was quelled. Hundreds of students were arrested; many were hurt. A student sympathy strike occurred, and Columbia closed early that spring.

In some spheres the radical movement became violent indeed. Factions of SDS and other New Left organizations proliferated, and some of those were determined to proceed on a course of their own. One group, whose members called themselves Weathermen after a line in a Bob Dylan song, sought to bring about revolution. In October 1969 it terrorized the police in the streets of Chicago but lost some of its momentum the next year when three members of the group blew themselves up while working with explosives in a house in Greenwich Village, New York.

The New Left became a vocal force in the 1960s, and it involved more and more students as the decade drew to an end. The protest brought some political change as it mobilized sentiment against the Vietnam War and ultimately undermined LBJ's base of support. Yet the protest also spawned other challenges to American society. The alienation and frustration first evident in the political sphere soon spread to a variety of other areas of American life and brought cultural change that was in many ways the most lasting of all.

The Counterculture

In the 1960s there was a general loss of faith in old norms. The protests exposed the emptiness of some of the old patterns, and many Americans, some politically active, some not, began to assert their own individuality and independence in new ways. Drawing on the example of the beats, the literary figures who had rejected conventional canons of respectability in the decade before, those who embraced the new counterculture sought new means of expression themselves.

Surface manifestations were most evident of all. The so-called hippies of the 1960s began to carry themselves in different ways. Men began to wear long hair and grow beards, to dress in simpler clothes, and to wear beads. Stressing spontaneity above all else, some rejected the demands of modern society and the patterns it involved and gravitated instead to living in communal groups where they were freer to function as they chose. Sexual norms began to change as people sought more open ways of communicating with each other and moved to divorce sex from its rigorous ties to family life.

Their example, shocking to some, soon found its way into the culture at large. More and more men, in certain areas at least, began to grow their hair long, to discard ties and jackets, and to experiment with other forms of dress. More colorfully clothed than ever before, they proved willing to see styles change from the traditional patterns that had predominated in the past. Women, too, embraced new fashions. Miniskirts or long dresses were appropriate for casual wear, and slacks and jeans became more common.

Sexual norms changed throughout America. Literature reflected the growing freedom, as federal courts ruled that books like D. H. Lawrence's *Lady Chatterley's Lover* were not obscene and many long-suppressed works began to appear. Nudity became more common on stage and screen. In the rock musical *Hair,* one scene featured the disrobing of performers of both sexes. Parietal rules, supervising the conduct of men and women together in campus rooms, went by the boards. With the pill providing a more effective method of birth control, there was an increasing willingness to experiment with new patterns of living together that would have been shocking a decade before.

Hallucinogenic drugs found their way into American life. Such drugs were nothing new. The beats had on occasion experimented with them, as had others, but now their use became far more common. One prophet of the drug scene was Timothy Leary, who, with Richard Alpert, was doing scientific research on LSD at Harvard University. Fired from their research posts for violating a pledge to the university health service not to experiment with undergraduates, the two men went on to promote the cause of LSD outside. As Alpert drifted from view, Leary became more aggressive in his assertions that drugs were necessary to free the mind. Dressed in long robes, he preached his message—tune in, turn on, drop out.

Another visible apostle of life with drugs was Ken Kesey of Oregon. While at Stanford, where he had gone to write after finishing college, he began participating in medical experiments at a hospital where he was introduced to LSD. With profits from a successful first novel, he bought a cabin and land near Palo Alto and surrounded himself with family and friends, who came to be known as the Merry Pranksters. In 1964 the group headed east in a converted school bus named "Furthur" that was painted psychedelic day-glo colors, wired for sound, and included a refrigerator filled with orange juice and "acid" that sustained the Pranksters on their trip.

Leary and Kesey may have been on the extreme fringe, but drug use did become more common in the United States. Marijuana became popular, even with some formerly staid members of the middle class, and students, old and young, experimented with a variety of substances in the search for liberation or experience in their lives.

Music became intimately connected with the changing scene. Folk music, with its gentle strains, was joined by the more hard-driving rock music that swept the country and the world. The Beatles were the major influence, as they took first England, then the United States, by storm. Other groups followed and carried the music to new ends. Mick Jagger of the Rolling Stones became an aggressive, sometimes violent showman on stage. Janis Joplin, a hard-driving, hard-drinking woman with roots in the blues, became a visible figure in the new rock world until her early death.

All strains of the counterculture came together at the Woodstock Rock Festival in August 1969 in Bethel, New York. Some 300,000 to 400,000 people showed up and covered the fields as they listened to major groups and enjoyed themselves for several days. It was a festive occasion, with people sharing drugs, stripping down to swim or parade in the sun, making love in the grass. No disruptive episodes occurred, and supporters of the changing scene heralded the start of a new era in the United States. But the potential for tragedy and turmoil always lurked beneath the surface at such events. At another festi-

Participants at the Woodstock music festival in August 1969. (*AP/Wide World*)

val at the Altamont Speedway in Livermore, California, in December 1969, the atmosphere turned sour. Without proper planning, the Rolling Stones hired members of the Hell's Angels motorcycle gang to serve as security guards at the concert. They ended up beating to death one man who ventured on stage and attacked others whose actions offended them. At final count the death toll stood at four. Despite the stress on spontaneity and doing one's own thing, there was a violent streak underneath that showed that the new society of peace and love had not yet arrived.

THE STRUGGLE FOR EQUALITY

During the 1960s a number of groups in American society began to make their voices better heard. Drawing on the example of blacks involved in the struggle for civil rights, they pressed for greater equality themselves with growing success. Women in particular made significant gains and watched their new movement forge ahead. Native Americans and Hispanics began to mobilize as well, though not quite as quickly.

The Women's Movement

The women's movement stemmed directly from the civil rights movement of the 1950s and 1960s. Women who had been involved in civil rights activity became increasingly discouraged about the gender discrimination they faced in the struggle. Men, black and white, held the policy positions, while women were relegated to more menial chores. They also felt sexually exploited by the men with whom they worked. Stokely Carmichael's assertion underscored their view. "The only position for women in SNCC," he said, "is prone."

As radical protest mounted, so did women's demands. By 1967 women who had been gaining experience in one liberation movement were ready to embrace another. Squelched at the National Conference for New Politics in Chicago in August 1967, a number of women made their grievances known the next week. "We hope our words and actions will help make women more aware and organized in their own movement through which a concept of free woman-hood will emerge," they said in a manifesto as they gave notice that they were ready to move toward their goals.

Women could take some satisfaction from Title 7 of the 1964 Civil Rights Act, which prohibited discrimination on the basis of sex as well as race and thereby gave legal backing to the struggle for equality. They could fall back on the National Organization for Women (NOW), formed in 1966 "to take action to bring women into full participation in the mainstream of American society now." But a full-blown movement had not yet emerged.

In 1967 a new spirit became visible. Having banded together and made their needs known, women began to branch out, to meet in small groups where problems could be raised and grievances aired. Countless women began to organize and take a closer look at their own lives.

A dramatic demonstration that a new feminist movement had arrived came in August 1968. Protesting the Miss America pageant, women crowned a live sheep to demonstrate their irritation with the object status given to the female body. They also loaded girdles, bras, curlers, and the like into a "free-

Demonstrators protesting the Miss America pageant in 1968. (*UPI/Bettmann Newsphotos*)

dom trashcan" to demonstrate they they no longer needed those items. Auctioning off a Miss America effigy, Peggy Dobbins declared, "Gentlemen, I offer you the 1969 model. She's better every year. She walks. She talks. She smiles on cue. *And* she does housework." Unfavorable media coverage only served to drive more and more women into the movement.

The Native American Struggle

Indians continued to organize, as they had at the start of the decade, to try to save what they could of their land. Some efforts ended in failure. Still, there were occasional moments of success. In 1967, the U.S. Court of Appeals ruled that the government had forced the Seminole Indians in Florida to cede their land in 1823 for an unreasonably low price. The Court directed the government to pay additional funds for the land taken 144 years before. That decision was a source of some satisfaction to the Indian population, although a decade and a half later the compensation had still not been paid.

But Native Americans were becoming more aggressive in pursuit of their own demands. The best reflection of that new spirit came in July 1968 with the founding of the American Indian Movement (AIM). Organized by George Mitchell and Dennis Banks, Chippewa Indians living in Minneapolis, AIM sought to help neglected Indians in the city. It managed to get Office of Economic Opportunity funds channeled to Indian-controlled organizations. It also established patrols to protect drunken Indians from harassment by the police. As its successes became better known, chapters formed in other cities, and served notice that a period of even greater insurgency lay ahead.

The Mobilization of Hispanic-Americans

Hispanics in America, Chicanos in particular, became increasingly aware of their own needs and of the way to meet those needs in the 1960s. With the establishment of the poverty program in the Johnson years, they hoped for improvement in their lot. But they soon found that most efforts were oriented toward the more vocal black groups, and they discovered that bureaucrats ignored people who did not make their voices heard. In 1966 and 1967, as the administration began to look into Mexican-American employment problems, Chicanos came to understand that without continuous efforts on their part, little would be done.

At the same time, they realized the importance of direct action of their own. César Chávez and the United Farm Workers movement served both as a source of inspiration and as an example of what had to be done.

Chávez, born in Arizona, was a labor organizer concerned with social justice and better conditions for the farm workers of the West. Establishing his own union, he concentrated on Mexican field hands who worked long hours in the fields for meager pay. By 1965 his organization had 1700 members and was beginning to attract volunteer help in the campaign.

César Chávez picketing on behalf of United Farm Workers. (*UPI/Bettmann Newsphotos*)

Chávez aimed first at the grape growers of California and launched a boycott to last until they met his demands. The Schenley Corporation and a number of wine companies came to terms, but others held out. In 1966, the Di Giorgio Corporation agreed to permit a union election, but when held, it proved fraudulent and left Chávez and his followers irate. Because California Governor Edmund G. Brown, Sr., needed the Chicano vote, he launched an investigation that resulted in another election. This time the United Farm Workers won.

Chávez became a national figure. Stories about him ran in the *Wall Street Journal* and *Life,* and his picture appeared on the cover of *Time* magazine. More important was the effect on the Chicano population in the United States. Chávez inspired activism on different fronts and gave a sense of hope to Chicanos throughout the land. Groups like the Young Citizens for Community Action formed in the cities and showed a determination to take matters into their own hands to bring about change. Militancy was on the rise.

THE SIXTIES IN PERSPECTIVE

As the decade came to an end, the most dramatic protests, both political and cultural, began to fade. Antiwar sentiment reached a fever pitch in the spring of 1970 when the struggle moved into Cambodia and beyond, but as the United States began to pull out its own forces, it began to decline. Some of the extreme militants like Abbie Hoffman and Jerry Rubin, who preached revolution while prancing about self-indulgently, no longer had center stage to themselves and drifted from sight. Hoffman went underground to try to escape a criminal charge; Rubin later surfaced in more respectable garb. Many, like Black Panther Bobby Seale, the focus of a major political trial as the next decade began, simply ran out of steam and tired of their effort. Some, like activists Sam Brown and Tom Hayden, sought to change society in more subdued ways.

Brown became head of ACTION, the agency coordinating VISTA and the Peace Corps; Hayden moved into reform Democratic politics and continued the battle from there. Others turned to making a living in mainstream America.

Why did the political activism of the New Left decline? Part of the reason lay with the very nature of political debate within the United States. The American party system provided little room for genuine controversy. Even more important, as English journalist Godfrey Hodgson observed, the left had "by the late 1950s virtually ceased to count in American political life." The old American left was fragmented and weak after the McCarthy period, and there was but a tenuous base on which the New Left could build.

Yet the movement had brought change. Slowly but surely the war in Vietnam came to an end. On the social front, it was clear that the United States was different than before. Sexual customs, patterns of music, and styles of dress were all bolder and more open than those before. Even as some of the fads faded and a number of the protests ran their course, new concerns began to emerge. The activism of the 1960s spawned other protests that came into their own in the years ahead.

The United States at the end of the decade was very different from the nation at the beginning. It had started the period with a general sense of confidence in the possibilities of American life and a belief that growth could continue forever and help bring about solutions to problems that generally seemed under control. The Great Society of LBJ moved toward the accomplishment of that end and brought the nation closer than ever toward the realization of its liberal goal. But a dangerous complacency was present at the same time, and even as the reform process unfolded, the challenges to American policy at home and abroad began to mount. By the end of the decade the consensus was in shreds. The reform impulse started to recede, even as concerned groups pointed out previously unperceived abuses in the nation itself. After the experience in Vietnam, there was far less agreement on America's mission and role in the world. The protest movement tore the United States apart and left real questions about its future course.

SUGGESTIONS FOR FURTHER READING

There are a number of useful treatments of the presidency of Lyndon Johnson. Doris Kearns, *Lyndon Johnson and the American Dream* (1976) is a readable analysis of Johnson's time in office by a political scientist and former White House Fellow. Rowland Evans, Jr., and Robert Novak, *Lyndon B. Johnson: The Exercise of Power* (1966) is a helpful assessment of the early years of Johnson's presidency. Hugh Sidey, *A Very Personal Presidency: Lyndon Johnson in the White House* (1968) is a journalist's view of the president. Eric Goldman, *The Tragedy of Lyndon Johnson* (1969) is the account of a historian who worked in the White House. Lyndon Johnson, *The Vantage Point: Perspectives of the Presidency* (1971) is the president's own rather flat account of his White House years.

On Great Society programs, see James T. Patterson, *America's Struggle Against Poverty* (1976) for perspective and Julie Roy Jeffrey, *Education for the Children of the Poor* (1976).

On foreign policy, see Philip L. Geyelin, *Lyndon Johnson and the World* (1966). Vietnam was the major foreign problem, and there is a vast literature on the war. George C. Herring, *America's Longest War: The United States and Vietnam, 1950–1975* (1979) is the best brief account of American policy in that struggle, particularly in the 1960s. Frances Fitzgerald, *Fire in the Lake* (1972) is an eloquent comparison of cultural differences and how they came into conflict. Chester Cooper, *The Lost Crusade* (1970) and Townsend Hoopes, *The Limits of Intervention* (1969) are also helpful. See, too, Neil Sheehan, ed., *The Pentagon Papers* (1971). For a more sympathetic analysis of the conduct of the war, see Guenter Lewy, *America in Vietnam* (1978).

The civil rights movement has also been extensively described. Harvard Sitkoff, *The Struggle for Black Equality, 1954–1980* (1981) is a useful starting point for the 1960s. Clayborne Carson, *In Struggle: SNCC and the Black Awakening of the 1960s* (1981) is a good treatment of one phase of the movement. Anne Moody, *Coming of Age in Mississippi* is the eloquent autobiography of a sensitive young black woman as she grew up in the South and became involved in the civil rights movement.

On the women's movement, Sara Evans, *Personal Politics: The Roots of Women's Liberation in the Civil Rights Movement and the New Left* (1979) provides a penetrating examination of the links between various reform movements in the 1960s. Shulamith Firestone, *The Dialectic of Sex: The Case for Feminist Revolution* (1970) is a radical feminist analysis of sex descrimination. Sara Davidson, *Loose Change* (1977) is a novel describing the lives of women in the 1960s.

On Native American questions, see Alvin M. Josephy, Jr., *Now That the Buffalo's Gone* (1982) for a good treatment of Indian struggles.

Rodolfo Acuña, *Occupied America: A History of Chicanos* (1981) is a helpful overview of Chicano affairs.

For the trials and tribulations of the 1960s, see William L. O'Neill, *Coming Apart: An Informal History of America in the 1960's* (1971); Milton Viorst, *Fire in the Streets: America in the 1960's* (1979); and Allen J. Matusow, *The Unraveling of America: A History of Liberalism in the 1960s* (1984).

On the growth of the counterculture, see Theodore Roszak, *The Making of a Counter Culture* (1968). Charles Reich, *The Greening of America* (1970) is useful as an example of a highly popular work of the period. Tom Wolfe, *The Electric Kool-Aid Acid Test* (1968) is a vivid account of the drug culture of the 1960s. Morris Dickstein, *Gates of Eden: American Culture in the Sixties* (1977) gives a sense of the ties between radical activities and the general culture in the 1960s. Kirkpatrick Sale, *SDS* (1973) focuses on the major radical political organization of the period.

chapter 7

The Nixon Years

The turbulence of the 1960s was apparent in the political sphere as the decade came to an end. As the election of 1968 approached, the specter of the Vietnam War remained, and so did the upheaval the conflict had caused. In that contest, Richard Nixon finally won the office he had long sought. He campaigned on the slogan "Bring Us Together" and claimed that with the proper support he could help heal the nation's wounds. Though Nixon began to extricate America from Vietnam in his first term, he proved unable to avoid further polarization by his actions at home and abroad. A carefully orchestrated reelection campaign ended in another electoral victory in 1972, but then his own personal and political ambitions brought him down. The Watergate affair shook the country once more, left it as disrupted as before, and demonstrated that the peace and prospertity Americans so desperately sought had not yet arrived.

NIXON'S VICTORY

Richard Nixon's career had already been a series of ups and downs when he eyed the presidency once more. Defeated in 1960, he refused to be written off, and he saw his fortunes revive as the Democratic party fell apart. With careful calculation, he planned his campaign to capitalize on the desire for stability he recognized, then structured his administration to ensure his own continued political success.

The Election of 1968

The election of 1968 was almost as tempestuous as the decade of which it was a part. The Democratic party in particular was in trouble as a result of the

Vietnam War. When Senator Eugene McCarthy of Minnesota came out squarely against the war, challenged incumbent LBJ in the New Hampshire primary, and almost won, the implications were clear. Americans were tired of the war, and their growing frustration undermined the president's strength. After Johnson's dramatic announcement that he would not seek another term, other Democrats jumped into the fray. McCarthy pressed on; Robert F. Kennedy, charismatic brother of the slain president, launched a bid for office that ended in his own assassination; and Vice-President Hubert Humphrey became the leading contender as the primary season wore on.

By the time the Democratic party convened in Chicago in the summer of 1968, it faced serious fragmentation. Party regulars wanted to close ranks, while insurgents demanded recognition of their position on the draft and the war. On the radical fringe, a number of groups pressed for confrontation as a way of dramatizing their concerns. The National Mobilization to End the War in Vietnam had a clear political goal. The Youth International Party envisioned a more fluid scenario. The Yippies spoke of putting LSD in the Chicago water supply, having thousands of people run naked through the streets, and disarming the police.

In Chicago the demonstrators came up against Mayor Richard Daley, the city's longtime political boss. He had the convention site, a hotel, protected by barbed wire and chain-link fencing and ordered troops to the scene. The first confrontations took place not long after the political gathering began, but the major incident came on the climactic evening when the convention nominated Hubert Humphrey. As thousands of demonstrating Yippies and others massed outside the hotel, the police sought to push them back, and in so doing lost control. The police went wild, clubbing demonstrators, newsmen, and bystand-

Peace demonstrators taunting the National Guard at the Democratic National Convention in 1968. (*AP/Wide World*)

ers indiscriminately, all in front of television cameras bringing the disruption to households throughout the United States. Inside the hall, Senator Abraham Ribicoff of Connecticut denounced the "Gestapo tactics on the streets of Chicago" as delegate polling took place. In the midst of the chaos, Humphrey won the nomination, but by that time it was not worth much.

Complicating the general election was the third-party campaign of Alabama Governor George C. Wallace, a southern demagogue who exploited racial tensions for his own ends. His deliberate appeals to segregationist sentiment in his own state had given him national exposure. Now, broadening his appeal to include working-class voters in the North as well as whites in the South he criticized the "left-wing theoreticians, briefcase-totin' bureaucrats, ivory-tower guideline writers, bearded anarchists, smart-aleck editorial writers and pointy-headed professors." There was considerable blue-collar resentment of the radical forces causing upheaval in America and of the middle-class elements that seemed to sanction the disruption. Wallace hoped to use that resentment for his own ends.

On the GOP side, the Republicans nominated Richard Nixon, who sought to capture the same constituency Wallace sought. Nixon now had another shot at the major political prize. Running for vice-president in 1952, he had almost been dropped from the ticket when charges of a slush fund surfaced, but he had saved his skin by appealing to the American people, claiming he had taken no illegal political gifts and citing his little dog Checkers as an example of the only kinds of presents he had accepted. That maudlin television performance had kept him politically alive and led to eight years as vice-president. After his loss to John Kennedy in 1960 and his subsequent defeat in a race for governor of California in 1962, however, Nixon seemed out of politics altogether. Indeed, he told the press on that latter occasion, "You won't have Nixon to kick around any more because, gentlemen, this is my last press conference." But after the Goldwater debacle in 1964, Nixon began to work hard for Republican candidates around the country and quickly built up a solid base of support. The front-runner in 1968, he easily won the nomination and seemed to be a changed man, a new Nixon ready to move easily to the top.

Nixon demanded law and order in America, implied he had a plan to end the war but refused to divulge the details, and ran a finely tuned campaign in which all appearances were carefully staged and nothing was allowed to appear out of control. No longer was Nixon as bitter or shrill as he had often appeared before. He remained stable, even aloof, and let his vice-presidential running mate, Governor Spiro Agnew of Maryland, take the offensive. Agnew, much like the Nixon of old, called Humphrey "squishy soft" on communism and declared tactlessly that "once you've seen one slum, you've seen them all." Yet even those comments did not break the momentum. Starting with a large lead, Nixon held on to the end. Humphrey seemed tarnished by being allied with Johnson and could not sever that connection. Though Humphrey crept closer as Johnson finally stopped all bombing of North Vietnam at the close of the campaign, it was too late. Nixon received 43.4 percent of the popular vote, not quite a whole percentage point more than Humphrey (George Wallace got the rest), but it was enough to give him an electoral majority and victory. The Democrats controlled both houses of Congress, but Nixon had the White House at last.

Nixon the Man

On his path to the top, Richard Nixon had fought hard and scrambled all the way. Born poor, he was determined to make it, and after entering politics he did. Yet the setbacks he suffered hurt him, and he constantly appeared to be scheming to right himself once again. Known to some as "Tricky Dick," he sought to put that image behind him as he practiced law in the years between 1962 and 1968. Still, as author and columnist Garry Wills pointed out, he appeared to be a mechanical man, planning his next step: "He is the least 'authentic' man alive, the late mover, tester of responses, submissive to 'the disciple of consent.' A survivor. There is one Nixon only, though there seem to be new ones all the time—he will try to be what people want."

Both in and out of office, Nixon was a shy, remote man who seemed to lack humor and charm. He could be awkward and stiff, unable to say the right thing at the right time. There was also, as speech writer Pat Buchanan later noted, "a side to his nature" that he strove to keep from public view. He embraced the political life, but never with the joy LBJ seemed to derive. Indeed, Nixon was most comfortable when he kept to himself. He enjoyed the company of a few wealthy friends and secluded himself when away from the White House at his estates in Key Biscayne, Florida, and San Clemente, California, both extensively refurbished at government expense. Even at work, he insulated himself whenever he could. He did not relish informal meetings with people and avoided the press when possible. He preferred written contacts to personal ones and appointed a staff that screened him as he wished. His administration was closed and secretive, for that best suited his style.

The Nixon Staff

Nixon's appointees gave him the support he needed. In his Cabinet sat all white, male Republicans generally sympathetic to his views. Some, like Secretary of Health, Education, and Welfare Robert Finch, were former political allies. Others, like Treasury Secretary David Kennedy or Postmaster General Winton Blount or Secretary of State William Rogers, had their roots in the corporate world. But for the most part Nixon worked around his own Cabinet. Other appointees in the White House came to play an even greater role. On the domestic side, Arthur Burns, a former chairman of the Council of Economic Advisers, and Daniel Patrick Moynihan, a Harvard professor of government (and a liberal Democrat), were the most important. In foreign affairs the major figure was Henry A. Kissinger, another Harvard government professor, with both talent and ambition, who directed the National Security Council staff and later assumed the post of secretary of state as his influence grew.

Yet still another tier of men in the administration insulated the president from the outside world and carried out his commands. None had public policy experience, but all shared an intense loyalty to their leader, a quality that Nixon prized above all others. Advertising executive H. R. Haldeman had worked on assorted Nixon campaigns and after the election became chief of staff. He viewed himself as a political mechanic, concerned most of all with Nixon's demands. Of his relationship with the president, Haldeman remarked, "I get done what he wants done and I take the heat instead of him." Working with Haldeman was John Erlichman, a classmate and friend from UCLA, later a lawyer in Seattle. At first he served as a legal counselor but gradually rose to the position of chief domestic adviser. Together Haldeman and Erlichman came to be known as the "Berlin wall." With little sensitivity to the broader political environment, they framed the issues and narrowed the options Nixon saw. Then there was John Mitchell, known as "El Supremo" by the staff. A bond lawyer from Nixon's New York office, he became a fast friend and manager of the 1968 campaign. In the new administration he assumed the post of attorney general and gave the president daily advice. He was determined to forge a powerful Republican machine, even if that meant skewing government policy for political ends.

FOREIGN POLICY

Nixon's real interest, as he assumed office, was foreign policy. Like John Kennedy, he was most intrigued with the foreign sphere and planned to play a major role himself in world affairs. "I've always thought this country could run itself domestically without a President," he once observed; he intended to turn his attention abroad.

Extrication from Vietnam

Nixon's first order of business was to extricate the country from Vietnam. The war had led to personal loss and economic disruption and had polarized the country. In the campaign of 1968, Nixon was well aware that public support for the struggle had waned, and he now began to move to bring the conflict to an end. In mid-1969 he announced what became known as the Nixon Doctrine, asserting that the United States would give aid to friends and allies but would not undertake the full burden of troop defense. To that end, he embarked on the policy of "Vietnamization," which involved removing American forces and replacing them with Vietnamese soldiers. Between 1968 and 1972 American troop strength dropped from 543,000 to 39,000, yet as the American political world applauded, the South Vietnamese proved unable to fight their own war.

Despite that effort, the quagmire engulfed Nixon. Much as he wanted to defuse opposition to the war, like LBJ he was determined not to lose it either. He therefore resumed bombing raids, kept many of them secret from critics, and in his own way widened the war. In April 1970, when a coup in Cambodia brought a sympathetic government, he announced that American and South Vietnamese troops were moving into Cambodia to clear out Communist enclaves there. The United States would not stand by as "a pitiful helpless giant" in the face of the perceived threat. That move brought chaos and civil war in Cambodia and renewed turbulence in the United States. Demonstrations on campuses began again, and some of them had tragic results. At Kent State University in Ohio, National Guardsmen shot four students to death and wounded nine others, even though the troops were in no danger themselves. At Jackson State University in Mississippi a similar tragedy occurred when policemen and highway patrolmen poured automatic weapon fire into a women's dormitory without warning. When they stopped, two people were dead, more wounded.

Nixon also authorized a similar incursion into Laos in 1971. But the forces this time were solely South Vietnamese, and Nixon claimed they proved the success of his phased American withdrawal. They took heavy casualties, however, and only severe bombing by the United States prevented further losses.

Vietnam remained a political football as Nixon ran for reelection in 1972. Negotiations were taking place, and just before voting day, Kissinger announced, "Peace is at hand." When South Vietnam seemed to balk at the proposed settlement, however, the administration responded with the most brutal bombing campaign of the war. Hanoi was hit hard; then North Vietnamese harbors were mined. Only in the new year was an agreement finally signed. Civil war continued for another two years in Vietnam, but after 12 years, the American role finally came to an end.

America's role was finished, yet the cost, both at home and abroad, was high indeed, for the struggle had lingered on unnecessarily, until extrication had the political effect the administration sought. Still, Nixon had accomplished what Lyndon Johnson had never been able to do, and the United States was free at last.

Body of a student in the road after shooting by the National Guard at Kent State University in Ohio in 1970. (*UPI/Bettmann Newsphotos*)

Détente

If Nixon's Vietnam policy was but a qualified success, in other areas his accomplishments were more impressive. The man who had made his career in Red-baiting crusades was able to deal imaginatively and successfully with the Communist powers, and in so doing he reversed the direction American policy had taken since the Second World War. Bypassing Congress, often bypassing his own Department of State, the president relied most heavily on National Security Adviser Kissinger, and together the two dealt in new ways with international affairs.

From the onset of the Cold War after World War II, American policy had been shaped to respond to the perceived Communist threat. Americans had viewed the Russians with distrust and dread, and after the Chinese Revolution of 1949, they had regarded the Asian Communists as part of the same monolithic plot to gain dominance over the entire world. Kissinger understood the real complexity of the situation abroad; he saw the futility of viewing the globe in bipolar terms. He also saw the tensions in the Communist realm, as when he observed, "The deepest international conflict in the world today is not between us and the Soviet Union but between the Soviet Union and Communist China." He helped Nixon restore better relations with both nations at the same time.

Nixon took the most dramatic steps in moving to open normal channels with the People's Republic of China. In the two decades since Mao Zedong's victory on the mainland, American policy had held that Jiang Jieshi's rump government on Taiwan was the rightful state, and there had been no diplomatic relations with the Communist regime. Slowly in 1971, perhaps with an eye on the forthcoming reelection campaign, the administration began to permit a

Richard Nixon and Chinese Premier Zhou Enlai during Nixon's visit to China in 1972. (*AP/ Wide World*)

selective softening of some of the most rigid stands. After the Chinese invited an American table-tennis team to visit the mainland, the United States began to ease some of the trading restrictions in force. In August, Nixon announced that he intended to visit China the next year, to be the first American president to do so.

Why did Nixon take such a bold step? In part he understood that the People's Republic was an established force that would not go away. Realistically, it had to be dealt with and not simply ignored. He saw the rest of the world moving to seat Red China in the United Nations and knew that the United States could no longer direct international opinion on that score. He felt too that he could use Chinese friendship as a bargaining chip when he dealt with the Soviet Union. At the same time, he had an eye on political realities at home. Nixon knew that he could open a dialogue with the Communists with relative impunity, for he had long been one of the most vocal critics of communism and could hardly be accused of being soft. He also knew that the coverage of his dramatic trip could not fail to give him a boost at home.

So Nixon went to China in February 1972. He met with Mao and with Zhou Enlai (Chou En-lai) talked about international problems, exchanged toasts, and saw some of the sights of the Asian land. Wherever he went, American television cameras followed and helped make the visit an overwhelming success. Formal relations were not yet restored, but the basis for diplomatic ties had been established.

Nixon meanwhile used that effort to seek rapprochement with the Soviet Union. He and Kissinger hoped to be able to play one Communist state against the other, and by and large they accomplished their aim. Several months after the China trip, Nixon visited Russia and was as warmly welcomed in Moscow as he had been in Beijing. After several cordial meetings, the president and Soviet Premier Leonid Brezhnev agreed to limit the number of missiles each possessed, to work together to explore space, and to ease long-standing restrictions on trade. Businessmen applauded the new policy, and most Americans seemed to approve of détente.

SALT I

The agreement to limit arms was an important first step toward control of the arms race. Strategic Arms Limitation Talks (SALT) had been going on for several years. Nixon had entered office determined to restore superiority over the Soviet Union but had come to recognize that sufficiency was an adequate standard by which to measure American might. Nixon saw a nuclear agreement as the centerpiece in the expanding network of contacts with the Soviet Union. He hoped that the more involved with the United States the Russians became, the more moderate they would be.

The SALT I treaty was an effort to limit offensive nuclear weapons. It included an "interim agreement" that set ceilings on the numbers of intercontinental ballistic missiles and submarine-launched ballistic missiles at 1972 levels. It also included an antiballistic missile agreement that restricted the development, testing, and deployment of such defensive systems. It limited each nation to two ABM complexes. An amendment two years later reduced the number to one.

The SALT I treaty benefited both the Soviet Union and the United States, even if it did little to limit the number of warheads each nation possessed. It demonstrated that agreement was possible and opened the way to further discussions in subsequent years.

Nixon's foreign policy efforts in general demonstrated tact and skill. He had a vision of a more stable world order and worked to bring that about. He encouraged Kissinger in his shuttle diplomacy efforts to bring peace to the Middle East. Well aware of the interconnections and links between actions in various parts of the globe, he used his Chinese and Russian policies to neutralize opposition to the phased withdrawal of American troops from Vietnam and so bought time to pursue Vietnamization on his own terms. The slow pace he encouraged there prompted criticism, but on other scores his foreign policy was a resounding success.

DOMESTIC AFFAIRS

While seeking international balance, the Nixon administration tried to promote a similar stability at home. Nixon recognized the growing discontent on the part of working-class and even many middle-class Americans with the fallout from the protest movements of the 1960s. He wanted to provide the nation with a new balance that would give him necessary political support. Nixon's approach rested on a determination to stabilize the troubled economy and to restore law and order throughout the United States.

Economic Policy

On the home front the Nixon administration never managed to overcome the problems it faced. Nowhere was that clearer than in the economic sphere. The American economy was huge—in 1970 GNP exceeded a trillion dollars—but it was unstable as well. Inflation, prompted by spending for the Vietnam War, remained a serious problem, even as unemployment continued to grow.

Nixon entered office intent on bringing inflation under control. Feeling that federal spending had gotten out of hand, he wanted to slow things down and encourage fiscal austerity, even at the cost of modest unemployment, as long as he could avoid recessions like those that had plagued the Eisenhower years. But he was resolved at the start to avoid economic controls, the kinds he had seen while working in the Office of Price Administration during World War II. "I will not take the nation down the road of wage and price controls, however politically expedient they may seem," he declared in 1970 as he embarked on a course of his own. He managed for a time to hold the money supply down, but he was less successful at monitoring spending levels and soon seemed to be losing control of the larger situation.

In traditional economic theory, unemployment and inflation were supposed to work against each other; inflation might be controlled at the expense of unemployment levels, and vice versa. Now both seemed to be rising hand in hand. Lawrence O'Brien, head of the Democratic National Committee, dubbed the new state of affairs "Nixonomics": "All the things that should go up—the stock market, corporate profits, real spendable income, productivity—go down, and all the things that should go down—unemployment, prices, interest rates—go up."

Since the game plan was clearly not working, Nixon reversed course. Though a devotee of the balanced budget, like most of his Republican predecessors, he nonetheless began to consider an expansionary economic policy to extricate the nation from its slump. The budget deficit for the 1970–1971 fiscal year was over $23 billion, and that was but $2 billion less than the record recently set under LBJ. As if to underscore his acceptance of the fact that government spending and budget deficits might be necessary in recession times, Nixon declared in early 1971, "I am now a Keynesian in economics." Critics quipped that Nixon's assertion was a demonstration that the doctrine was dead.

Not long thereafter, in the summer of 1971, Nixon also imposed economic controls. The United States was running a trade deficit—paying out more than it got for its imports and services performed abroad. Inflation had reached the then intolerable level of 5 percent and did not simply cause disruptions at home but also made American products more expensive abroad. The president felt he had to act. He decreed a 90-day freeze on wages, prices, and rents and imposed a 10 percent tax on imports. In the fall, under phase 2 of the plan, he created a number of agencies to monitor somewhat less restrictive controls. For a time the new policies seemed to work. The trade balance appeared to improve, and inflation was checked for a while. But soon pressure from both business and labor interests undermined the process of control, and the inflation rate began to soar again—all the way up to 8.3 percent in 1973. Had Nixon held on more strongly, he might have maintained control, but he did not. With matters still unstable, the Arab nations of the Middle East began to cut back on oil production and to raise prices. Another war in the Middle East encouraged the Arab actions, and soon the industrialized nations of the world, so heavily dependent on oil, began to feel the devastating effects. Inflation rose still faster than it had earlier, with consequences that became even more disruptive than before.

Public Policy

The Nixon administration's record was shaky elsewhere on the home front. As he entered office, Nixon faced a standoff with the legislative branch, for both houses of Congress were solidly Democratic. Not since 1849 had a new president faced a Congress squarely in the opposition camp. Much of the story of the domestic side involved congressional efforts to go in one direction while the Nixon White House sought to go in another.

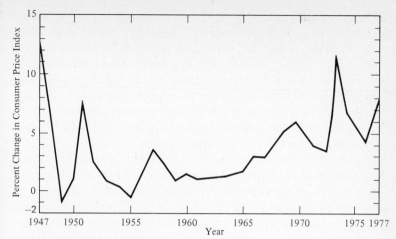

Inflation during the postwar years.

The Democratic Congress in Nixon's first term wanted to continue the liberal approach of the Kennedy-Johnson years. Lawmakers extended the Voting Rights Act of 1965, increased spending for food stamps and other domestic programs, and authorized social security gains to help the elderly. At the same time, they responded to growing pressures for action on the environmental front.

The White House was less interested in that basic approach. Nixon felt he represented a different constituency, and he was determined to respond to its demands. In part his assessment rested on the analysis of Kevin Phillips, a campaign aide, whose book *The Emerging Republican Majority* pointed to important political changes that had occurred. Phillips argued that the Democratic party was slowly losing the solid base established in the New Deal years. A new conservatism was growing among Americans disturbed by the turbulence and change experienced in the past few years. Working-class voters and southern whites in particular were worried by racial ferment and concerned that their own gains might be endangered. Approached in the proper way, relatively conservative Democrats could be won over to the Republican cause and could buttress the growing strength in the Sun Belt—from Florida to Texas to California.

The Republican approach to the question of welfare showed both the nature of the appeal and the ambiguities of the general approach. Nixon, always with an eye on reelection, knew he had to do something about a rapidly expanding welfare program that was threatening to get out of hand. The government's Great Society approach entailed spending more and more in the face of growing conservative cries that it was inefficient, unnecessary, and aimed at discouraging people from trying to work. In the 1968 campaign Nixon exploited that hostility and used the growing frustration to his own advantage. But in office what should he do?

The president knew he had to tread carefully. He needed to avoid alienating his Republican base, even as he sought to win over traditionally Democratic blue-collar workers. To get them, however, he had to reassure them that whatever changes were in store, the Republicans would not dismantle the parts of the welfare state on which they relied. A solution to the problem of what to do came from domestic adviser Moynihan, who urged Nixon to follow the example of former British leader Benjamin Disraeli, a conservative with a concern for the poor. Having criticized the policy of "pouring billions of dollars into programs that have failed," Nixon now endorsed a work-incentive program that was expensive but provided some sort of direction out of the mess. The Family Assistance Plan guaranteed a minimum of $1600 to a family of four. With food stamps, the level could rise approximately $800 more. Out to discover those welfare cheaters who were taking unfair advantage of the system, the plan required all participants to register for job training and to accept employment when found. Proponents sought to make it more profitable to work than to subsist on the public rolls. Socialist Michael Harrington called the plan "the most radical idea since the New Deal," but the program would have cost a great deal, and in the end the money question probably killed it. Conservatives felt the plan went too far, while Democrats raised a variety of other objections for political ends. Though the House of Representatives passed a bill setting up the program, the measure expired in the Senate. Still, Nixon had not lost anything in the process. Conservatives may have been marginally disgruntled but had nowhere else to go, and the president had now taken real steps to win over a new set of constituents to his side.

Civil Rights

Nowhere was Nixon's effort to reconstruct his base more evident than in the area of civil rights. Viewing everything in political terms, Nixon felt that he had little to gain by trying to court blacks. Republicans had missed out on that segment of the vote in 1960 when he had first sought the presidency, and little had changed eight years later when he had gotten barely 5 percent of the black tally. Furthermore, trying to court the black electorate could endanger the white southern vote. Nixon had won part of the South in 1968, George Wallace most of the rest. The Republicans felt that with the proper southern strategy, they could make the South secure.

Attorney General John Mitchell was really the architect of the administration's plan. He saw things as author Kevin Phillips did and hence directed government policy to secure the support of southern whites, whatever the expense to blacks. The civil rights movement had run its course, the White House believed. There was no need to press for further black gains.

The administration went to great lengths to cultivate the white South. Senator Strom Thurmond of South Carolina, renegade Democrat in 1948 and now a convert to the Republican party, was Nixon's most ardent southern supporter, and great pains were taken to maintain his support. One of Thurmond's aides served on the White House staff as a spokesman for the region. A directive forbade any statements by administration officials that might appear hostile to the South.

The administration moved even further in the same direction. At the very start of his first term, Nixon sought to reduce the appropriation for fair housing enforcement. In the first year the Justice Department, under Mitchell, tried to prevent extension of the Voting Rights Act of 1965. In the face of vigorous NAACP protest, Congress went ahead with the extension, but the administration had made its point. Then, when Thurmond and others pushed for the easing of federal desegregation guidelines, the Justice Department acted again. In Mississippi the administration saw to it that some deadlines were moved back and made its modest effort look like a major retreat. When the NAACP appealed the matter, the Supreme Court ruled unanimously that the school system had to be desegregated at once. Nixon disagreed with the decision, and while that failed to change anything, it again demonstrated to the South that he was sympathetically inclined.

Nixon also entered the growing controversy over busing to achieve racial balance. Busing became a highly charged issue in the Nixon years. Transporting students from one area to another to attend school was nothing new. Busing, in fact, had usually been viewed by parents as an educational advantage, for children could be moved from small schoolhouses to better schools. By 1970, over 18 million students, almost 40 percent of the school population in the United States, rode buses to school. Yet when busing became tangled with the question of integration, it became a touchier issue.

The busing question first surfaced in the South, where it could be used to break down racial barriers. The matter came to a head in North Carolina, in the Charlotte-Mecklenburg school system. The 550-square-mile district had over 84,000 students in more than 100 schools. Twenty-nine percent of the pupils were black, and they were concentrated primarily in one section of the region. When voluntary integration efforts proved unsuccessful, a federal judge ruled that the district was not in compliance with the latest Supreme Court decisions. In 1971 the Supreme Court itself ruled on the case and said that district courts had broad authority to order the desegregation of school systems—by busing, if necessary.

Earlier Nixon had stated his opposition to such busing. Now, despite the Supreme Court ruling, he sought a moratorium, or even a restriction, on busing as a desegregation device, but he was unsuccessful in that effort. More and more southern cities were obliged to set up transportation plans to integrate their schools.

Resistance was fierce, particularly in the North, when the busing mandate reached there. In many northern cities, schools were as rigidly segregated as in the South, largely due to de facto residential segregation in the concentrated ghettoes. In Boston, the effort to integrate proved rockier than anywhere else. In 1973, despite a state measure eight years earlier requiring districts to desegregate any schools more than half black, 85 percent of the blacks attended schools that had a black majority. More than half were in schools that were 90 percent black. In June 1974 a federal judge ordered busing to begin. The first phase, involving 17,000 pupils, was to start in the fall of that year, the second phase the following fall.

Elementary school shifts went easily. Reassigned high school students had more trouble. A white boycott at South Boston High cut attendance from the anticipated 1500 to less than 100 on the first day. Buses bringing in black students were stoned, and some riders were injured. White South Bostonians felt that they were being asked to carry the burden of liberals' racial views, and they were angry at having to do so. Racial episodes in a number of high schools led to the flight of white students whose families either enrolled their children in private institutions or fled the city altogether. Busing was a bitter issue, one that reflected the still volatile nature of the quest for equal rights.

During the Nixon years there were occasional civil rights gains. The administration supported a scheme known as the Philadelphia Plan, which sought to end discrimination on federal building projects. Unions involved were required to accept as apprentices certain quotas of black youths and then to guarantee them union membership when the training was done. It was a step forward in opening the labor market, and one the courts approved.

On balance, however, the record was weak, for that fit the political plan. Nixon himself once declared that "there are those who want instant integration and those who want segregation forever. I believe that we need to have a middle course between those two extremes." But given the continued resistance to racial change in some parts of the country, modest progress meant no progress at all. Still, Nixon never viewed himself as a racial bigot. Rather he saw himself as a man who would do whatever was practical to assist in racial affairs, but practical could easily mean different things at different times. At one point the president told James Farmer, a black leader appointed to the post of assistant secretary of health, education, and welfare, that he only wanted to do what was right for blacks. "I care," he said. "I just hope people will believe that I *do* care." Hope though he might, he was among blacks the most unpopular president of the postwar period.

Law and Order

Nixon's social and political approach was reflected in his determination to restore law and order to the land. In the wake of the protest movements of the 1960s, a backlash had begun to grow as Middle Americans increasingly voiced their irritation with the chaos they saw. Crime rates seemed to be rising as drug use spread. Permissive attitudes towards sex seemed to flaunt old codes. Nixon's strategy was to exploit the divisions as part of his larger campaign. Both in word and in deed, his administration intended to cultivate those white conservative groups who felt change had gone too far, in an effort to restore the old verities.

One phase of the campaign was rhetorical alone. Nixon himself denounced protesters when demonstrations occurred. "Bums," he called the students at one point. More and more, however, his vice-president took the lead, just as Nixon had done in the Eisenhower years. Spiro Agnew had a gift for jugular attack, and in his speeches he often struck hard. "Ideological eunuchs," he called the students in one repeated phrase, "parasites of passion" in another. Opposition elements made up an "effete corps of impudent snobs" who did untold damage to the nation.

At the same time, John Mitchell used the Justice Department to demonstrate that the administration was concerned with the values of Middle Americans disturbed by the upheavals taking place. Just as the attorney general was instrumental in slowing down the civil rights process with legalistic ploys, he also stepped up the campaign on crime, even at the expense of individuals' constitutional rights. Mitchell personified the new aggressive approach.

Mitchell directed the administration's effort to reshape the Supreme Court. In his first term, Nixon had the extraordinary opportunity to name four judges to the Court, and he was determined to appoint men who shared his views. The first appointment was that of Warren Earl Burger, as Chief Justice, to replace Earl Warren, who was stepping down after 16 years at the top. Burger was a moderate who faced no difficulty in the Senate confirmation process.

Subsequent appointments reflected the southern strategy and conservative approach. Nixon sought a strict constructionist as well as someone acceptable to the South and so chose Clement Haynesworth of South Carolina for the Court. Haynesworth had gone to Harvard Law School and was now chief judge of the Fourth Circuit Court of Appeals. Opposition soon developed when conflict-of-interest charges surfaced. Coupled with allegations that his decisions showed an antilabor, anti-integration bias, they resulted in Senate rejection of the nomination. Irate, Nixon branded the charges "brutal" and "vicious" and determined to appoint someone with similar views.

His next choice was G. Harrold Carswell of Florida, from the Fifth Circuit Court of Appeals, and Carswell too ran into trouble. He was singularly unqualified for the Supreme Court. His intellectual ability was challenged by lawyers and legal scholars, who pointed to the large number of his decisions reversed on appeal to higher courts. Racial bias seemed clear when a speech he had made in 1948 expressing his belief in white supremacy appeared. To the charges of mediocrity, all Senator Roman Hruska of Nebraska, one of his supporters, could manage was, "Even if he were mediocre, there are lots of mediocre judges and people and lawyers. They are entitled to a little representation aren't they?" That argument did not carry, however, and Carswell went down to defeat.

In the end Nixon appointed Harry Blackmun, Lewis F. Powell, Jr., and William Rehnquist, all able and qualified for the positions, all apparently inclined to tilt the Court in a more conservative direction. In the next few years the Court did begin to ease the burden of the prosecution in cases it heard, as it shifted somewhat from the direction the Warren Court had taken in protecting defendants' rights. The Court also upheld laws banning pornography if they mirrored community standards and thereby brought to a halt the process of liberalization that had been taking place.

On other scores, however, the Court failed to move as the president had hoped. It ruled against the government in school desegregation cases, upheld busing as an acceptable alternative, and argued that the death penalty as then in force was unfair and had to be changed. This Court, as others, followed its own bent, though a shift to the right remained apparent.

SOCIAL MOVEMENTS

As the nation struggled with its problems in governmental spheres, millions of Americans struggled to cope with new issues in their own lives. The 1960s had generated an assortment of movements and groups that continued to flourish in the years that followed. A healthy and strong women's movement expanded rapidly. Hispanics and Native Americans became more assertive in their demands for equality. Other groups became concerned with environmental and consumer causes. People began to see that change was possible if sufficient pressure was applied.

The Women's Movement

Women mobilized, fought for gains, and achieved some of their objectives. As Helen Reddy declared in "I Am Woman," a popular song recorded in 1971:

> I am woman, hear me roar
> In numbers too big to ignore,
> And I know too much to go back to pretend
> 'Cause I've heard it all before
> And I've been down there on the floor,
> No one's ever gonna keep me down again.

The perception of the role of women was beginning to change. In the early 1970s, a Yankelovich survey noted that in a two-year period the number of college students who felt women were oppressed had doubled, and the numbers continued to rise. Women headed for new careers. The proportion of women beginning law school tripled between 1969 and 1974.

Several publications helped the women's movement gain momentum. Gloria Steinem, author of a regular political column in *New York* magazine, banded together with several other women in 1971 to found *Ms.* magazine. *Ms.* succeeded beyond their wildest dreams. In the first eight days the 300,000 copies of the preview issue sold out, and the magazine was on its way. As the founders observed, they had "tapped an emerging and deep cultural change that was happening to us, and happening to our sisters." *The New Woman's Survival Catalogue* provided advice of all kinds to its readers. *Our Bodies Ourselves,* a handbook published by a women's health collective, encouraged women to understand their own bodies and sold 850,000 copies between 1971 and 1976. The new books and magazines were radically different from older women's magazines like *Good Housekeeping* and the *Ladies' Home Journal.* Those publications aimed at women at home and focused on their needs. The newer publications explored the frustrations of working women and gave women interested in liberation a forum of their own.

The women's movement was decentralized, diffuse, and often internally divided. Some women worked for incremental reform and modest progress. More radical feminists demanded wholesale restructuring of the society.

Groups like the National Organization for Women (NOW) pressed for equal employment opportunities, child-care centers, and abortion reform. Both in and out of NOW, women concerned with legal questions and symbolic changes worked for passage, then ratification, of the Equal Rights Amendment (ERA) to the Constitution. Passed by Congress in 1972, it read: "Equality of rights under the law shall not be denied or abridged by the United States or by any State on account of sex." Thirty of the required 38 states ratified it quickly. A few others followed, and final approval seemed but a matter of time.

Meanwhile, other women insisted on more radical approaches. Some demanded fundamental changes in sexual identity to end male domination and exploitation. Shulamith Firestone, in *The Dialectic of Sex* in 1970, called for "the freeing of women from the tyranny of their reproductive biology" and the spreading of childbearing and child-rearing functions to all members of the society. Other socialist feminists argued that capitalist society itself was responsible for women's plight and claimed that only through the process of revolution could women be freed.

Not all women embraced the movement they saw growing around them.

Marching for ERA. Marchers include Representative Bella Abzug, Gloria Steinem, Dick Gregory, Betty Friedan, Representative Barbara Mikulski, and Representative Margaret Heckler. (*AP/Wide World*)

> So what had been achieved in the
'60s

Marabel Morgan was one who insisted that a woman's place was at home by her husband's side. The comfortable and secure wife of a Florida attorney, she generalized from her own experience when she argued that "it is only when a woman surrenders her life to her husband, reveres and worships him, and is willing to serve him, that she becomes really beautiful to him." In *The Total Woman* in 1973, she spelled out the "4A approach": accept, admire, adapt, appreciate. Substantial numbers of women listened to the message. As of 1975, 500,000 copies of the hardcover edition had been sold, and 77 followers spread her message in group meetings throughout the country.

Political opposition came from Phyllis Schlafly, who led a nationwide effort to resist ratification of the Equal Rights Amendment. Author of several books, including one supporting conservative presidential candidate Barry Goldwater a decade before, she was adamant about the ERA. "It won't do anything to help women," she said, "and it will take away from women the rights they already have, such as the right of a wife to be supported by her husband, the right of a woman to be exempted from military combat, and the right, if you wanted it, to go to a single-sex college." Women, she believed, already had legal backing enough for their rights and needed no more.

Native Americans and Hispanic-Americans

As women pressed for greater opportunities, other groups mobilized more effectively as well. The American Indian Movement (AIM), founded the year before Nixon took office, gave Native Americans a platform and a focus as they pushed their own cause.

The new militant mood became visible in November 1969, when a number of Indians seized Alcatraz Island in San Francisco Bay. Pointing to the Fort Laramie Treaty of 1868, which permitted male Indians to file homestead claims on federal lands, the occupiers took over the island, which now housed a defunct federal prison, declared surplus property five years before. They protested the inability of the Bureau of Indian Affairs to "deal practically" with questions of Indian welfare and remained on the island until 1971, when federal officials moved them off.

The next year, militants launched the Broken Treaties Caravan to Washington. For six days insurgents occupied the building of the Bureau of Indian Affairs. Then, in 1973, AIM took over the South Dakota village of Wounded Knee, where in 1890 the U.S. 7th Cavalry had massacred the Sioux. The reservation surrounding the town was mired in poverty. Half of the families there were on welfare. Alcoholism was widespread. Eighty-one percent of the student population had dropped out of school. The occupiers wanted to dramatize such conditions and to draw attention to the 371 treaties leaders claimed the government had broken. Federal officials encircled the area, and when AIM tried to bring in supplies, they killed one Indian and wounded another. The confrontation ended with a government agreement to reexamine the treaty rights of the Indians, although little of substance was done. Still, the episode reflected increasing Indian activism and determination not to be pushed around.

Native Americans on guard at Wounded Knee, South Dakota, in 1973. (*UPI/Bettmann Newsphotos*)

Hispanics in America also mobilized for their own ends. Some protests took place in the schools. In March 1968, 10,000 Chicano students had walked out of five high schools in Los Angeles. Their actions prompted other walkouts in Colorado, in Texas, and in other parts of California, to demand Mexican teachers, counselors, and courses. At the university level, Chicano activism led to the establishment of Mexican-American studies programs throughout the West and Southwest. They offered degrees, built library collections, and provided Chicanos access to their own past.

At the same time, other forms of organization took place. The Young Chicanos for Community Action began to take a paramilitary stance. Its members became identified as the Brown Berets and formed chapters throughout the Midwest and Southwest. Some Chicanos began to organize politically. José Angel Gutiérrez helped mobilize Chicanos in his hometown of Crystal City, Texas. In the fall of 1969, when students protested conditions at the local high school and then walked out, a citizens' organization guided by Gutiérrez stepped in to develop a spirit of solidarity. From that group emerged the La Raza Unida political party, which began to play a major role in the area and successfully promoted Chicano candidates for political office.

Chicanos joined in the general protest against the Vietnam War. Because the draft drew most heavily from the poorer segments of society, the Chicano casualty rate was far higher than that of the general population. In 1969 the Brown Berets organized the National Chicano Moratorium Committee and staged antiwar demonstrations. They argued that this was a racial war, with black and brown Americans being used against their Third World compatriots. Some of the rallies ended in confrontations with the police.

Aware of the growing demands of Hispanic-Americans, the Nixon administration sought to diffuse their anger and win their support. Political analysts saw that if Nixon had carried 5 percent more of the Chicano vote in Texas, he would have won the state. Looking toward reelection, they advised an effort to bring Chicanos into the Republican camp. By dangling political positions, government jobs, and promises of better programs for Mexican-Americans, they attempted to draw the Chicanos to their side. The effort paid off, as Nixon received 31 percent of the Hispanic vote in 1972. Rather than reward his Chicano followers, however, the president cut back the poverty program begun under LBJ.

Disillusioned and discouraged, Chicanos could take some comfort from a Supreme Court decision in 1974 declaring that schools had to meet the needs of children with a limited grasp of English. That decision led to federal funding of bilingual education. On the political front, however, the major lesson for Chicanos was that even small gains demanded strenuous organization and even then could not always be guaranteed.

Other Movements

As Native Americans, Hispanics, and others pursued their own demands, a number of new movements emerged and gained momentum. An environmental movement that emerged in the mid-1960s grew rapidly. A Gallup poll revealed that while only 17 percent of the public considered air and water pollution to be one of the three major governmental problems in the middle of the previous decade, that figure had risen to 53 percent by 1970.

The roots of the modern environmental movement lay with a series of articles and then a book, *Silent Spring,* published by Rachel Carson in 1962. She took careful aim at chemical pesticides, particularly DDT, which had increased crop yields and allowed more successful farming, yet had disastrous side effects that had been ignored. Americans became increasingly concerned about ecological questions as they grew more aware of the pollutants around them.

Concern mounted in 1969 when it was discovered that thermal pollution from nuclear power plants was killing fish in rivers. DDT was threatening the very existence of the bald eagle, the nation's symbol. A massive oil spill off the coast of southern California turned white beaches black and wiped out much of the marine life in the immediate area of the disaster.

The environmental movement took different forms. Some people pressed for preservation of unspoiled areas, but far more exerted pressure on legislative and administrative bodies to frame the kinds of regulations necessary to ease the problems. Congress passed a series of important measures. The Water Quality Improvement Act, Clean Air Act, and Resource Recovery Act all began to bring pollution under control by mandating changes in both business and consumer practice. Capping the structure was the new Environmental Protection Agency, created in 1971, which had the authority to enforce the measures by bringing suit against violators of the standards set.

Related to the environmental movement was a growing consumer movement dating from the 1970s. Americans throughout the twentieth century, and particularly in the 1950s, had become increasingly attracted to fashionable clothes, home furnishings, and electrical and electronic gadgets, their appetites whetted by mass advertising. In years past Congress had established a variety of regulatory efforts to protect citizens from sellers eager to make a profit in unscrupulous ways. In the 1970s a strong consumer movement developed, aimed at protecting the interests of the purchasing public and making business more responsible to consumers.

Ralph Nader headed the new movement. He had become interested in the issue of automobile safety while a student at Harvard Law School and had pursued that interest as a consultant to the Department of Labor in Washington, D.C. His book, *Unsafe at Any Speed: The Designed-in Dangers of the American Automobile,* published in 1965, argued that many cars were coffins on wheels. Head-on collisions at even low speeds, he showed, could easily kill, for cosmetic bumpers could not withstand modest shocks. He singled out the Chevrolet Corvair as "one of the nastiest-handling cars ever built" because of its tendency to roll over in certain situations. Angered by his charges, General Motors hired a private detective to find something compromising in his life. Nader sued the giant corporation and won several hundred thousand dollars, which he poured back into his cause. His efforts paved the way for the National Traffic and Motor Vehicle Safety Act in 1966.

Nader's efforts attracted volunteers. In 1968 there were nine "Nader's raiders," in 1969 a hundred. They turned out critiques and reports and, more important, provided an example for the country at large. At all levels of government—city, state, and national—consumer-protection offices began to monitor the complaints that Americans were now willing to make. More and more people became aware of their rights and determined to end consumer exploitation.

While some Americans worked to change the system through political action, others rejected the idealism of the 1960s and devoted themselves to "doing their own thing," according to a popular phrase. Social commentator Tom Wolfe termed the 1970s the "Me Decade" in a lengthy report for *New York* magazine. Millions of Americans began to look inward rather than outward. Books like Eric Berne's *Games People Play,* published in 1969, popularized transactional analysis, a therapeutic approach focusing on interpersonal relationships. The Esalen Institute in Big Sur, California, offered encounter sessions to those who could afford to come to the center for a week. Still another approach was taken in the Erhard Seminars Training (est) program. Whatever the program, participants were encouraged to face their own feelings as squarely and honestly as they could, and screams and sobs, moans and groans became common sounds in the sessions. The whole effort was aimed, in Wolfe's words, at "changing one's personality—remaking, remodeling, elevat-

ing, and polishing one's very *self* . . . and observing, studying, and doting on it."
People were encouraged to strip away the excess baggage tied on by society or
self "in order to find the Real Me."

While many Americans sought salvation in narcissistic quests, increasing
numbers became involved in mystical religious movements that promised internal peace of a different sort. Some embraced transcendental meditation. Others
became involved with Zen. Cults proliferated, as the Hare Krishna group, the
Unification Church of the Reverend Sun Myung Moon, the Children of God,
and a host of other groups drew people, mostly young, into their midst.

WATERGATE

As American society changed and Americans embraced new causes, political as
well as personal, the Republican administration sought to capitalize on the
fragmentation for its own ends. Looking toward reelection throughout his first
term, Nixon hoped to appeal to a middle-class constituency irritated by the
radical activists and self-indulgent individuals who had either brought or capitalized on the upheaval of the past few years. Sparing no expense, the president
relied on a group of fiercely loyal aides who were prepared to do anything for
him. In their enthusiasm, they transgressed the bounds not simply of propriety
but of the law as well. The Watergate affair was a direct result of their excessive
approach. The cover-up that followed could not be contained, and eventually it
brought them all down.

Siege Mentality in the White House

Nixon and his aides wanted to create stability on the foreign front as they tried
to restore prosperity at home, but the course was not always clear. Protests
marred the effort to end the commitment in Vietnam, inflation and recession
kept the economy out of control, and fragmenting forces in Congress and out
seemed to threaten the administration's goals. Gradually there developed a
feeling in the White House that the administration should do whatever was
necessary to perpetuate its own command.

The White House staff was dominated by a sense of siege. Nixon surrounded himself with people who insulated him from the outside and reflected
his own view that real vigilance was necessary to protect him from the forces
that sought to bring him down. One of the most vocal was Charles W. Colson,
special counsel and important aide. He termed himself a "flag-waving,
kick-'em-in-the-nuts, anti-press, anti-liberal Nixon fanatic."

Colson played an important part in developing the enemies list, which
recorded prominent figures viewed as unsympathetic to the administration. It
included politicians like Edward M. Kennedy, Edmund Muskie, and Walter
Mondale, members of the media like Daniel Schorr, and public performers like
Jane Fonda, Dick Gregory, and Steve McQueen. Ultimately 300 names appeared on the list, with 20 marked as the most serious threats. Then the prob-

lem became to decide, as young White House lawyer John Dean wrote, "how we can maximize the fact of our incumbency in dealing with the persons known to be active in their opposition to our Administration. Stated a bit more bluntly—how we can use the available federal machinery to screw our political enemies." All kinds of things were possible, tax investigations included, to harass those singled out.

At the same time, the administration pursued an even more extensive program to squelch dissent. Committed to a policy of law and order, Nixon and his aides were willing to use extraordinary means to achieve their ends, and often the efforts made proved more destructive than the activities they were meant to control. When suspicions were aroused that the National Security Council staff was speaking too freely to the press, wiretaps were placed on the phones of some of the people thought to be involved. Nixon was particularly irate when stories of the secret bombing of Cambodia began to leak out, so he had the phones of selected reporters tapped, too.

Far worse, however, was the effort to coordinate intelligence activities within the United States. Both the FBI and the CIA had for some years been illegally following the activities of militant Americans at home. They had wire-tapped phones, opened letters, and infiltrated meetings of those deemed sus-pect. Now Nixon seemed willing to pay even less attention to civil liberties in the United States. Dissent, he felt, was getting out of hand; campus distur-bances like the one at Kent State were undermining the stability of the land. In mid-1970 he called together the top members of the intelligence community, including Richard Helms of the CIA and J. Edgar Hoover of the FBI, and sought to enlarge and extend the actions they could take. Presidential aide Tom C. Houston laid out a new plan that in effect allowed law enforcers to dispense with the law. He proposed permitting interception of mail, free entry to private homes, and a host of other activities. Even FBI director Hoover, already overzealous in combatting perceived subversion at home, was appalled. Such flagrant disregard for the law was simply not possible, he argued, and the plan was set aside.

While that effort came to naught, other ventures with the same goals were tried. Most significant was the formation of the group of "Plumbers" to stop government security leaks. The background lay in the newspaper publication of the Pentagon Papers in June 1971, after Defense Department official Daniel Ellsberg turned the secret history of the Vietnam War over to the press. Nixon and Kissinger were furious, and the Justice Department sought a Supreme Court order restraining publication but failed in the quest. Now administration leaders were determined to take whatever steps necessary to prevent further leaks.

With John Erlichman at the top, the White House set up its own investi-gation unit. One recruit was E. Howard Hunt, a former CIA agent with 23 years in the agency and a specialist in assorted dirty tricks. He also had a fertile imagination, which he used in the dozens of spy novels he authored under different names. Another member of the team was G. Gordon Liddy, a one-time member of the FBI, assistant district attorney, and recent Treasury Department employee. He was a fiercely loyal partisan who was willing to do anything without flinching.

Together Hunt and Liddy set out to find out whatever they could about Ellsberg in an effort to discredit him and his work. Acquisition of a CIA profile failed to show much, but since rumors were circulating about his private life, the Plumbers decided to check the files of the California psychiatrist Ellsberg had been seeing. Those records were confidential, of course, but Erlichman approved the necessary break-in and burglary "if done under your assurance that it is not traceable." Hired Cubans carried out the plan but never found the incriminating material they sought. In time the Plumbers group became less active as the major members took posts in Nixon's reelection campaign.

CREEP and the Election of 1972

As Nixon's first four years drew to an end, the Committee to Re-elect the President (CREEP), headed by John Mitchell, moved into gear. It launched a massive fund-raising drive, aimed at collecting as much money as it could before reporting funds and amounts became necessary under a new campaign-finance law. That money could be used for any purposes, and indeed some was channeled into payments for the performance of various dirty tricks aimed at disrupting opponents' campaigns. Other funds financed an intelligence branch within CREEP. Liddy was chief of the new unit, which included Hunt as well.

In early 1972 Liddy and a number of others proposed an elaborate scheme to wiretap assorted Democrats and to try to compromise them at their nominating convention. Twice Mitchell refused to go along, on the grounds that the plan was risky and would cost too much. Finally, after two months, Mitchell approved a modified version of the plan to tap the phones of the Democratic National Committee at its headquarters in the Watergate complex in Washington, D.C. The former attorney general, top legal official in the land, had authorized breaking the law.

The first effort at wiretapping failed. A second attempt on the evening of June 16–17 worked better but involved serious mistakes. Some of the people engaged were inside men who worked for CREEP. They carried with them cash that could be traced to the committee. In the process of breaking in, they carelessly taped locks horizontally rather then vertically so that the tape could be seen, and even did it the same way again when a security guard removed it on a routine inspection tour. At that point the guard called the police, and the men installing the tape were caught in the act.

A serious setback had occurred, but Nixon and his aides thought it might be kept from view. Every effort was made to play the matter down, head off the investigation, and allow the campaign to take its appointed course.

The Republicans seemed to be in good shape, for the Democrats were still in a state of disarray after the debacle of 1968. A number of the potential candidates had serious problems they could not overcome. Massachusetts senator Edward Kennedy still faced the stigma of the Chappaquiddick affair, in which a woman in his car drowned under questionable circumstances. George Wallace, an independent in 1968 now seeking the Democratic nomination, survived an assassin's bullet but was paralyzed for life. Finally, in a convention marked by far more open rules than before, liberal senator George McGovern of South Dakota won the nomination. While he had the support of vocal pressure groups who now had a greater say, he lacked the backing of union elements or urban machines so important to Democratic success in the past.

Branded as the candidate of the radical fringe, McGovern never had a chance. Nixon had put together a new majority by his southern strategy and law-and-order stance and had defused the Vietnam issue as well. In November he won a major victory at the polls. He received 47 million popular votes to McGovern's 29 million, and took the electoral college by 521 to 17. He got traditional Republican support, even as he cut into areas where the Democrats in the past had been strong, and showed significant strength among blue-collar workers, union members, and southern voters. The mandate seemed clear as he began his second term.

Cover-up and Catastrophe

Despite Nixon's huge reelection victory, the Watergate break-in and its effects could not be set aside. When the apprehension of the burglars first occurred, the top members of the administration had to decide what to do. The FBI was tracing the money to CREEP, and the link might become visible at any time. On June 23, 1972, Nixon had authorized the CIA to call off the FBI on the grounds that national security was involved. Though not involved in the planning of the break-in, the president had become party to the cover-up. During the campaign he had authorized payments of hush money to silence Hunt and others implicated in the mess. Publicly he had proclaimed that a thorough internal investigation revealed that "no one in the White House staff, no one in this administration, presently employed was involved in this very bizarre incident." Top members of the administration, Mitchell included, perjured themselves in court to shield the higher-level officials who were in fact involved.

After the election, in early 1973, the trial of the Watergate burglars took place, and all either pleaded guilty or were found guilty in the end. At sentencing time, however, the judge was not satisfied that justice had been done and asserted that evidence indicated that others too had been involved.

A pair of zealous reporters, Bob Woodward and Carl Bernstein of the *Washington Post,* were following a trail of leads on their own. Even before the election they had begun to publish pieces about the secret funds at CREEP and about the political intelligence and sabotage campaign. They continued their pursuit as the case began to unfold.

At the same time, a Senate Select Committee on Presidential Activities undertook a thorough investigation of the entire Watergate affair. The staff was not sure what it was looking for at first, yet soon a more complete picture emerged. James McCord, one of the convicted burglars, testified and moved the process along. Newspaper stories provided further leads, and the official investigation in turn provided new material for the press. Faced with rumors that the White House was actively involved, Nixon finally decided that he had to release Haldeman and Erlichman, his two closest aides, in an effort to save his own neck. Praising them on nationwide TV, he proclaimed that he would take the ultimate responsibility for others' mistakes for "there can be no whitewash at the White House." But even that was not enough, and the investigation ground inexorably on.

In May 1973 the Senate committee, chaired by Senator Sam J. Ervin of North Carolina, opened public hearings, televised as the earlier McCarthy hearings had been, and they had a dramatic effect. Presidential aide John Dean, seeking to save himself, testified that Nixon knew about the cover-up. Other staffers also made significant revelations before the committee. The most dramatic disclosure came when one aide revealed the existence of a secret taping system in the president's office that recorded all conversations. Other presidents had taped some things from time to time, but Nixon's system was far more complex and elaborate than theirs and could help verify what truth there was to the growing rumors that he had been party to the cover-up all along.

In an effort to underscore his own honesty, Nixon acceded to the appointment of a special prosecutor in the Justice Department to look into the affair. Archibald Cox, Harvard Law School professor, received the post and immediately began to seek access to the tapes. Nixon's refusal to release them led to a confrontation with the White House that reached its climax in October 1973. Nixon insisted that Cox be fired. When the new attorney general refused and resigned instead, Nixon moved down the Justice Department hierarchy until he found someone to carry out his command. He accomplished his immediate aim but lost considerable support as a result of the "Saturday Night Massacre," as the episode was called.

By that time Nixon was clearly in trouble. His 68 percent approval rating in February dropped to 40 percent in July and continued to slip. With the Ervin committee hearings under way, more and more Americans began to believe that the president had at least some part in the cover-up and should take responsibility for his acts. After the firing of Cox, *Time* magazine ran an editorial headlined "The President Should Resign."

At about the same time, the administration suffered still another blow. Vice-President Spiro Agnew, the spokesman for law and order who had mobilized Middle America against the radical young, was accused of accepting bribe money even while in national office. He had once declared, "I have often been accused of putting my foot in my mouth, but I will never put my hand in your pockets." His disclaimer notwithstanding, the evidence pointed clearly to his guilt, and he had to resign. Nixon's choice for vice-president was House Minority Leader Gerald Ford of Michigan, but even that selection, popular on Capitol Hill, could not turn the administration's fate around.

The struggle over the tapes continued, despite Cox's departure. Nixon sought to stem the tide by appointing another special prosecutor, Leon Jaworski of Texas, but he too pressed on as Cox had done. Nixon then tried to prove his innocence by releasing edited transcripts of some of the White House conversations. Even without the ultimate damning evidence, the record of angry and vindictive talks in the Oval Office further eroded Nixon's support. Facetious stories circulated about the president's efforts to decide what he could do. In one, later related by Sam Ervin, Nixon went around to the monuments of his predecessors to get advice. From George Washington came the injunction to tell the truth, but Nixon said he could not. From Thomas Jefferson came the suggestion to go to the people, but Nixon felt he could no longer do that. Finally from Abraham Lincoln came the ultimate advice. "Richard," he said, "go to the theater."

Nixon did not have much choice. There had been numerous demands for his impeachment, and after the Saturday Night Massacre the process of preparation began. In late July 1974 the House Judiciary Committee, made up of 21 Democrats and 17 Republicans, began to meet and debate the case. By a 27 to 11 tally on the question of obstruction of justice, it voted to impeach. By a 28 to 10 vote on the article accusing the president of abuse of power, it called for impeachment. By a smaller margin it recommended impeachment for refusing to obey a congressional subpoena to turn over his tapes. The full House of Representatives still had to vote for impeachment before it took effect, and then the Senate would have to preside over a trial. But for Nixon the handwriting was on the wall.

After delaying briefly, on August 5 Nixon finally obeyed a ruling of the Supreme Court and released the tapes. In them evidence of the president's complicity in the cover-up was so clear that even his most ardent supporters could not ignore it, and his ultimate resignation became but a matter of time.

Vice-President and Mrs. Gerald Ford with President and Mrs. Richard Nixon as Nixon prepared to resign the presidency in August 1974. (*AP/Wide World*)

Four days later, on August 9, 1974, the extraordinary episode came to an end as Nixon became the first American president ever to resign.

Why Watergate?

Though Nixon was gone, a number of questions still remained. Why did the Watergate break-in occur in the first place? And why did the president risk all in a cover-up he knew was wrong?

It is still not clear precisely what the Republicans hoped to find at the Democratic National Headquarters. There have been assertions that they were trying to discover ties between the McGovern forces and the Castro regime in Cuba. There have been other charges that they were looking for links between billionaire Howard Hughes and top Democratic officials in the hope that some sort of dirt could be uncovered for use in the campaign. But nothing is certain, and the aims remain obscure.

In a larger sense, however, the whole scheme was related to Nixon's commitment to winning at any cost. He had lost one election by a razor-thin margin in 1960 and won another by a similar close count in 1968. The Republicans had not done particularly well in the midterm contests of 1970. Now, convinced that every advantage helped, the reelection forces were determined to do whatever was necessary to gain the victory they sought. The efforts made to discredit opponents and the dirty tricks used were all part of that approach.

Also involved was the sense that the president could do no wrong. Nixon, of course, was hardly the first president to take advantage of his role. Yet he carried the imperial presidency to a new extreme. He enjoyed the trappings of luxury and lived well at the top. He sought to have the White House guards uniformed to be more like their counterparts in England. In cartoons as time went on, he appeared as "King Richard," monarch of the land. He had far more assistants than his predecessors in office, and his first term saw the cost of operating the executive office rise from $31 million to $71 million. In foreign affairs he launched secret bombing campaigns on the grounds that he had the constitutional right as commander in chief to do whatever was necessary in the war. At home he impounded funds appropriated by Congress for given ends and simply refused to spend the money to carry out the legislative will.

Nixon, in sum, greatly enlarged the prerogatives of the president and accrued powers even more avidly than his predecessors. He surrounded himself with subordinates who shared his assumptions and were eager to respond to his commands. They viewed themselves as tough and aggressive aides with a clear mission to perform and were unwilling to let anything stand in the way. Self-centered in their stance, they were also often amoral in their approach. Though many of them were lawyers, they proved willing to overlook legalities in the pursuit of their own personal and political ends. That, as much as anything else, accounts for the willingness to try to hide the truth after the discovery of the Watergate affair. The risks of coming clean were too great, for that might have jeopardized the ultimate aim. The hang-out option was considered and ignored in favor of a fabric of lies that proved far more destructive in the end.

Nixon, used to crisis in his political career, gambled one last time from what he considered a position of strength—and in so doing lost all he had won.

THE NIXON YEARS IN PERSPECTIVE

How should Nixon's presidency be judged? The Watergate affair was clearly the most widespread and disturbing political scandal in American history. In the end, 378 officials, including top-level Cabinet officers and presidential aides, either pleaded guilty or were indicted for the things they had done. Many spent time in prison for their crimes. The Watergate episode drew attention away from the radical fringe and riveted it on politicians who might be suspect. Was morality possible, Americans asked, in the political realm? Nixon, who wanted to rebuild the Republican party and restore its strength, ended up doing serious damage to his own cause. The majority he sought was, for a time, a casualty of his troubles.

Still, there were accomplishments before the scandals brought the administration down. On the domestic side, Nixon had experimented more boldly with economic measures than other leaders facing like problems, and if his efforts did not always succeed, it may have been because of his reluctance to try any one policy for a more sustained period of time. On the foreign front, the record was even better. The policy of détente with former Communist foes was a major step forward and showed real insight into the dynamics of international affairs. Better relations with the Russians were useful to all. The opening to China was the kind of bold and dramatic step that his forerunners had been afraid to take. After two decades of tension, the slow process of normalization of relations had begun.

In a variety of ways, Nixon left his mark. Eager for power, he used some of his authority for important ends. But then, in the ultimate crisis of his political life, he undermined his own cause and brought himself down. Nixon took office in the wake of the turbulence of the 1960s with the hope of restoring stability to the United States. Instead he caused still further disruption.

SUGGESTIONS FOR FURTHER READING

On the Nixon presidency, Rowland Evans, Jr., and Robert D. Novak, *Nixon in the White House* (1972) offers the best assessment of public policy and politics in the first term. John Osborne, *The Nixon Watch* (1970) and two sequels, *The Second Year of the Nixon Watch* (1971) and *The Third Year of the Nixon Watch* (1972), provide good coverage of administration efforts and policies by a noted journalist. Richard Nixon, *RN: The Memoirs of Richard Nixon* (1978) is his own account of his life and his achievements. Garry Wills, *Nixon Agonistes: The Crisis of the Self-Made Man* (1970) is a scathing account of Nixon's earlier period. Bruce Mazlish, *In Search of Nixon* (1972) is a psychoanalytical assessment.

On politics, see Kevin Phillips, *The Emerging Republican Majority* (1969) for a sense of changing patterns. For the election of 1968, Theodore H. White, *The Making of the President, 1968* (1969) is helpful.

On foreign policy, see Henry Kissinger, *White House Years* (1979) for the detailed account of the national security adviser, then secretary of state.

For the Watergate affair, J. Anthony Lukas, *Nightmare: The Underside of the Nixon Years* (1976) provides the background necessary to understand the scandal and places that crisis in the proper perspective. Carl Bernstein and Bob Woodward, *All the President's Men* (1974) is the vivid story by two journalists of how they helped unravel the Watergate scandal and reveal White House involvement. John Dean, *Blind Ambition: The White House Years* (1976) is a memoir by one of the White House staffers involved in the crisis.

Arthur M. Schlesinger, Jr., *The Imperial Presidency* (1973) is a very useful account of the growth of presidential power that culminated in the excesses of the Nixon administration.

On women's issues in the 1970s, see William Chafe, *Women and Equality: Changing Patterns in American Culture* (1977) and Peter Gabriel Filene, *Iim/Her/Self: Sex Roles in Modern America* (1975).

chapter 8

The Search for Stability

In the years following the Watergate affair, the United States sought to reestablish its stability and its course. The political world was in a state of turmoil, and that upheaval reverberated throughout the society as a whole. Could any politician be trusted to guide the nation in an honest and straightforward manner? Could the country pursue its national interest in a way that avoided the crises of overinvolvement abroad? Could the nation heal the rifts at home that continued to threaten to tear it apart? Those were disturbing questions, ones for which there were no easy or immediate answers. The healing process would take patience and time, at the very point that new problems, domestic and foreign, emerged to trouble the people of the United States.

Guiding the process of transition was a man who suddenly found himself thrust into the presidency. As the economy spiraled downward and the world outside wondered just how the United States would right itself, Gerald Ford sought, with but limited success, to reassert the confidence that had sustained the nation in the past. He was followed two and a half years later by Jimmy Carter, a Democrat elected largely in reaction to the eight years of Republican rule. His troubled term showed that the nation remained in transition as it struggled with questions of bureaucracy, economy, and social purpose at home and abroad. Then came the Republican restoration, as Ronald Reagan took office in 1981. Appealing to a conservative constituency that resented the more radical reflections of social change, he mounted a major campaign to restrain the growth of the welfare state. He also demonstrated a determination to resist Communist pressure abroad in a way that revealed the lingering legacy of the Cold War.

THE FORD INTERLUDE

Gerald Ford assumed the presidency in the midst of what he called "our long national nightmare." He understood the implications of the scandal and the degree to which it had rocked the United States, and he sensed too that this was a time for "communication, conciliation, compromise and cooperation" both with the nation's citizens and with Congress. His own actions, however, disrupted the course he had set for himself.

Gerald Ford

As he took office, Ford was a reassuring figure, for he was, by all accounts, a decent and popular man. In a long congressional career that began after World War II, he eventually became House minority leader and was well liked by those with whom he worked. He was unassuming, unpretentious, a Middle American who clung to the traditional virtues and believed that hard work in the business world and elsewhere should be rewarded. To his followers he conveyed a sense of trust, and they felt a burst of relief when Nixon chose him as vice-president in 1973.

Still, there were some doubts about his abilities then and when he became president the next year. Lyndon Johnson's comments were the most cruel. Aware of Ford's background as a member of the University of Michigan's champion football team in the 1930s, LBJ claimed that Ford acted as if he had played too long without a helmet. He also declared, in a remark cleaned up by his aides, that "Jerry Ford is so dumb he can't walk and chew gum at the same time." Other critics were kinder, yet their barbs still made the same point. Richard Rovere, a noted journalist, wrote in the *New Yorker* when Ford became vice-president: "That he is thoroughly equipped to serve as Vice Pres-

Secretary of State Henry Kissinger with President Gerald Ford. (*Kennerly, Gerald R. Ford Library*)

ident seems unarguable; the office requires only a warm body and occasionally a nimble tongue. However . . . neither Richard Nixon nor anyone else has come forward to explain Gerald Ford's qualifications to serve as Chief Executive." Ford was hardly as limited as critics charged, yet even a close friend said, "Now I wouldn't put Jerry in charge of the Department of Creation." Ford himself in his own modest way acknowledged his limitations as he was sworn in. "I am a Ford, not a Lincoln," he said.

Those who had watched Ford in Congress over the years had a keen sense of the conservative stance he took. Fiercely partisan, he voted the Republican convictions he shared with his constituents in the Grand Rapids, Michigan, district he represented throughout his career. Over the years he had opposed federal aid to education, the poverty program, and mass transit. He had finally voted for the Civil Rights Act of 1964 and the Voting Rights Act of 1965, but only after the weaker substitutes he had favored had gone down to defeat. He had harped on the law-and-order issue before Nixon had made it his own; in 1966 Ford had declared, "How long are we going to abdicate law and order—the backbone of civilization—in favor of a soft social theory that the man who heaves a brick through your window or tosses a fire bomb into your car is simply the misunderstood and underprivileged product of a broken home?" He was a consistent proponent of spending for defense and supported Nixon in his approach to Southeast Asian affairs. In the 90th Congress, his votes fell with those of conservative Republicans and southern Democrats 63 percent of the time, and as Nixon found himself deeper and deeper in trouble, Ford was one of his most faithful followers.

Taking over as president, Ford knew that he had to act quickly to restore confidence. Yet the nation seemed to be on his side; there was a vast sense of relief that the storm had been weathered and better times lay ahead. *Time* magazine pointed to "a mood of good feeling and even exhilaration in Washington that the city had not experienced for many years."

Ford destroyed that base of support by his pardon of Richard Nixon barely a month after Nixon's resignation in disgrace. Other members of the Nixon administration faced indictment and imprisonment for their roles in the assorted misdeeds. But the former president himself, even before a hearing, was to go free for any crimes committed while in office. Though Ford obviously hoped that his magnanimous gesture would help heal the nation's wounds, in fact it only led people to wonder what kind of bargain had been struck when Nixon resigned, and it raised serious questions about the new president's judgment and ability as he faced the problems ahead. Now Ford was booed just as Johnson and Nixon before him had been, and he too had to leave speaking engagements from back doors to avoid angry demonstrators who organized to protest what he had done.

Foreign Affairs Under Ford

In foreign policy, the United States under Ford followed the basic outlines laid down in the Nixon years. The opening to China, the extrication from Asia, and the consolidation of European ties were under way, and the new administration simply maintained the sense of direction Nixon had established. Providing the guidance and the continuity as well, Henry Kissinger remained as secretary of state. He continued to play an enormously influential role, particularly in Ford's first months, in offering background, laying out options, and directing top officials toward those notions he favored himself.

The conflict in Vietnam lingered on into the spring of 1975, yet by that time the United States was out of the war and finally, after its major investment in money and lives, managed to remain uninvolved when the North Vietnamese moved to consolidate their control over the entire country in 1975. The president called for another $1 billion in aid, even as the South Vietnamese were abandoning arms and weapons in ungainly retreat, but Congress refused to go along. Republican supporters hailed Kissinger's approach to Asian affairs over a period of several years for having freed the United States from the quagmire in which it had become caught. Critics, on the other hand, pointed out, in the words of the *New Republic,* that Kissinger brought peace to Vietnam the same way Napoleon brought peace to Europe: by losing.

In other areas the administration showed an impulsive desire to act. In May 1975, Cambodian forces captured the *Mayaguez,* an American merchant ship, cruising nearby. When protests went unanswered, the United States responded by sending 350 marines to attack an island where the crew was thought to be. The Cambodians were evidently already preparing to return both ship and crew, and lives were unnecessarily lost, yet in the aftermath of the Vietnamese defeat Kissinger and Ford could claim that they had responded with vigor and strength and had not let the nation be pushed around. Their justification notwithstanding, the raid was a clear case of overkill in which the response was hardly commensurate with the risks or desired ends.

On a variety of fronts Ford encountered resistance from a Congress determined to reassert its priorities after seeing the erosion of its power to executive gain. The war in Vietnam had encouraged the growth of the imperial presidency, and looking at the consequences, Congress decided that it was time to stand firm. The War Powers Act, passed over Nixon's veto in 1973, provided the legislative branch with the authority to oversee intervention abroad and to call a halt if it saw fit. Congress asserted that power to forbid moving back into Cambodia and Vietnam and asserted its prerogative again to refuse to provide aid in Turkey and Angola, where trouble threatened too.

In some areas, however, the record was strong. With revolutions unfolding and colonial regimes falling all the time, some sort of alternative approach to African affairs was overdue, and the nation began to make overtures to black Africa that promised a new course. Strategic Arms Limitation Talks (SALT) continued and at least gave hope for nuclear disarmament at some indeterminate time. Ford accepted the Helsinki accords pledging East and West to cooperate economically and to promote the cause of human rights, continued pursuing the opening to China, and elsewhere maintained the spirit of détente, even while rejecting the term. In the Ford years American foreign policy tended to be reactive as it followed lines already laid down, yet the country remained at peace, avoided major confrontations, and continued tentatively to redefine a role for itself abroad.

Domestic Affairs

The record on the domestic front was worse. Ford took office at a turbulent time, and his administration made little progress in settling either economic or social issues by the end of his brief term. As in the foreign field, the president approached his position with a decidedly conservative bent. He had priorities and convictions that guided him, constrained him, and often threw him into confrontation with a Congress ready to assert its own authority once more.

Economic problems were most severe as Ford became president. Inflation hovered at a record rate of 11 percent a year, with consumer prices going up at an even faster pace. The unemployment level was 5.3 percent and rising, and gross national product was dropping at the same time. Home construction had stalled as interest rates soared, and the stock market was falling. Nixon had sought to bring the economy under control, but his reluctance to follow any one course through for an extended time and his increasing preoccupation with the Watergate crisis doomed his program. Inflation and stagnation proceeded along in tandem, in apparent violation of old economic rules, and that curious state of affairs led humorous commentators to come up with new descriptive terms: "stagflation" and "inflump." Not since Franklin Roosevelt assumed office in the depths of the Great Depression had a new president faced economic difficulties so severe.

Ford's approach was to try to cajole. Much like Herbert Hoover after 1929, he sought to restore confidence and to persuade the public that conditions were bound to improve. His first effort was the "Inflation Fighters" campaign, in which businesses that froze prices for six months would be awarded IF flags, and the government would pledge to buy only from firms cooperating in the plan. But the scheme was informal and short-term and soon gave way to another plan to promote citizen participation instead.

The WIN campaign called on Americans to "Whip Inflation Now." By coordinating the small personal actions of millions of people, the administration hoped to bring the problem under control. Ford asked families to wear red and white WIN lapel buttons, to save rather than spend a portion of their income, and to plant vegetable gardens—like the World War II victory gardens—to challenge rising prices in the stores. The whole plan was hokey from the start. It had no substantive machinery to back it up, hardly struck at the root causes of the problem, and soon drifted from view.

Another approach was to strike at budget deficits, perceived to be the forces fueling inflation as they grew. Substantial tax increases and slashes in federal spending were proposed, but then Congress rejected that conservative approach and endorsed an antirecession spending program of its own. Faced with a coflict in his own administration, Ford, like Nixon before him, shifted course and made what one aide called a 179-degree turn. He embraced a multi-billion-dollar tax cut and higher unemployment benefits—in short, a budget that met Keynesians' demands. There was modest recovery for a time, yet the inflation level remained high, and 8.9 percent of the population was still out of work. The economy was only marginally better when Ford left than when he assumed command.

Approaches in other areas were much the same. At a time when oil prices were rising and oil shortages were threatening to throw the entire economy out of control, the nation slogged along its traditional path with little guidance at the top. When the Federal Energy Administrator complained about the lack of a realistic policy and proposed a tax to bring consumption down, he lost his job. The alternative followed was an oil import surtax, which Congress resisted and an appeals court later ruled illegal. In the midst of political squabbling, not much of substance was done.

Tied to the energy question was Ford's view that troublesome controls mandating clean water and air had to be relaxed to make it easier to generate power. To that end, in opposition to some of his own environmental staffers, he vetoed a strip-mine control bill and expressed his disapproval of a clean air measure, too.

In the civil rights arena, he asked his own attorney general to examine the possibility of supporting antibusing advocates in a Boston court case. He later accepted the sound advice that the idea be dropped.

When he had a chance to proclaim amnesty after the Vietnam War and welcome draft evaders back into the fold, his plan was harsher than expected. Offering only conditional amnesty, it proved to be an unsuccessful approach to a problem that still remained. In six months, of 126,900 eligible, only 22,500 applied.

On all fronts Ford took a conservative approach, consistent with his view of the limitations on what government could do. He continued to see things through the eyes of his constituents of the past, even though his base was now the country at large. The sense of decency remained, but the qualifying restrictions could not be denied. His first press secretary, Jerald F. ter Horst, summed it up best of all: "If he saw a schoolkid in front of the White House who needed clothing, he'd give him the shirt off his back, literally. Then he'd go right in the White House and veto a school-lunch bill."

As a result, Ford often seemed at odds with the legislative branch. He vetoed 66 bills that came to him from the Democratic Congress, and while that rate was lower than that of FDR, it still was high indeed for someone who was trying to promote harmony in government. He rejected bills creating a consumer-protection agency and those stimulating education, housing, and health programs. Always his stress was on the passive approach. In response to his actions, Congress overrode a higher percentage of vetoes than it had since the days of Franklin Pierce in the 1850s, yet the outlines of the stalemate remained.

THE CARTER YEARS

Caretaker president that he was, Ford at first foreswore any intention of seeking reelection himself, then discovered he enjoyed the office and decided to seek a term of his own. But the aftermath of Republican scandal lingered on, and there was consequently a delay in the political reorientation that had begun to occur in the Nixon years.

The Election of 1976

As Ford campaigned in 1976, it was clear that he had liabilities he was unable to overcome. In his early months in office, perhaps as surprised as the country as a whole with the turn of events, he had not appeared "presidential," and though his image improved, he never did manage to capture the imagination of the nation with his addresses and talks. Hardly a captivating speaker, he was fond of gestures that were rubbery at best, and, in the later observation of Alistair Cooke, the noted English commentator on the American scene, "he always seemed to be battling gamely with a language he had only recently acquired."

Ford did manage to turn aside a primary challenge by Ronald Reagan, and he won the Republican nomination and faced Jimmy Carter, former governor of Georgia. Carter hoped that by capitalizing on his role as an outsider he could win America's confidence and its vote. Starting off as a relative unknown, he waged a skillful primary campaign and, to many people's surprise, became the Democratic nominee.

Carter seized on the backlash of the Watergate affair. He stressed that he was not from Washington and that, unlike many of those mired in past scandal, he was not a lawyer. Underscoring his own personal integrity, he told voters, "I will never lie to you."

Carter began with a lead but managed to dissipate it as voters questioned whether he was a real leader who could take charge. Ford hurt his own cause by his capacity for bloopers, particularly when he declared on nationwide television that there was no Communist domination in eastern Europe and seemed unaware of the trials and tribulations of the Cold War. One Chicago observer remarked that the election was like the Indianapolis 500, with people waiting to see who crashed next.

In the end, most elements of the old Democratic coalition held, and Carter finished on top. He won a 50 percent to 48 percent victory in the popular vote and secured a 297 to 240 margin in the electoral college. He was successful with labor and with black voters. He captured most of the South, after Nixon's incursions in the elections before, and did reasonably well with Catholics. He split the industrial North, but despite some losses there, he still had enough strength to secure the victory he sought.

Jimmy Carter

Jimmy Carter stood in stark contrast to his recent predecessors in the White House. Rooted in the rural South—he came from a Georgia town of 600 people—he was the first chief executive from that region in well over a hundred years. Though he had turned to politics in later years, he had not embraced the profession at the start of his career. He was a graduate of the Naval Academy, where he had been trained as a manager and an engineer. He was by nature a private person, not wholly comfortable with the pomp and incessant political activity of Washington. He hoped from the start to take a more modest approach to his office and thereby to defuse the imperial aura it had come to have. Rigorously ethical and committed to his born-again faith, he was determined to put his own stamp on his new post.

Early indicators seemed to identify Carter as a reform Democrat tied to his party's goals. When he accepted the Democratic nomination in June 1976, he demanded "an end to discrimination because of race and sex." He challenged the "political and economic elite" that had long held sway and sought a new approach to providing a solid base of support for the poor, weak, and old.

In his appointment policy he followed through on those goals. Of 1195 full-time appointees, 12 percent were women, 12 percent were black, and 4 percent were Hispanic. In the case of Hispanics and blacks, the administration was at least moving closer to reflecting the percentages in the population at large; in the case of women, there was clearly a long way to go. Still, Carter had taken important first steps. In the judicial sphere he nominated four times as many women judges as all previous presidents combined.

In other areas, however, there were signs of a more conservative approach. Carter had called for a new partnership of business, labor, and government, but that was not forthcoming. Increasingly, he lost political support, which had not been very strong from the start. The election itself had been close, and while Carter had prevailed, he had run more poorly than other Democrats in 1976. Consequently, they owed him little, and though they were ready to give him a chance at first, it was not long before support began to wane.

Carter's own proclivities came into play as Washington relationships began to break down. Surrounded by southern, largely Georgian, advisers, Carter conveyed a sense of disdain for the occupants of Capitol Hill. He was uneasy with the congressional process and found it difficult to bargain effectively in ways necessary to break legislative logjams. When persuasion failed to work, he had none of Lyndon Johnson's wheeling and dealing skills to make intransigent politicians follow his lead. He was equally uncomfortable with members of the press, and, as he began to falter, they responded by being less likely to give him the benefit of the doubt.

Carter suffered, too, from traces of scandal in an administration that prided itself on being pure. The first trouble arose when Bert Lance, director of the Office of Management and Budget, came under fire for questionable banking practices in the past. Lance was a Georgia banker who had been director of transportation there in Carter's gubernatorial days. He was Carter's trusted friend, one of the few people the president took into his confidence. The first person nominated for a Cabinet-level post, he played an important part in the administration's initial year.

Now, however, he stood accused of having allowed large bank overdrafts for insiders and double use of collateral for loans. Whatever the legalities, there was widespread suspicion that something wrong was going on and evidence enough to demand further examination. Carter came to his friend's defense, but he finally had to conclude that for political reasons Lance had to go. In the process, however, significant segments of the country began to believe that the president had tried to protect his assistant too much, and this hurt his own reputation for honesty and integrity.

The other affair involved the president's brother Billy, a flamboyant character who too often stole the spotlight. Irreverent and unpredictable, he relieved himself in public once, made anti-Semitic comments on occasion, and generally proved an embarrassment to the White House. Then he accepted over $200,000 in "loans" from friends in Libya as he cemented his relations with the proterrorist Middle Eastern state, and it appeared as though family connections were intruding on diplomatic affairs. This time it was not so much Jimmy Carter's integrity that was at stake as his judgment in allowing his brother to take advantage of his position and profit from it in questionable ways.

The Carter administration was troubled from beginning to end. The promise of fresh faces and a new start could only carry so far. The pledge to maintain standards of conduct higher than before often proved difficult to keep. Carter struggled on but had an increasingly difficult time in both the domestic and the foreign spheres.

Foreign Affairs in the Carter Years

Carter enjoyed his greatest success in foreign affairs, but even there the record was mixed. Guided by Cyrus Vance, the moderate secretary of state, and Zbigniew Brzezinski, the more hawkish national security adviser, the president made some significant breakthroughs but also suffered some humiliating defeats.

The major achievement came in his effort to help bring peace to the Middle East. The situation there had long been volatile, with Israeli and Arab forces fighting a series of bitter wars. Most recently there had been hostilities in 1967, then again in 1973. After the last war Henry Kissinger had engaged in widely touted "shuttle diplomacy" to bring about a partial disengagement, but the situation was far from resolved. Carter at first hoped to deal with Middle Eastern affairs in an international conference, but when Anwar el-Sadat of Egypt and Menachem Begin of Israel began dramatic negotiations on their own, Carter agreed to follow that approach. In September 1978, as the effort stalled, Carter invited the two Middle Eastern leaders to Camp David in the Maryland hills. There, practicing personal diplomacy of the most effective sort, Carter helped bridge the gap and provided the impetus that led to a peace treaty in March 1979. After 30 years of fighting, Israel and Egypt were no longer at war. Israel began to withdraw from the occupied Sinai peninsula, while Egypt extended diplomatic recognition and the chance for friendly relations at last.

There were other accomplishments in the late 1970s. At Carter's urging, in April 1978 the Senate finally ratified two treaties returning the Panama

Canal to Panama by the year 2000. The United States had long controlled the canal it had earlier built, yet the presence of a foreign power in Panama had irritated both Panamanians and other Latin Americans, who resented the strong power to the north. In the agreements, accepted after bitter Senate debate by the margin of a single vote, the United States reserved the right of unilateral military intervention if necessary to keep the canal clear and priority of passage if a foreign crisis ensued. Those guarantees gave the United States all the security it needed and cleared the air in Latin America at the same time.

Carter also proved successful in following up on Richard Nixon's Asian initiatives and establishing formal ties with the People's Republic of China. The United States had been moving in that direction for several years, and Carter now took the final steps. The Chinese were interested in modernization of their country and sought assistance after decades of trying to work alone. The American administration hoped to use relations with China as a way of keeping the Soviet Union on guard, even as American businessmen eagerly eyed the Chinese market of nearly a billion people. As each power pursued its own goals, three decades of friction came to an end.

Relations also improved with black Africa. There much of the credit went to Andrew Young, an articulate and outspoken black minister and former congressman whom Carter appointed ambassador to the United Nations. As new African states emerged and black interests finally came to the fore, Young helped persuade the president that the United States should stand back and let matters take their course. Young played an important part in shaping a less abrasive American policy, even as he forged closer ties with representatives of the developing lands. When Carter visited Nigeria and Liberia in March 1978, hundreds of thousands of people lined the streets to cheer a new friend.

With the Soviet Union, however, the administration traveled a rockier course. The Russian-American relationship, the main diplomatic concern since World War II, encountered major ups and downs in the latter part of the decade. Carter assumed office with détente at high tide. In his first year in office he could declare that the United States had finally escaped its "inordinate fear of Communism" and could further cement solid ties with the Soviet state. But then administration initiatives complicated the task, and Soviet ventures in turn finally left the more moderate policy in shreds.

One complicating factor was Carter's honest dedication to a policy of human rights. UN pronouncements had long echoed the theme, and it had been most recently underscored in the 1975 Helsinki accords. Now Carter called his human rights approach not simply a declaration but "the soul of our foreign policy." No compromise was possible, he asserted. "Our commitment to human rights must be absolute." Noble as the new campaign was, it proved difficult to put into practice. The president did establish a Bureau of Human Rights in the State Department to institutionalize the more assertive approach. He also spoke out in support of Soviet dissidents under fire for expressing their views, but while that demonstrated to the world at large the depth of the commitment he felt, it also weakened the fragile fabric of détente.

In particular, it contributed to the early trouble in reaching agreement on arms limitation, through a SALT II treaty between the two major powers. Misjudging the Russians as his administration took over the negotiations that had been proceeding in the Ford years, he offered new weapons-reduction proposals that went a good deal further than before. That jolt, coupled with Russian irritation at Carter's public support for internal critics of Soviet affairs, threw matters into a tailspin and delayed progress for a year. In the end, though, Carter backed off, patient negotiation triumphed, and a SALT II agreement was reached in Vienna in June 1979. Far more complicated than the first Strategic Arms Limitation Treaty, it had avid proponents and opponents as it awaited ratification by the Senate of the United States.

That process was immeasurably complicated by the Soviet invasion of Afghanistan six months later in December 1979. The Russians had exercised dominance over Afghanistan for the past year and a half and were now moving to assert more effective control. Carter responded by calling the Soviet action the most serious threat to world peace since World War II. He exaggerated, of course, for while the invasion could not be condoned, it was certainly no worse than Russian moves elsewhere in the world in the 35 years since the war. Still, in response the president postponed presenting SALT II to the Senate, sought more defense spending, and called for an American, and possibly world, boycott of the Olympic Games scheduled for Moscow in the summer of the next year. The ineffectual boycott took place, SALT II sat on the back burner, and by the end of the Carter administration it seemed that détente was effectively dead.

If Carter stumbled in his handling of Soviet-American affairs, he fell flat in his effort to defuse a major crisis with Iran. The long-standing problem was the shah of Iran, whom Americans had long considered a friend and defender of stability in the Persian Gulf. Carter himself took that approach when he visited Tehran at the end of 1977. He and others, however, overlooked the corruption and abuse in that Middle Eastern state. Ironically, Carter's assertion of human rights helped focus discontent on the misdeeds of the shah. Opposed by fervent religious forces on the one hand and radical critics on the other, the shah lost control in January 1979 and had to leave his land. In his place now sat the Ayatollah Ruholla Khomeini, an old Islamic priest who had been living in exile in Paris and who took over the leadership of a new Islamic regime.

Carter's major blunder came when, on the advice of Henry Kissinger and others, he admitted the shah to the United States for medical care in October 1979. Within a few days, armed and angry Iranian students seized the American embassy in Tehran and held 53 Americans hostage to ensure that a series of demands were met. Foreign-service personnel have always faced the risk of attack, but their capture became a national cause. Embattled already on all fronts, Carter helped focus attention on affairs in Iran, and citizens around the nation responded to his lead. He broke relations, froze Iranian assets in the United States, and sought to stand firm in the face of mounting pressure at home and abroad. An ill-fated commando raid failed to bring the hostages home, and the administration instead had to engage in protracted negotiations to try to secure their release. In the end an agreement was reached, but not until the day Carter left office were the prisoners finally freed. The Iranian crisis preoccupied Carter in his last year and was but one indication of the difficulty he had on all fronts.

Domestic Affairs

Every bit as troublesome were his ventures in domestic matters, particularly in economic affairs. Inflation had been on the rise for over a decade when Carter took power, but after a recession from 1974 to 1976, the rate hovered at 4.8 percent and seemed under control. Afraid of a return of the recession, Carter pursued an expansionary policy as the government spent more than taxes brought in. To help meet mounting deficits, which reached peacetime records in the Carter years, the Federal Reserve Board authorized increasing the money supply, and before long inflation, in double-digit figures, was wholly out of control. Carter sought to counter in 1979 by slowing down the economy and cutting the deficit to more manageable levels. The cuts fell largely on social programs and only demonstrated the distance Carter had put between himself and reform Democratic goals.

Yet even his effort to cut back was not enough. In January 1980, when Carter released a new federal budget showing still high total spending levels, the financial community suddenly realized how desperate the situation had become. Bond prices fell and interest rates mounted, and there seemed no sure sense of what to do. No longer was there confidence that this was but a passing phase that would be over in a year or two. The mood of optimism seemed irretrievably lost. "To say that there was any economic policy is almost an act of charity," economist Robert J. Samuelson noted as Carter left office. "What was most consistent about the Carter administration was its inability to make a proposal in January that could survive until June." The economic problems were not of Carter's making, to be sure, but he seemed only to make them worse. Like his predecessors, he was not really sure what to do, and his vacillating course helped bring him down.

He was similarly troubled in his effort to deal with the mounting energy crunch in the United States. Again the problem was not of his making; the Arab world had been increasing oil prices inexorably since 1973, and there was no end in sight. Yet a growing dependence on foreign oil—over 40 percent of the oil used was imported by the end of the decade—was a cause for alarm. The first scare, as a result of the Arab embargo in 1973, had led to no long-range policy, as the United States responded on a haphazard basis and hoped the problem would go away.

In April 1977 Carter presented a full-scale energy program, which he called the "moral equivalent of war." Critics used the acronym MEOW to describe the plan, and after his agressive start, the president himself seemed to back off. Proposals became bogged down in Congress, not to emerge for 26 months. Eventually the program committed the nation to move from oil dependence to reliance on coal, possibly even on sun and wind, and involved as well the hope that a new synthetic fuel corporation could help meet energy needs.

Nuclear power, another alternative, seemed less attractive as costs rose and accidents occurred.

Parts of the Carter program made sense, yet on balance the president never conveyed a sense of leadership. Carter seemed to reverse course often and to wander from one point to another instead of taking a consistent approach. Too often he appeared to have no legislative strategy at all, no priorities that he would communicate to Congress and then follow up as he took command. As columnist Tom Wicker observed at the end of Carter's four years, "He never established a politically coherent administration." That was largely because Carter was less comfortable as a politician, more comfortable as a problem solver and engineer. Like Herbert Hoover, he was a technocrat in the White House; like Hoover, his approach was wanting.

Carter managed to alienate not only Congress but also the public at large. A man with a razor-sharp mind, he could not communicate easily with his constituents and win them to his side. Though he sensed at first the nation's post-Vietnam wariness of inspiration and sought to take a more subdued approach, in time he realized that his office demanded more, yet he was never able to spark the public mood. He was, Alistair Cooke later observed, "the most intelligent, best informed and dullest Presidential speaker since Woodrow Wilson." With his singsong speech and humorless approach, he provided no spark at all. As journalist and author Hedrick Smith noted as early as the end of his first year, "His greatest shortcoming so far has been his failure to rouse the nation with the lift of a driving dream." That shortcoming only hurt more as time went on. By the summer of 1980 his disapproval rating had reached 77 percent, making him the most unpopular incumbent president in recent American history.

THE REAGAN REVOLUTION

Though Jimmy Carter had hoped that his election would herald the reestablishment of Democratic control, after four years the American public seemed ready for still another change. Watergate was now past, and the Republicans regrouped in an effort to point the nation in a more conservative direction.

The Election of 1980

Carter sought reelection in 1980, and after a struggle with Senator Edward M. Kennedy, brother of the slain president, Carter won the Democratic nomination again. But in the general election he had to face Ronald Reagan, who won the Republican nomination at last, as well as Congressman John Anderson and a number of others making challenges of their own, and for Carter the going was rough.

Reagan, an actor, then governor of California, inherited the conservative mantle of Barry Goldwater and the ever-growing right. His soothing manner notwithstanding, Reagan had a gift for making inapproriate remarks that detractors loved to cite. In 1976, as he bowed out of the campaign for president, a *New York Times* review pointed to his earlier comment on the poor scuffling for free food: "It's too bad we can't have an epidemic of botulism." It quoted his prior remark on Vietnam: "We should declare war on North Vietnam. We could pave the whole place over by noon and be home for dinner." In 1980, at the Democratic convention, Reagan's comment that fascism was "the basis for the New Deal" was held up for scorn, as was his claim that 80 percent of all air pollution was caused by plants and trees. But Reagan could be more persuasive than that, as when he called the Carter administration "a litany of broken promises." He also showed a certain wit when he quibbled with Carter over economic terms: "I'm talking in human terms and he is hiding behind a dictionary. If he wants a definition, I'll give him one. A recession is when your neighbor loses his job. A depression is when you lose yours. A recovery is when Jimmy Carter loses his."

In the campaign, Reagan began with an enormous lead and held it till the end. The Iranian crisis continued to rankle, and the economic crisis did Carter in. In 1976 Carter had asked, in his campaign autobiography, "Why not the best?" but as he held himself out again in 1980, a former speech writer commented that his performance as president showed why that was not enough. In November Reagan scored a landslide victory, garnering a 51 to 41 percent popular margin and a 489 to 49 triumph in electoral votes. He also led the Republican party to control of the Senate for the first time in years. Reagan won the Northeast, the South, and most areas in between. He split the Jewish

President Ronald Reagan soon after taking office in 1981. (*UPI/Bettmann Newsphotos*)

vote and the working-class vote, and though he missed out on the black vote, which went to Carter as before, he had more than enough strength elsewhere to carry him along.

Reagan and the Outside World

In the field of foreign affairs, Reagan was determined to assert American interests more strongly than Carter. Rooted in the Cold War tradition, he believed in spending freely for defense and in standing up to the Soviet Union in pursuit of American goals. He criticized his predecessor for a policy of aimless drifting and was determined to take a more pointed approach. To assist him in the formulation and conduct of foreign policy, Reagan appointed General Alexander Haig, former chief of staff in the Watergate White House, who had managed to survive the scandal and now sought to exercise authority on his own. When Haig proved overly contentious and ambitious, George Shultz, secretary of the Treasury under Nixon, took over as secretary of state.

Reagan moved quickly in a number of areas. Though he spoke of economy on government, he proposed unprecedented defense spending. Over a five-year period the administration sought a military budget of $1.5 trillion dollars to expand American capabilities. Arguing that the nation was otherwise vulnerable, the president insisted that spending for arms—both nuclear and conventional—had to increase.

The administration also took the view that a nuclear war could be fought and won. Discounting the scenario that showed cataclysmic destruction in the event of nuclear war, it insisted that the nation could indeed prevail. Asked whether American institutions could survive a nuclear struggle with the Soviet Union, Louis O. Giuffrida, head of the Federal Emergency Management Agency, said, "I think they would eventually, yeah. As I say, ants eventually build another anthill." Deputy Under Secretary of Defense for Strategic and Theater Nuclear Forces T. K. Jones revived the dormant notion of civil defense. "Dig a hole, cover it with a couple of doors and then throw three feet of dirt on top . . . ," he advised. "It's the dirt that does it. . . . If there are enough shovels to go around, everybody's going to make it."

While promoting defense spending and nuclear superiority, the administration abandoned the SALT approach to arms reduction and argued that a different alternative was necessary to preserve American might. The president proposed that Russia destroy certain missiles in return for an American pledge not to deploy new weapons in Europe, but the Soviet Union balked at that wide-open suggestion so different from the careful and detailed negotiation that had accompanied all past steps. On both sides, the arms race continued and military budgets soared.

In its first few years in office, the Reagan administration showed growing concern with instability in Central America, particularly in El Salvador, where left-wing guerrillas fought against a repressive right-wing regime. Fearful that another nation might follow Cuba's Marxist example, the United States increased its aid to the antirevolutionary El Salvador government, heedless of a similar course followed years before in Vietnam. It also channeled support to Nicaraguans in exile who vowed to overthrow the Socialist government in that country.

In foreign affairs the Reagan team proved more rigidly ideological than other recent administrations. It took stands that invited confrontation and often echoed approaches taken in the early Cold War years. Like Jimmy Carter, Ronald Reagan had no past grounding in diplomatic issues, but he had strong convictions, and the policies that unfolded reflected those views.

Domestic Affairs

Reagan had equally strong views about domestic policy. Rooted in Middle America, he fervently believed in the American dream. He looked back nostalgically at a world of heroes and heroic deeds, where a man could make his own mark through his own efforts. He had played and won by the rules of the system; others should do the same.

Faced with a collapsing economy that seemed out of control and a federal establishment that continued to grow, Reagan moved to reverse the twentieth-century movement toward what conservatives charged was the federal government's management of every aspect of American life. Upon taking office, he announced that he intended to reduce government spending by eliminating "waste, fraud and abuse." Concerned about the federal deficit, he committed himself to a balanced budget before the end of his term and demanded cuts, particularly in social programs he viewed as unnecessary.

At the heart of his program was the notion of supply-side economics, which held that the reduction of taxes would encourage business expansion, and that in turn would lead to a larger supply of goods to help stimulate the system as a whole. "Reaganomics," promoted during the campaign, promised an economic system that would work.

To allow for tax reduction and military expansion, the administration began to make huge cuts in social programs. Public-service jobs, mandated under the Comprehensive Employment and Training Act, were eliminated. Unemployment compensation was cut back. Medicare patients were required to pay more for their share of health costs. Welfare benefits were lowered, and food stamp allocations were reduced.

The Republicans worried about entitlements—programs that assisted Americans who met a basic standard of eligibility. Costs for social security, the largest of those programs, had been rocketing, and there was genuine fear that commitments might not be able to be maintained. When Reagan hinted at cuts there, however, a howl of protest ensued, and he dropped the issue until a later time.

While making social cuts, the administration also managed to push through its tax-cut package. As finally passed, a 5 percent cut went into effect on October 1, 1981, with further 10 percent cuts set for July 1, 1982, and July 1, 1983. Americans enjoyed the added funds the cuts gave, yet Reaganomics did not seem to work as planned. Largely as a result of the huge defense expenditures, the annual budget deficit grew even larger—approaching $200 billion—and led Congress to push for a number of tax increases as a way of trying to impose some control. Yet critics questioned whether that makeshift approach would help much in the end.

Related to the economic program was Reagan's pronounced effort to reduce the regulatory apparatus of the federal government. The president was dedicated to cutting programs wherever he could, for both financial and philosophical reasons. Part of that effort involved his promotion of a "New Federalism" that projected a massive shift in responsibilities from the federal to the state level. Critics charged that the proposal was simply a backhanded way of moving programs from one place to another and then eliminating the funds. His support notwithstanding, the program never really got off the ground.

As president, Reagan took a decidedly conservative approach to social issues as well. He willingly accepted the support of the New Right and spoke out for prayer in the schools. He endorsed the campaign against abortion. He was less supportive of minority rights and appeared dubious about affirmative-action programs. Though questions of economy and budget took precedence, particularly in his first few years, he made clear where his sympathies lay. He knew the constituency to which he wanted to appeal.

The Election of 1984

In 1984, Ronald Reagan sought a second presidential term. His opponent was Walter Mondale, who had served as Jimmy Carter's vice-president. Mondale received the Democratic nomination only after a bitter primary campaign with the Reverend Jesse Jackson, a black activist, and Gary Hart, a liberal senator from Colorado. Mondale tried to unite his fragmented party by boldly supporting Geraldine Ferraro for the vice-presidency, and she became the first woman ever to receive a major party's nomination for one of its top posts.

Reagan relied on his show business background as he ran an upbeat, buoyant campaign. His appearances sometimes included fireworks and swarms of tiny parachutes holding miniature American flags. His unofficial campaign song was "I'm Proud to Be an American." His message to audiences was: "You ain't seen nothing yet."

Mondale hammered away at the huge and growing budget deficit. He criticized the president's approach to foreign policy while contending that he could be equally tough toward the Soviet Union. He claimed Reagan was following a "cocoon strategy" by relying on media blitzes rather than dealing with the issues that troubled the land. Mondale's approach proved unsuccessful. He seemed colorless and unexciting himself, and by mid-September he trailed Reagan in the polls by 18 percentage points.

Mondale's campaign enjoyed a momentary upswing after the first televised debate. Invoking the image of John F. Kennedy, Mondale appeared articulate and aggressive. Reagan, by contrast, seemed unsure of himself and tired by the end of the debate. Viewers wondered whether the 73-year-old president was fit for another term. Reagan, however, regained command in the second debate. He defused the age issue when it arose by smiling and saying, "I am not going to exploit my opponent's youth and inexperience, not at all."

In the voting, Reagan scored a landslide victory. He received 59 percent of the popular vote to Mondale's 41 percent, and enjoyed a 525 to 13 vote in his favor in the electoral college. He lost only Minnesota, Mondale's home state, and the District of Columbia. Although disappointed, the Democrats took some consolation in regaining two seats in the Senate and maintaining control of the House of Representatives. Reagan seemed to have scored a personal victory as millions of Americans endorsed his soothing and optimistic approach. Whether his victory heralded a more general shift in favor of the Republican party remained to be seen.

THE CONTINUING STRUGGLE FOR EQUALITY

Though support for social reform was not always forthcoming from the White House, groups that had struggled for equality in past years were not about to cease their efforts. The women's movement remained very much alive, as did the campaigns for the rights of blacks, Hispanics, and Native Americans.

The Women's Movement

Women viewed the accomplishments of the women's movement with a sense of satisfaction. Betty Friedan, whose book *The Feminine Mystique* had reflected a pervasive discontent two decades before, observed in 1983, "I am still awed by the revolution that book helped spark. . . . I keep being surprised, as the changes the women's movement set in motion continue to play themselves out in our lives—the enormous and mundane, subtle and not so subtle, delightful, painful, immediate, far-reaching, paradoxical, inexorable and probably irreversible changes in women's lives—and in men's."

Changes had indeed occurred. Affirmative action had made jobs for women more accessible. Women made tremendous gains in such diverse fields as coal mining, where the percentage of women rose from 0.001 to 11.4 between 1973 and 1979, and banking, where the percentage increased from 17.6 to 33.6 in the ten years after 1970. Similar advances could be seen in other areas. According to the U.S. Census Bureau, in 1980, 45 percent of mothers with preschool children held jobs away from home. That figure was four times greater than it had been 30 years before. More day-care centers existed, allowing women greater flexibility in getting out and finding work. At the same time, fathers were playing a greater role in their children's lives.

Women now enjoyed greater opportunities to train for the professions. Title 9 of the Education Amendments of 1972, which barred sex bias in federally assisted education activities and programs, had a profound effect. Colleges now admitted far more women to law, medical, dental, and business schools and dropped restrictions that kept husbands and wives from teaching at the same schools. The same measure changed the nature of intercollegiate athletics. Big Ten schools, which spent hundreds of thousands of dollars on men's programs, in 1974 spent an average of $3500 a year on women's sports. That was no longer legal, and while complete equity remained a distant goal, women got a greater share. By 1980, 30 percent of the participants in intercollegiate athletics were women, twice the total before Title 9 had become law.

In the tenth anniversary issue of *Ms.* magazine, in the summer of 1982, founding editor Gloria Steinem noted the differences a decade made. "Now, we have words like 'sexual harassment' and 'battered women,'" she wrote. "Ten years ago, it was just called 'life.'" Other examples followed: "Now, rape is defined as a crime of violence—and victims are less likely to be raped again by the law." Perhaps best of all: "Now, we are becoming the men we wanted to marry. Ten years ago, we were trained to marry a doctor, not be one."

The signs of change were evident on all fronts. Thanks to the activities of Steinem and countless others, an old girls' network, like the proverbial old boys' network, began to develop, with connections that helped ambitious women get ahead.

In politics women were more active than ever before. Jane Byrne succeeded Richard Daley as mayor of Chicago. In Houston and San Francisco women held the same office. Far more women served in state legislatures and in Congress in Washington. Women made their voices heard in other ways, too. In the election of 1980, analysts observed a gender gap. Women, for the first time, voted significantly differently than men. Men voted for Ronald Reagan by a margin of 56 to 36. Women, alarmed by his hard-line foreign policy and opposition to the Equal Rights Amendment, voted for him by a much smaller margin of 46 to 45.

In late 1982 a film about a man who dressed as a woman to get a job became one of the major hits of the season. *Tootsie,* starring Dustin Hoffman, was a funny film with a serious side. Posing as Dorothy Michaels, Michael Dorsey, a rather unpleasant man, challenged sexual harassment, argued with male chauvinists at work, and became a real battler for women's rights. In the process, Dorothy came across as a much nicer person than Michael had ever been. When he finally reverted to being himself, Betty Friedan noted, "the sensitivity he acquired, sharing woman's experience, made him a much better, stronger, more tender man."

Yet women still had to worry about their roles and rights. Despite changes in their portrayal by the media, something of the sex-appeal image remained. Women forged new careers but still had to struggle against the old stereotypes. They were increasingly disturbed about pay differentials. In 1982 women employed full time received 62 cents for every dollar paid to men. Increasingly, they began to demand not simply equal pay for equal work but equal pay for different jobs that had comparable value.

Women who were relieved when the Supreme Court legalized abortion in 1973 discovered that the issue remained very much alive. The number of abortions increased dramatically in the decade following the decision. By some estimates there were 10 million lawful abortions, or one for every three births. In response, "pro-life" forces mobilized as never before. Nellie Gray organized a march on Washington every January 22 to call attention to the anniversary of the *Roe* v. *Wade* decision. "It's murder, pure and simple," she said. "Abortion means killing babies." Opponents lobbied to cut off federal funds that allowed the poor to obtain the abortions the better-off could pay for themselves; they insisted that abortions be performed in hospitals and not in less expensive clinics; and they worked to reverse the original decision itself. Though the Supreme Court, which included the first woman in its history, reaffirmed its judgment in 1983, protest continued.

Agitation over the ERA became more intense. Ratification of the Equal Rights Amendment had been taken for granted after its favorable vote in Congress in 1972, so much so that no ratification strategy was thought necessary. Despite its quick ratification by a large number of states, the momentum stalled before the required number had been reached. Even with an extension in the deadline granted in 1979, the amendment failed to generate the necessary support. Phyllis Schlafly and others maintained their highly effective opposition campaign and gained the support of women who felt threatened by the changes they saw occurring and of men, particularly in state legislatures, who had long been uncomfortable with the women's movement as a whole. By mid-1982 ERA was dead. The extended deadline had passed, and ratification would have to await reintroduction of the measure.

Women could nonetheless applaud their gains. Yet some worried that too great a sense of self-satisfaction could make further change harder to obtain. A growing number of young women who enjoyed the fruits of the movement sought to avoid the feminist label and shunned involvement in militant campaigns. Others remained active, convinced that only with continued pressure would further change occur.

The Movement for Black Rights

Like the women's movement, the black movement pressed forward, but progress came more slowly than in the decade before. Although gains were evident, there were also growing signs of reluctance in the society to maintain the pace of progress, as well as growing efforts on the part of groups that felt threatened to reverse the direction of the past few years.

On all fronts, blacks became more visible. Between 1970 and 1980 the black population increased 17.3 percent, almost three times the rate of increase of the white population. Federal affirmative-action guidelines brought more blacks into schools and universities, into professions and industries. Black political candidates won mayoral elections in major cities, including Detroit, Los Angeles, and Chicago. In the election of 1982, the number of black representatives in Congress increased.

Still, in many areas, entrance to a school or profession did not lead to advancement. "The issue in the 1980s is not so much getting black people in the door or onto that first rung," said Roderick Plummer, an official at Chemical Bank. "It's about pushing people through the ranks, giving them policymaking involvement and the responsibilities and the pay that go along with it." Blacks in positions of prominence often found themselves on the spot. Horace Edwards, the black chairman of Arco Pipeline Company, observed that "what I have found in my career at Arco is being constantly required to prove my worth, over and over again." At almost every crucial juncture, "a new boss or a supervisor starts with some preconceived ideas" that had roots in racial prejudice.

Other difficulties came as whites protested the consequences of racial progress in their own lives. In 1973 and 1974 Allan Bakke, a white, applied for admission to the medical school at the University of California at Davis. Rejected both times, he sued on the grounds that a racial quota reserving 16 of 100 places for minority-group applicants was a form of reverse discrimination and violated the Civil Rights Act of 1964. In 1978 the Supreme Court ordered Bakke's admission to the medical school, but in a complex ruling involving six separate opinions, the Court upheld the consideration of race in admissions policies, even while arguing that rigid quotas could no longer be imposed. The decision received widespread attention but failed to make much difference. Black enrollment in universities peaked at 9.3 percent of the total in 1976 and by 1980 had dropped to 9.1 percent, just what it had been in 1973. Affirmative-action programs continued in much the same way they had operated before.

Throughout the United States, even as progress slowed, signs of solving America's ancient racial dilemma occurred. In mid-1983, in Indianola, in the heart of the Mississippi delta, blues artist B. B. King returned to a festive homecoming. Playing for the people he grew up with, his audience cut across race and class lines. In the socially stratified town, where racial discrimination remained, blacks and whites came together for the first time to listen to the music and dance to the blues. It was hardly a crucial moment in the larger order of things, but it was a reflection that patterns were shifting at last.

Hispanic-Americans

Hispanics in the United States, their numbers swelling, began to play an increasingly important role in American affairs. According to the 1980 census, there were 14.6 million Hispanics, up 61 percent from the 9 million a decade before, and the figures did not include the millions in the country illegally. Hispanics made up the fastest-growing minority group and promised soon to overtake the blacks as the largest minority.

Despite population gains, economic conditions remained grim for many Hispanics. While the median family income for non-Hispanic families reached $16,284 in 1979, for Mexican-Americans it was $11,421, and for Puerto Ricans about $8300.

Language difficulties and other problems of adjustment plagued Hispanic children in the schools. Richard Rodriguez, an articulate Chicano who went on to do graduate work in English, recalled the shock at coming to school and having to cope with a new language. His experience paralleled that of newcomers from virtually all immigrant groups throughout the history of the United States. "All my classmates certainly must have been uneasy on that first day of school," he wrote. "But I was astonished." He heard the nun in the parochial school he was attending pronounce his name in English—the first time that had ever happened—and found he had to cope with new questions that had never concerned him before.

Richard Rodriguez learned English well—so well, in fact, that he became caught up in school and in the race to succeed. Like other immigrant children, he found himself growing away from his family, using one form of expression with his parents and relatives and another with the world outside. In time he came to understand how "I had been educated away from the culture of my mother and father," how as he moved ahead there was no moving back; that was the price that had to be paid.

There was a movement to implement bilingual education in the schools to make the educational process more meaningful to students who spoke Spanish in their daily lives. Despite such efforts, many Hispanics still encountered serious difficulties. In the nation as a whole, only 30 percent of the Hispanic high school students graduated, and less than 7 percent completed college.

Still, there were indications of change. Affirmative-action efforts helped Hispanics as well as blacks, and a growing network of Hispanic educators and programs promised to ease the way for future students. "Ten years ago, there was no national Chicano academic community," declared Arturo Madrid, president of the National Chicano Council on Higher Education, in 1982. "Now we have a professional presence in higher education." A colleague estimated that there were 5000 Chicano faculty members in 1980, compared to 2000 a decade before. Chicanos found themselves, like members of other minority groups, moving from the ranks of the "missing persons" to positions as "the onlys," where, Madrid noted, they served as "the only Chicano dean of this or the only Chicano professor of that." But in time, as more joined forces, their voices were better heard.

In the same way, Hispanics began to play a greater political role. Rudy Ortiz served as mayor of San Antonio in 1978. In 1983 Colorado state legislator Federico Peña was elected mayor of Denver. In New Mexico Governor Toney Anaya called himself the nation's highest elected Hispanic and moved to create a national "Hispanic force." As the United States neared the national election in 1984, recognition grew that large concentrations of Hispanics in states like California, Texas, Florida, and New York could make a major electoral difference. That gave them a political influence they had not enjoyed earlier.

Native Americans

The Native American community also became more vocal. Continuing to show the militance that had surfaced in the late 1960s and early 1970s, Indians served notice that they were serious about looking out for themselves.

In the decade between 1970 and 1980, the Native American population increased by 72 percent. Roughly half of those continued to live on reservations, but even they learned to function in non-Indian society as they asserted rights long ignored. From the few hundred Indians in college in the early 1960s, the number swelled to tens of thousands by 1980. That created a network of educated Indians in industries and professions, as well as a mood of determination to press on with tribal and personal goals.

One major struggle involved an Indian effort to hold on to a land base. For years tribes had been pushed off their land by federal and state governments and had been able to do little to preserve what they had. In the 1970s, when New York State tried to condemn a section of Seneca land for a superhighway running through part of the Allegany Reservation, Senecas went to court. In 1981 the state finally agreed to give them state land elsewhere and a cash settlement in return for an easement through the reservation. That decision gave notice that land seizure could not be taken for granted and provided encouragement for Indian efforts in Montana, Wyoming, Utah, New Mexico, and Arizona to resist similar incursions.

In the same way, Native Americans reasserted long-abused water rights. In the northern plains, as in the southwestern desert, water was in increasingly short supply, and fierce struggles raged in the 1970s and 1980s over that precious commodity. As farmers and ranchers fought larger conglomerates, the Indians insisted that their voices, too, be heard. One such struggle involved Pyramid Lake in the Sierra Nevadas. That lake, which explorer John C. Frémont once termed "a gem in the mountains," served the Paiute Indians, but their rights notwithstanding, they watched the lake shrink and fish die when a federal irrigation project went into effect years before.

Native Americans could take some encouragement from a landmark water-rights case in 1973, in which a federal court ruled that the government must implement its obligation as trustee to protect Indian property. In the 1980s, 70 years after the filing of the first lawsuit, the issue finally reached the Supreme Court. The Justice Department acknowledged injustice done in the past and began work to help bring about some form of change. With a growing determination not to be turned away, the Paiute effort reflected the larger Indian effort in the United States. For, as that case dragged on, other struggles around the country showed that water rights were fundamentally important to Indian tribes and could no longer be denied.

Another effort involved the reassertion of fishing rights. In the Northwest, as in other parts of the nation, Nisquallies, Puyallups, Muckleshoots, Chippewas, and others argued that they had long-standing rights to fish where they chose, without worrying about the intrusive regulations of the states. Despite pressure from other fishermen, a series of court cases provided Indians with at least some of the protection they sought on the basis of old treaty rights and once again showed that aggressive pursuit of their own goals could make a difference.

NEW MOVEMENTS AND GROUPS

As older groups continued their campaigns for equality, other groups formed and made their voices heard. New immigrants arrived in America with needs of their own. Consumer advocates stepped up the campaign that had just begun. Vietnam veterans demanded material and emotional support after their sacrifice in the war. Homosexuals sought the same freedom from discrimination that women and racial minorities wanted. Some of those groups were more successful than others, both in achieving their own goals and in parrying the thrusts of groups that opposed the changes they sought.

The New Immigrants

In the 1970s and 1980s, the United States admitted new immigrants from a variety of foreign nations. The Immigration and Nationality Act amendments of 1965—part of the Great Society—authorized America to accept immigrants impartially from all parts of the world, not primarily from western Europe according to the system created in the 1920s. Between 1930 and 1960, 80 percent of America's immigrants came from Europe or Canada. Between 1977 and 1979, 16 percent came from those areas, while 40 percent each came from Asia and Latin America.

Foreign crises fueled the influx. From 1975 on, the United States accepted more than half a million Indo-Chinese refugees. In 1980, more than 160,000 arrived. That same year, the nation admitted 125,000 Cubans and Haitians who arrived in southern Florida. The total of all immigrants in 1980 was 808,000, the highest in 60 years.

Millions of others arrived illegally. As Latin American nations grew and as economic conditions deteriorated, more and more people looked to the United States for relief. In the mid-1970s, Leonard Chapman, commissioner of the Immigration and Naturalization Service, estimated that there might be 12 million foreigners in the nation illegally. Although official estimates were lower, Attorney General William French Smith declared in 1983, "Simply put, we've lost control of our own borders."

The United States was a melting pot once again. In Los Angeles, Koreans, Vietnamese, and Cambodians competed for jobs and apartments with Mexicans, blacks, and Anglos, just as other groups contended with one another in New York City in the early years of the twentieth century. Throughout the country, in Miami, in Houston, in Brooklyn, the languages heard in the schools and on the streets changed, as did the very complexion of the society.

Not well organized, the new immigrants usually began with any jobs they could find as they started the slow process of working their way up the economic ladder. They took whatever help was available, and they became an increasingly visible part of the United States.

Consumer and Environmental Activists

Other groups were more vocal as they pursued their own interests. The consumer movement, sparked by Ralph Nader in the 1960s, continued its efforts despite Republican attempts to dismantle the regulatory apparatus that had been erected. For consumer advocates, such actions caused serious concern. In 1982, for example, Congress rejected a relatively weak Federal Trade Commission rule that would have required used-car dealers to tell prospective buyers of known problems with the automobiles being considered. Opponents of the

FTC measure contended that it would have raised the price of a used car. In the face of press protest and consumer criticism over that and similar issues, Congress slowly began to shift course. The Consumer Federation of America proved willing to play politics, and 77 of 94 congressional candidates it endorsed won. By early 1983 pollster Louis Harris announced to a meeting of the Consumer Assembly that by a 55 to 36 percent margin, the public rejected "the notion that the consumer movement has run out of steam." By an 80 to 15 percent margin, Harris went on, Americans felt that "unless they keep fighting, consumer groups may begin to lose what they have achieved."

Still other activists continued to agitate about the state of the environment. Fears of pollution and contamination grew stronger as people learned more about substances they had taken for granted in the past. In 1978 the public became alarmed about the harmful effects of toxic chemicals dumped in the Love Canal section of Niagara Falls, New York. A few years later attention focused on dioxin, one of the poisons in the Love Canal case, which now surfaced in other areas in even more concentrated form. Dioxin—a by-product of the manufacture of herbicides, plastics, and wood preservatives—remained active when released in the environment and seemed almost to defy control. Thousands of times more potent than cyanide, it was one of the most deadly substances ever made.

Dioxin gained national attention as a result of problems in Times Beach, Missouri. The suburb of St. Louis had sprayed its unpaved streets with waste oil in the early 1970s as a way of controlling dust. The oil later proved to be contaminated, and, after floods at the end of 1982, the contamination spread throughout the town. Finally, the Environmental Protection Agency ordered a $33 million buy-out of all homes and businesses in the area. But the problem did not stop there. Other sites in Missouri, New Jersey, and California became the scenes of scares. Americans began to wonder just what regions might be safe.

Acid rain was another source of concern. In the eastern United States and southeastern Canada, industrial and automobile emissions had contaminated the atmosphere enough to kill fish, corrode building surfaces, and damage the

Dead fish from Lake Michigan washed ashore in Chicago. (*AP/Wide World*)

leaves of plants and trees. After extensive monitoring of ecological disruptions, the National Academy of Sciences made the connection between the troubles and polluted rain. Only later, in mid-1983, did the Reagan administration acknowledge the problem, but it had no easy answer about what to do.

Environmental activists were also concerned about nuclear power. Once hailed as the solution to all of America's energy needs, nuclear plants fell on hard times, particularly after a disastrous accident at a reactor at Three Mile Island, Pennsylvania, in March 1979. There a faulty pressure-relief valve led to a loss of coolant that was initially undetected by operators at the plant, who refused to believe indicators showing something seriously wrong. Part of the nuclear core became uncovered, part began to disintegrate, and the surrounding steam and water became highly radioactive. An explosion releasing radioactivity into the atmosphere appeared possible, and thousands of residents of the area began to flee. The scenario of nuclear disaster depicted that year by Jack Lemmon and Jane Fonda in the film *The China Syndrome* seemed more real all the time. The worst never occurred, and the period of maximum danger passed, but the plant remained shut down and filled with radioactive debris, a monument to a form of energy now deemed more potentially destructive than any ever known.

In the aftermath of the Three Mile Island episode, public confidence in nuclear energy fell. Long-standing doubts spread, as nuclear power proved far more expensive and dangerous than advertised. In the period after 1972, 102 projected plants were canceled, and no new plants were ordered after 1978. In 1983 the nuclear industry suffered another jolt. The Washington Public Power Supply System, which had sold $2.25 billion in bonds to finance two new reactors as part of a five-reactor complex, found that huge cost overruns made further construction unfeasible. After extensive efforts to bail out, the system succumbed in the largest municipal bond default in history. Two of the other plants were mothballed when analysts realized that the energy to be produced was not needed. Existing utilities around the country continued to operate, but antinuclear activists were winning in their struggle to make society safer in the atomic age.

Vietnam Veterans

Another group more vocal than before was the contingent of Vietnam veterans home from the war. America's role in the Vietnam War had ended in 1973, but the aftereffects lingered on. Increasing numbers of veterans began to call attention to Agent Orange, widely used to defoliate trees in Southeast Asia. It contained dioxin, among other things, and caused contamination that lasted indefinitely. Former soldiers with a variety of medical ailments now sought compensation and care for the debilitating results of their service. Some problems were physical; others were psychological. Delayed stress syndrome was a major complaint, and it emerged in various ways among former soldiers who could not get the war out of their minds.

Veterans particularly complained about having done what was asked in combat, only to return to a society that had soured on the struggle and treated them unsympathetically. Almost a decade after the United States extricated itself from the war, the nation erected a memorial in the capital to the Americans who had lost their lives. But even that gesture was surrounded by controversy.

In response to growing pressure for some kind of monument, a nationwide competition was held to choose a design. Maya Ying Lin, a 22-year-old Yale University student, triumphed over thousands of other entrants with a design for two large black granite walls forming a V. On those walls would be inscribed the names of the 57,939 American dead. The memorial that emerged was simple and stark, so much so, in fact, that some veterans argued that it seemed to make a political statement about the conflict without honoring the dedication of those who died. In response to their complaints, the government's Fine Arts Commission agreed to add a 50-foot flagpole and a larger-than-life statue of three soldiers. Disagreement then raged about where those additions should go. Finally the Fine Arts Commission voted to place them at the side of the memorial in a grove of trees.

With the monument complete, the Vietnam Veterans Memorial Fund sponsored a five-day tribute in October 1982 in Washington. It began with the reading of the names of the Americans who died in Vietnam, included a parade down Constitution Avenue, and culminated with the dedication of the monument.

The parade was a festive affair. Men appeared with beards and ponytails, looking very much like their antiwar contemporaries 15 years before. People wandered in and out of line as they saw and embraced old friends. Marching in the nation's capital before vast crowds, they sensed they had finally gained long-overdue recognition.

For some veterans the memorial seemed to put the Vietnam War behind the nation once and for all. It signified an end to the tremendous conflict at home that for them had lingered on. Many problems still remained, but as America honored those involved, living and dead, it became easier to look ahead to other concerns.

The Elderly

The elderly also became increasingly vocal in the mid-1970s. Elderly people made up the fastest-growing generation in modern America. Between 1900 and 1980, as the population of the country as a whole tripled, the number of people over 65 rose by a factor of 8. In the 1970s alone, the group over 75 grew by more than 37 percent. Behind the rapid increase was the steady advance in medical care which in the twentieth century increased life expectancy from 47 to 73 years. Americans watched Bob Hope celebrate his eightieth birthday, George Burns, even older, continue to act, and Ronald Reagan, over 70, govern the country. They became aware of what columnist Max Lerner called "the aging revolution," which promised to become the most lasting of all of the social movements changing the United States.

The elderly raised new issues in a nation beset by hard times. Many wanted to continue working and resented mandatory retirement ages that drove them from their jobs. Pleading their cause was Representative Claude Pepper of Florida, the octogenarian head of the House Select Committee on Aging, who declared, "I am like an old hickory tree. The older I get, the tougher I get." Legislation in 1978 raised the mandatory retirement age from 65 to 70. That helped older workers but had a serious effect on employment opportunities for younger workers waiting for their chance when older counterparts moved on.

Generational resentment over jobs was compounded by the troubles faced by the social security system established half a century before. As more and more Americans retired, the system became hard-pressed to make the payments due and still remain solvent without assistance from the general governmental fund. In the early 1980s it appeared that the entire system might collapse. A temporary solution, in part involving higher taxes for those still employed, and a later age for qualifying for benefits, rescued the fund, but further hard decisions down the line were postponed.

At an intensely personal level, American families faced difficult decisions about how to care for older parents who could no longer care for themselves. In years past, the elderly might naturally have come into their children's homes, but attitudes and family patterns had changed. Children were fewer than in earlier generations, and as women gravitated to jobs outside, they were less able to assist in the care of a parent. Sometimes nursing homes or similar residences became necessary, but the decision to place a parent under institutional care was often excruciating.

Homosexuals

Homosexuals of both sexes became more visible in the United States. There had always been those more comfortable with the "gay" life style, but American society as a whole was unsympathetic, and many homosexuals as a result kept their preferences to themselves. In the 1970s, in response to social gains by various groups and sexual liberation in general, gays became more open. A nightlong riot in response to a police raid on the Stonewall Inn, a homosexual bar in Greenwich Village in New York, helped spark a new sense of consciousness, and a movement for gay rights began.

Throughout the decade homosexuals made vast gains. By 1980 an estimated 20 percent of the population of San Francisco was homosexual, and sizable gay communities existed in Los Angeles, New York, and most other major cities. In 1973 the American Psychiatric Association ruled that homosexuality should no longer be classified as a mental illness, and that decision was overwhelmingly supported by the membership as a whole the next year. In 1975 the U.S. Civil Service Commission lifted its ban on employment of homosexuals.

Still, gays who chose to live more open lives faced agonizing decisions. In early 1982, Dan Bradley, head of the national Legal Services Corporation, announced his own homosexuality. In so doing, he spoke of the extensive earlier efforts he had made to hide that fact. "I subscribed to *Playboy* magazine— I must be the only man who subscribed to it but never read it—just to make

A gay rights parade on Fifth Avenue in New York in 1983. (*AP/Wide World*)

sure that when people came to my house there was evidence of my straightness," he said. "I'd make up names of women and told people I had a lot of 'dates'—all sheer fabrication, all lies." Though he was single, he wore a wedding ring for seven years. Far more comfortable once he "came out of the closet," Bradley left his former job and traveled around the country in an effort to promote passage of a gay civil rights bill.

Homosexual women as well as men became more open. A lesbian movement developed, sometimes but not always involving women active in the more radical wing of the women's movement in general. Lesbians, like male homosexuals, insisted on the same freedom from discrimination that other groups sought.

Not all Americans were sympathetic. Churches and other religious groups often discriminated against gays. In 1982 James Tinney, a Pentecostal preacher who had announced his homosexuality three years before, was excommunicated from the Church of God in Christ as he prepared a revival meeting for gays in Washington. In Atlanta a Metropolitan Community Church, part of a gay denomination, was burned after a series of attacks by vandals. Throughout the country Americans became concerned about AIDS (acquired immune deficiency syndrome), a new disease that seemed to strike homosexuals who had numerous partners more often than any other group. Suddenly the new freedom of the 1970s and 1980s seemed to have a darker side.

The Moral Majority

Another group that sought to change society in its own way was the so-called Moral Majority. Upset by what they saw as evidence of ethical decline, members wanted to revive the values they contended had made the country strong.

The Moral Majority was concerned about social conditions. Particularly troubling was an increase in crime. Between 1970 and 1980 the murder rate rose 30.8 percent, the robbery rate 42 percent, the burglary rate 56.2 percent, the assault rate 78.9 percent, and the rape rate 98.9 percent. Drug use seemed to be on the rise. Marijuana was not simply a fad but an institution for a certain segment of society. Cocaine use, too, appeared widespread. In 1982 Don Reese, a football player, confessed in a cover story in *Sports Illustrated* that "cocaine arrived in my life with my first-round draft into the National Football League in 1974. It has dominated my life ever since." He went on to declare that "cocaine can be found in quantity throughout the NFL," and subsequent disclosures substantiated his charge.

Moral Majority members were also disturbed by the vocal efforts of other groups to promote their own interests. They feared the increase of homosexuality, objected to abortion, and felt it was time to strike back with a united voice of their own. Led by the Reverend Jerry Falwell of Virginia, the Moral Majority reflected the growth of evangelical Protestantism in the United States. The movement showed, too, the growth of conservative strength in American political debate. The right had momentarily seized control of the Republican party in 1964. Now the religious right proved better organized. Though it was hardly a majority at all, but rather a highly vocal minority, it relied successfully on modern communication and fund-raising techniques to take aim at liberals who disagreed on crucial issues. In 1980 the movement played an important part in the election of Ronald Reagan and others who shared his views. Members hoped that the Republican victory would enable them to translate their vision of America into the law of the land.

THE RECENT PAST IN PERSPECTIVE

As the United States approached the midpoint of the 1980s, the nation remained unsure about what direction it should take. Economic and political troubles had left their mark. Americans had suffered from economic disruption at just the point when they sought relief from the trials of Watergate and Vietnam. They groped for answers to the questions that concerned them in all phases of their lives. The certainties of the immediate post–World War II years were gone. In economic, social, and political affairs, Americans were less sure about the course to take.

No longer were they confident about their ability to guide the economy. As stagnation and inflation proceeded at the same time, they began to question the ideas of John Maynard Keynes, who had suggested that aggressive fiscal policy could break downward cycles and promote economic health. Economic leadership in the 1970s and 1980s seemed lacking. Nobel Prize winner Friedrich A. Hayek, looking at the performance of economic advisers, said that "one sometimes feels that untaught common sense would probably have done better." The monetary and fiscal tools employed in the past were no longer effective. The decade of the 1970s was, *The Economist* of London noted, "a bad decade for economics." There was now a general recognition that fine-tuning the economy through short-term monetary and fiscal adjustments no longer worked effectively. The 1980 midyear review of the economy by the Joint Economic Committee of Congress said just that in a bipartisan conclusion to its examination of the recent state of affairs.

Despite progress by women and various racial and ethnic minorities in obtaining equality in American society, significant problems remained. Yet as Americans looked ahead, they were less sanguine than they had been in the past about the prospects for further change. The mood of social reform that had propelled the quest by assorted groups had run its course. Radical upheaval in the 1960s had made a real difference and had encouraged major change. But by the 1970s, even as various groups continued to press their causes, a backlash in the society slowed the process down.

Finally, Americans were less sure than they had been that government could provide the leadership the country needed or that the president could guide the nation in the direction it chose to go, for the presidency had become an impossible job. As Reagan took office, *Newsweek* asked, "Can anyone do the job?" Increasingly jealous of its contracting authority, Congress was determined to fight back, and legislative stalemate was often the result. Further complicating the situation was the incredible growth of bureaucracy. To make matters worse, special-interest groups often ingratiated themselves with government staffers who were determined to go their own way, whatever their directions from above. With expectations so high yet constraints so great, analysts wondered if there was any way out. Senator Gaylord Nelson of Wisconsin once told a story that supported his view that so much had gone wrong with the presidency in recent years that no one in the office could perform well. He spoke of Leo Durocher, the colorful manager of the Chicago Cubs, who put a rookie in center field for the end of a baseball game. The rookie quickly dropped a fly ball, made a poor throw, and allowed the opposing team to tie the score. An irate Durocher pulled the rookie out and installed himself in the field, whereupon he dropped a fly ball and lost the game. Furious, he grabbed the unfortunate rookie and screamed, "You've got center field so screwed up no one can play it." Had the presidency reached that state?

Beset with problems, Americans became obsessed with a quest for solutions. One reflection of that quest was *Time* magazine's 1982 nomination of the computer as its "man of the year." As microcomputers found their way into millions of American homes, *Time* seemed to imply that machines alone might help people understand the changing world and its demands. Another reflection of the search was the public response to E.T., a curious little space creature starring in a 1982 film that became the top moneymaker in movie history. E.T., in all his innocence, seemed to provide a contrast to adult society so filled with problems that people lost sight of larger goals. Americans embraced the extraterrestrial being as if he might be able to provide the direction they sought.

Whether with computers or with creatures from beyond, Americans girded themselves in the 1980s as they embraced a scaled-down version of the American dream. They had weathered chaos and crisis after the more comfortable post–World War II years and had watched their society change. In the new decade their society was still adjusting, and many of the emerging patterns were still unclear. Yet Americans were nonetheless ready to use whatever resources they could to move on. Less naive than before, they were prepared to affirm their destiny once more.

SUGGESTIONS FOR FURTHER READING

For the brief presidency of Gerald Ford, John Hersey, *The President* (1975) is a perceptive treatment by one of America's best-known authors. Richard Reeves, *A Ford, Not a Lincoln* (1975) is an even more penetrating account of how Ford functioned as president. For Ford's own story, see Gerald R. Ford, *A Time to Heal: The Autobiography of Gerald R. Ford* (1979). Also useful is Jerald F. ter Horst, *Gerald Ford and the Future of the Presidency* (1974).

On Jimmy Carter, there are a number of useful accounts. Jules Witcover, *Marathon: The Pursuit of the Presidency, 1972–1976* (1977) tells the story of Carter's quest for office. James Wooten, *Dasher* (1978) gives a sense of Carter, as does Betty Glad, *Jimmy Carter: From Plains to the White House* (1980). Also useful is Jimmy Carter, *Keeping Faith: Memoirs of a President* (1982), his own assessment of the White House years.

On Ronald Reagan, Lou Cannon, *Reagan* (1982) is a veteran reporter's account of Reagan's background and early years as president. Lawrence I. Barrett, *Gambling with History: Reagan in the White House* (1983) is another journalist's view of Reagan and his accomplishments.

Andrew Hacker, ed., *U/S: A Statistical Portrait of the American People* (1983) is a helpful compilation of demographic trends based on the 1980 census.

Christopher Lasch, *The Culture of Narcissism: American Life in an Age of Diminishing Expectations* (1978) provides one view of modern American culture.

Richard Rodriguez, *Hunger of Memory: The Education of Richard Rodriguez* (1982) is a sensitive autobiographical account of growing up Hispanic in the United States.

Alvin M. Josephy, Jr., *Now That the Buffalo's Gone* (1982) carries the story of American Indian struggles up to the most recent period.

INDEX